# Venus in t

In this second edition of the remarkable, and now classic, cultural history of black women's beauty, *Venus in the Dark*, Janell Hobson explores the enduring figure of the "Hottentot Venus" and the history of critical and artistic responses to her by black women in contemporary photography, film, literature, music, and dance.

In 1810, Sara Baartman was taken from South Africa to Europe, where she was put on display at circuses, salons, museums, and universities as the "Hottentot Venus." The subsequent legacy of representations of black women's sexuality—from Josephine Baker to Serena Williams to hip-hop and dancehall videos—refer back to her iconic image. Via a new preface, Hobson argues for the continuing influence of Baartman's legacy, as her image still reverberates through the contemporary marketization of black women's bodies, from popular music and pornography to advertising. A brand new chapter explores how historical echoes from previous eras map onto highly visible bodies in the twenty-first century. It analyzes fetishistic spectacles of the black "booty," with particular emphasis on the role of Beyoncé Knowles in the popularization of the "bootylicious" body, and the counter-aesthetic the singer has gone on to advance for black women's bodies and beauty politics.

By studying the imagery of the "Hottentot Venus," from the nineteenth century to now, readers are invited to confront the racial and sexual objectification and embodied resistance that make up a significant part of black women's experience.

**Janell Hobson** is an associate professor of women's studies at the University at Albany, State University of New York, USA.

# Venus in the Dark

Blackness and Beauty in Popular Culture

*Second Edition*

JANELL HOBSON

Routledge
Taylor & Francis Group

NEW YORK AND LONDON

Second edition published 2018
by Routledge
711 Third Avenue, New York, NY 10017

and by Routledge
2 Park Square, Milton Park, Abingdon, Oxon, OX14 4RN

*Routledge is an imprint of the Taylor & Francis Group, an informa business*

First edition published by Routledge 2005

*Library of Congress Cataloging-in-Publication Data*
Names: Hobson, Janell, 1973– author.
Title: Venus in the dark : blackness and beauty in popular culture / Janell Hobson.
Description: Second edition. | London ; New York : Routledge, 2018. |
    Includes bibliographical references and index.
Identifiers: LCCN 2017040645 | ISBN 9781138237612 (hardback : alk. paper) |
    ISBN 9781138237629 (pbk. : alk. paper) | ISBN 9781315299396 (ebook)
Subjects: LCSH: Women in popular culture. | Human body in popular culture. |
    Women, Black. | Beauty, Personal—Social aspects.
Classification: LCC HQ1233 .H63 2018 | DDC 306.4/613—dc23
LC record available at https://lccn.loc.gov/2017040645

ISBN: 978-1-138-23761-2 (hbk)
ISBN: 978-1-138-23762-9 (pbk)
ISBN: 978-1-315-29939-6 (ebk)

Typeset in Minion
by Apex CoVantage, LLC
Printed and bound by CPI Group (UK) Ltd, Croydon, CR0 4YY

# CONTENTS

# ILLUSTRATIONS

## Disclaimer

# FOREWORD

When I chose to focus my dissertation on the icon of the Hottentot Venus, embodied by South African native Sara Baartman, my adviser was far from appreciative. She was a staunch literary historian whose primary research goals focused on the recovery and reclamation of black women's historical voices—especially those voices that were most resistant to the prevailing stereotypes surrounding black female sexuality. I was adamant in my decision, however, since the icon addressed for me issues of race, gender, physicality, beauty, sexuality, and transnationality—subjects that I found compelling for research. In the end, I received a stern warning that I would be perpetually associated with a fetish and a subject matter that would prove difficult in transcending its fetishization.

The dissertation eventually became the book *Venus in the Dark,* and, twelve years after its publication, the scholarship on Sara Baartman—as well as the academic and popular discourse on the iconography of the Hottentot Venus—has remained vibrant. There is the compelling work of Priscilla Netto, Mansell Upham, Deborah Willis, Harvey Young, Natasha Gordon-Chipembere, and Simone Kerseboom, in addition to biographers Rachel Holmes and Clifton Crais and Pamela Scully.[1] Cultural producers have also contributed their own ruminations on Baartman's legacy, including burlesque dancer Akynos Shekera, visual artists Beth Consetta Rubel, Frederick Mpuuga, Brian Kirhagis, and Camil Williams, as well as playwrights Meghan Swaby and Charly Evon Simpson.[2] Even

Suzan-Lori Parks's *Venus* received an off-Broadway revival in 2017. Such conversations exist within a larger framework of impressive literature and cultural works exploring the complex racialized sexualities and sexual histories and representations of women of African descent. Despite all this, or perhaps *because* of this discourse, Baartman's life still exists in gaps and silences, often overwhelmed by the predetermined image of the Hottentot Venus.

In tracing a history that included no letters, poems, or narratives "written by herself," the quest for Baartman led me to the remnants of her body in 1999 as I quite literally stumbled upon her skeleton (before it was finally removed and returned to South Africa for burial on August 9, 2002) and the plaster cast molded by the anatomist Georges Cuvier at the Musée de l'Homme in Paris, as well as various early nineteenth-century sketches, paintings, and cartoons—the latter already a distortion of the historical figure etched within contexts not always perceptible to a twenty-first-century audience. It is precisely this last point why certain scholars, writing on Baartman, discussed the wisdom of excluding such visuals in their publications. I would find out, first hand, the reasons for such caution, as the responses to my scholarship on the Hottentot Venus over time have proven to be both complex and problematic. Consider the few examples below detailing reactions to the different presentations that I have delivered on this work, or even to the ways that other scholars have tried to elicit this history:

- At a job talk based on my dissertation research—which I had just completed—a white doctoral student responds to my subject matter during Q&A by remarking on her own research on the history of flight attendants, stating that my lecture helped explain why black flight attendants needed their own uniforms that could accommodate their supposedly big behinds, instead of the regulated ones fitted for white attendants.
- After this same job talk, I was cornered by a future black colleague who proceeded to chastise me for perpetuating racist logics (as the white doctoral student's comments suggested) that viewed black

women as inherently different due to our bodies; she worried that my lecture reiterated the worst stereotypes of black womanhood, which her own research on "respectable" black club women in late nineteenth-century and early twentieth-century New York sought to counter.

- At a speaking engagement highlighting "emerging scholars in women's studies," an elderly white woman scholar consulted me afterwards, wanting to know if the plaster cast of Baartman's body—shown in my slide show—didn't "prove" that there was something inherently "strange" and "abnormal" about the size of Baartman's buttocks. She at least was racially conscious enough to ask me this question privately, and not during the public Q&A session; however, she was *not* conscious enough to know this line of thinking was inappropriate.

- At an international conference, African and mixed-race scholars, who were members in the audience for a panel on which I presented, engaged in a heated debate about the proper spelling of Baartman's first name, as well as the power of language to diminish the individual, as the Dutch name "Saartjie" literally translates as "little Sarah." I was then interrogated about my own scholarly choices in naming Baartman and was subsequently accused of perpetuating colonialist logics as a U.S.-based scholar writing on an indigenous South African woman from the past.

- Years later, at a national conference, I would find myself in a similar heated debate, this time as an audience member responding to a white anti-porn feminist scholar who invoked the specter of the Hottentot Venus in a presentation on racist and misogynistic portrayals of black men and white women in interracial porn. Before she examines her subject matter, she begins with an early photograph (perhaps dating in the late nineteenth or early twentieth century) of an African woman in "tribal dress" whom she mislabels Sara Baartman, the "Hottentot Venus." This image supposedly represented black sexuality as "primitive" and "hypersexual," themes that categorized interracial porn. That the photograph didn't even feature the African woman in the usual pornographic poses that emphasize the size of her buttocks (she was depicted in a frontal pose, so no signification of her size even existed within these visual parameters) suggests the presenter's misreading of Venus iconography, not to mention her presentation's focus had nothing to do with black women's sexuality as she was only interested in black men and white women in pornography. Baartman, and black women by extension, was simply invoked to represent the "basest" in human sexuality. Her stunned response when I and several other black feminist scholars in the audience called her out on her flawed scholarship indicates the ways that present-day scholars and audiences are unconscious of their dehumanizing gaze and the reduction of Baartman's history to objectification and devaluation.

Such incidents reinforce Baartman's fiercely debated status as a theoretical subject, whether in the way her iconography elicits racialized sexism from present-day audiences who configure her—and women of African descent by extension—as racially and sexually "deviant," or in the way marginalized communities contest the politics of who gets to study African subjects. They also call into question my own decision to study Hottentot Venus imagery, which I had hoped the racial and sexual oppression that Baartman's history represents could be historically confronted and then subverted for our own present-day contexts.

While I still highlight visual representations of Baartman in my scholarship and teaching, I now do so strategically, with more detailed scripts that invite audiences to recognize their own subconscious racial readings that may cause them to reduce or re-objectify Baartman, or I often deliberately present images of Baartman through verbal counter-narratives that describe Baartman as "beautiful" and as "normal" in the contexts of cultures that praise and recognize a woman's well-endowed body. This work needs constant subversion and re-orientation. As such, Baartman's history insists on new ways of knowing her life story beyond the iconicity of the "Hottentot Venus," which continues to oversimplify ideologies of race, gender, and sexuality, especially when situated in theories of embodiment.

Regarding this subject, some have expressed concerns that my work reinforces both a gendered and racially essentialist understanding of and U.S.-centric context for the black female body when situating

Baartman's history in a comparative framework with African American women.[3] Specifically, in *Venus in the Dark,* I invoked the black/white binary in my articulations of Baartman's history, which does not address the specific racial hierarchy within South Africa that distinguishes and subsequently denigrates the Khoekhoe from "black" Africans. While such comparisons can become reductive, I nonetheless contend that my use of "black" to situate Baartman within the imaginary of "black women's bodies" is a political choice since this racial category, already socially and politically constructed—despite various color hierarchies that exist—is invoked, not to erase the local specificities and struggles of different marginalized groups, but instead to interrelate us within the rubrics of a diasporic community of "blackness." Such communities might exist in the geopolitical spheres of what Paul Gilroy calls the "Black Atlantic"[4] or elsewhere on the African continent and other locations. The various black women in the diaspora who have reclaimed Baartman within a history of "black womanhood" do so in solidarity with a shared history of racial and sexual objectification and embodied resistance.

Such expressions of solidarity might create a simplified view of the Hottentot Venus as a convenient historical analogy for understanding contemporary iconography. However, we need not discard the analogy between the Hottentot Venus and present-day fetishistic spectacles of black women's bodies because such comparative frameworks illuminate trajectories and the development of phenomena over time. Baartman's history maps onto African American women's bodies in specific ways: from the way Cuvier, who examined and wrote about her, directly influenced scientists who would project similar racist and misogynistic arguments about free and enslaved African American women, to the ways that present-day visual culture perpetually signifies on images from the past, sometimes to reinforce similar ideologies or to confound them. The problematic legacy of white supremacy requires our confrontation with history and its racialized construction of black female sexuality, even when, as black feminist porn studies scholar Mireille Miller-Young argues, such legacies "inform our fantasies, which means that sometimes our fantasies are ugly and include our own subjection."[5]

In view of this legacy, Baartman has become a consistent stand-in for black women's sexualities since contemporary rhetorics often insert Baartman's body into historical narratives or into contemporary scenarios by way of suggesting a comparative reading of black women's bodies—especially when the "big booty" is discussed. This explains why Cleuci de Oliveira, writing for the feminist blog Jezebel, highlighted Baartman as the "Original Booty Queen"[6] to comment on present-day "booty queens" like reality television star Kim Kardashian, or why feminist scholar Gail Dines draws on the "Hottentot Venus" to criticize the hyper-sexualization of Nicki Minaj's cover art and music video for her 2014 hit song "Anaconda,"[7] an immediate historical connection I too have invoked and have further nuanced in chapter 6, added to this edition of *Venus in the Dark.* This begs the question: can a black woman (or black-adjacent as some might read Kardashian) emphasize her well-endowed behind without conjuring the ghost of the Hottentot Venus? Such "ghost stories," as Crais and Scully argue, have already distorted the legacy of Baartman, much less others who have followed in her wake.

In *Patient,* a collection of poems on the history of enslaved women who were subjected to medical experimentations by gynecology founder J. Marion Sims, poet Bettina Judd recalls how she is often expected to address Baartman's story even though her research is specifically focused on those women who encountered Sims. As Judd writes, "Questions that lean toward the body sometimes trip over the dead."[8] Here, she imagines Baartman responding to her question—"Where would you like for me to put you?"—with an undistinguished laugh or sigh. That Judd conjures up Baartman's ambiguity in her response gestures toward her own assertion that Baartman must now be put to rest, lest we "trip over her body" in our attempts at theorizing the subjects of black women's histories and black women's sexualities. Baartman represents the paradox of being a woman who is perpetually hailed and named, although she is neither truly seen nor heard.

These critical interventions and complications of Baartman's history prompt another question: How do we begin to authenticate the subjectivity of someone like Baartman? Crais and Scully suggest that we start with her history at the Cape of South Africa to contextualize her culture, her sense of ethnic identity, and her survival strategies as an African woman living in the wake of colonialism (Crais and Scully, 10). The results of their research into her point of origin have revealed that Baartman was perhaps a full decade older than we may have believed, thus making her a much wiser woman when she embarked on her journey to Europe. They also discovered that she possessed the cosmopolitan sophistication of an urban dweller, even though her marginalized status in a colonial outpost subjected her to traveling to England in the slave hold of a ship. Baartman's history is far more complicated than many of us have imagined.

However, we rarely begin the story with Sara Baartman but instead with the "Hottentot Venus," upon her arrival in London on the sideshow stage of Piccadilly Circus in 1810. Because of this, we cannot help but foreclose on Baartman's subject status, as occurred with the French-language film, *Venus Noire,* by Tunisian-French filmmaker Abdellatif Kechiche.[9] The irony of this retelling is the way that Kechiche consulted with historians Crais and Scully, whose biography on Baartman places her South African story at the center;[10] yet his film fails to center Baartman's agency or to begin her story at the Cape. Although Kechiche approached Baartman's story through his own sympathetic lens as a postcolonial immigrant to France, he is unsuccessful in re-imagining her own perspective and her own voice. The result is a film that reduces Baartman to her body and in which she remains silent for most of the story.

There are moments when Baartman, played by Afro-Cuban actress Yahima Torres, registers shock, sadness, and resentment, but these emotions are secondary to the focus: the racist dehumanizing gaze of her white European audiences, the real subjects in this film. Indeed, in one sexually explicit scene, Baartman is shown displaying her pubic area—the subject of scientific examination, with regards to curiosity around her rumored "Hottentot apron"—for the amusement of a white Frenchman copulating with a white prostitute. Interestingly, apart from sexually humiliating displays of her exhibition, Baartman is never shown engaging in sex acts, even when the film implies her descent into prostitution toward the end of her life. Despite her troubling of inter-racial sexual taboos—or perhaps because of it—the film itself never violates this forbidden desire of contact. Merely signifying sex via her embodied presence, Baartman can only function as the sign of racial otherness.

Incidentally, in both the London and Paris shows, the center attraction depicted in the film includes a "danse sauvage" (savage dance) that Baartman performs. Given that historical documents usually emphasize Baartman's singing and playing of musical instruments in her performances, Kechiche's choice of imagining her performance through her "danse sauvage" places Baartman squarely in a tradition of white consumptive spectacles of black dancing bodies.[11] This cinematic imaginary is much like the improvisational performances of Josephine Baker, whose nude primitivist spectacles (which also included her own "danse sauvage") transformed her into a Parisian sensation during France's colonial 1920s—a subject I analyze further in chapter 4. Given the ways that Baartman remains silent throughout the film, we are not even privy to Baartman's "singing" voice; we instead witness her dancing in a stereotypically wild and frenzied way before her white audiences.

*Venus Noire* gestures toward a counter-narrative, but more often, Kechiche does not move beyond her objectified body to discover her story. It begins with her plaster cast—presented by Cuvier before a scientific audience—and ends with documentary footage of the transfer of Baartman's remains from France to South Africa in 2002. Such bookends foreclose on Baartman as primarily that of object and scientific specimen. Kechiche's film is less about Baartman and more about the titular *Venus Noire* since Baartman is not quite *seen* nor is she *heard*. Her history subsequently demands a re-centering of an African woman's perspective and a decolonized narrative of resistance—one that perhaps exists beyond Kechiche's imagination.

Curiously, this film premiered at the Venice Film Festival in September 2010, exactly two hundred years after Baartman's arrival in London and, incidentally, one month after South Africa's Department of Arts and Culture unveiled a model for the Sarah Baartman Centre of Remembrance, to serve as a memorial and museum in Hankey, Eastern Cape, near Baartman's burial site. Unfortunately, Baartman's burial spot has been subject to different acts of vandalism, one widely reported back in April 2015 when some imagined the violation occurred in retaliation for the despoiled statue of British colonialist Cecil Rhodes at the University of Cape Town, which took place earlier that year.[12] Baartman's history remains entangled with the struggles of South Africa and the world at large while her own dignity still faces assault.

Such struggles reveal the power and politics of history, as well as who gets to tell and preserve that history and how such histories are intrinsic to transnational systems of oppression that continue to subjugate women of African descent—whether in failing to pay the proper respect to an historical figure, exploited and abused in the past and present, or in recognizing those women today who still battle for the world's respect. And yet, Baartman's image as the Hottentot Venus reverberates in the global circulation of black women's bodies, which sustain the marketability of everything from popular music to pornography to advertising. It is within this contemporary context that I situate this new edition of *Venus in the Dark,* which includes a new chapter that provides a retrospective on the iconography of black sexualities that specifically speaks to the early millennial zeitgeist as much as it deconstructs the palimpsest of an era two centuries past. These iconographic echoes might suggest that, despite the local struggle to fix a specific memorial site for her, Baartman's "Centre of Remembrance" already exists in the porous, temporal zones of global culture.

# ACKNOWLEDGMENTS

*This latest edition would not be possible without the support of my new editor at Routledge, Alexandra McGregor, who convinced me that the issues explored in this book are still relevant and worth revisiting, Kitty Imbert for working with me on the new edits, and Kinitra Jallow and Donna Young for reviewing my newest drafts. In the spirit of the original edition, I continue to call out those who supported me from the very beginning.*

This book is the culmination of all the support that I have received from family, friends, and colleagues who bear their stamp on my personal and intellectual growth. First and foremost, I dedicate this book to my mother, Jeanette Hobson, whose love, support, generosity, and influence throughout my life made it possible for me to pursue doctoral studies, to trust in my ideas, and to reach out to others in confidence and acceptance. I also dedicate this book in memory of my uncle Maurice Woodley (1948–2004), whose pride in my accomplishments, appreciation for good arguments, and fatherly influence will be missed.

There are several friends and colleagues who helped in the shaping of this book. I am grateful for the critical input of Vivien Ng, Ime Kerlee, Mark Anthony Neal, Stefanie Samuels, Lisa B. Thompson, Sylvia Roch, Rachel Jean-Baptiste, Jerry Philogene and Cherine Johnson, who read chapters at different stages of my writing. I especially appreciate the guidance and support of Mark, Vivien, and Marjorie Pryse during my attempts at publication. I thank my editor at Routledge, Matthew Byrnie, for his feedback and dedicated work on my book, and I also thank my graduate assistants, Shahin Kachwala and Alison Kenner, for their diligent work in assisting me with the indexing.

My study has benefited greatly from the input of my dissertation committee, whose intellectual influences are marked throughout this project. I am indebted to Kimberly Wallace-Sanders, whose seminar on "The Black Female Body in American Culture," taught during the spring semester of 1999 at Emory University, provided me with a topic for which I have become passionate. Her seminar also provided me with valuable sources for this project; particularly, her grant proposal assignment proved most useful when I turned it into an actual proposal for research in Paris on Sara Baartman and proceeded to base this project on that scholarship, made possible through Emory University's Women's Studies Summer Research Grant.

I am also grateful to Beverly Guy-Sheftall, whose work on black and "Third World" women introduced me to significant ways in which I could privilege and center the lives of such women in my scholarship. I especially appreciate her responses and criticisms. Thanks are also due to Pamela Hall, whose advice, talks, and enthusiasm for this project have been a major help and push forward in completing it. I especially thank my adviser, Frances Smith Foster, for her constant support, which has taken on such forms as providing me with publication outlets, fostering in me an appreciation for diligent and responsible research, patiently reading through my ideas, and entertaining my efforts to create an interdisciplinary feminist work.

I'm grateful to my colleague Namita Goswami for encouraging me to pursue our idea to go to Paris and search for Baartman. Of course, this dialogue would not have taken place without the help of Frances Wood, whose conversations and suggestions have added so much to my perspectives on the subject of black women, and Nia Sherry Turner, both of whom offered us a ride to a Sweet Honey in the Rock concert, where the Paris trip was brainstormed in 1999.

Many others have been supportive to me during the dissertation stage, including several faculty members, staff members, and colleagues.

I am indebted to the help and patience of Women's Studies staff members at Emory University: Lee Ann Lloyd, Linda Callaway, and Berky Abreu. I thank Natasha Barnes, Randall Burkett, Mark Sanders, Judith Bettelheim, and Barbara McCaskill for their supportive and provocative conversations, as well as Rosemarie Garland Thomson and T. Denean Sharpley-Whiting for their thoughtful and helpful correspondences.

I also extend thanks to my friends Derrick Barrett, Aronica Gloster, Sibelle Reina, and Sharon Spencer Rollins, all of whom remain constant in my life and have expressed enough interest in my work to assure me that I have a potential audience beyond the discipline.

Furthermore, this project would not have been complete without the assistance of those whom I encountered on my way to and in Paris: Thomas Besch, for assisting me with the contact of the libraries there and with the Musée de l'Homme; William Barrett—with my mother's aid—for assisting me with the contact of the South African embassy in Paris; Lincoln Marais, serving as the first secretary of the South African Embassy at the time, who not only provided updates on the political concerns over the remains of Baartman but offered great hospitality and friendship during my stay; and especially Philippe Mennecier, at the Musée de l'Homme, for providing significant information and documents on Baartman.

Thanks also to the library personnel at the Musée de l'Homme, the Muséum d'Histoire Naturelle, the Bibliothèque Nationale de France, the Robert W. Woodruff Library, the M.E. Grenander Special Collections at the S.U.N.Y. Albany Library, and the Library of Congress—the latter where I was privileged to study, made possible through a Faculty Research Award Program grant awarded by the University at Albany.

Finally, I thank Sara Baartman, in whose memory I hope this project will honor and illuminate her enduring legacy.

# 1

# RE-PRESENTING THE BLACK
# FEMALE BODY: AN INTRODUCTION

Few could argue that any other black female icon in history rivals the "Hottentot Venus" for overexposure. First embodied by famed South African Sara (or Saartjie)[1] Baartman, a Khoisan woman who was brought to England and France for public exhibition between 1810 and 1815, the Hottentot Venus came to symbolize both the presumed ugliness and heightened sexuality of the African race during her era. In this century, Baartman became a national symbol when her remains were repatriated to her country of origin and laid to rest in 2002.

Before this grand display of national pride and restoration, Baartman's body had been exhibited in nineteenth-century freak shows to display her "large" buttocks, and it remained on display posthumously at the Musée de l'Homme in Paris until the late twentieth century. She was subjected to scientific experimentation when celebrated anatomist, Georges Cuvier, dissected and preserved her brain and genital organs to highlight distinct racial and sexual differences between the African and European "races." Such actions framed the development of scientific racism, which impacted later projects, such as European imperialism, eugenics, and acts of genocide. Given the centrality of this figure, and the woman behind the icon, we may recognize this particular narrative and iconographic history as one of utmost urgency in any discussions of race, gender, and their intersectional oppressions.

However, this is neither a biography on Sara Baartman, nor a historical investigation into the events surrounding this dehumanizing spectacle. Instead, this study explores how the "Hottentot Venus" figure has shaped representations of blackness and beauty. Moreover, it examines how contemporary artists, scholars, and interest groups in our own times have reconfigured Baartman, the woman behind the image, and other black female subjects to interrogate a visual legacy of imperialist iconography. Such imagery often requires an "aesthetic of resistance,"[2] which moves beyond simple counter-rhetoric that celebrates race or gender difference.

Although I delve into parts of Baartman's life history (what can be gleaned from the sparse historical record) and provide historical contexts in which her show emerged, my aim is primarily to articulate a transnational black feminist discourse that situates the Hottentot Venus figure in the larger realm of black diasporic identity, aesthetics, and politics. As an African American woman with parental lineage in the primarily black anglophone Caribbean, my own views on the subject of beauty, race, and difference are shaped by a diasporic culture that accepts as normative, as beautiful and desirable, what was otherwise once characterized by dominant cultures of the West[3] as a medical, "disabling" condition of "steatopygia" (a term for "protruding buttocks" that was used to describe Baartman). In other words, from a black cultural viewpoint, to *not* be endowed from behind is to be "lacking" in some way. And, although I'm not suggesting that this view can be fairly compared to European perspectives from the early nineteenth century, I think we may need to consider our own early-twenty-first-century attitudes toward black female bodies—their shapes, their sizes, their skin tones—and their potential as beauty subjects. We should especially consider this when commenting on Baartman's history.

For instance, one can read present-day scholarship in Western academia that investigates the Hottentot Venus exhibition and still find contemporary authors describing Baartman as "fat-arsed" or as someone who "suffered" from steatopygia.[4] Interestingly, a significant body of literature on this subject utilizes the historical and racially encoded term "steatopygia" as if this feature on any person indicates an anatomical anomaly or disability. When we reproduce a nineteenth-century ideology of race science that has no basis in our present day, we inadvertently corroborate certain theses of racial and sexual deviance.

Even when we move beyond the literature of Baartman, we still find this ideology of deviant black female bodies reiterated in contemporary popular culture. It is thus in the spirit of black feminist thought and practice that I wish to redeem black women's bodies and the figure of the Hottentot Venus beyond the discourse of racial alterity. Other works have contributed significantly to this project[5]; therefore, I do not present myself as someone who is more capable of achieving this goal. Feminist standpoint theory—as articulated by such scholars as Nancy Hartsock, Sandra Harding, and Patricia Hill Collins—suggests that our positions (i.e., our identity politics) shape our "ways of knowing," thus framing our academic approaches to a subject.[6] As Uma Narayan points out, however, none of us can successfully claim ourselves as "Authentic Insiders" with deep, prior knowledge based in biology (or sociology for that matter).[7] Moreover, when Audre Lorde addresses the goal of women "redefining difference" in their identity politics, she specifically asserts that:

> [It] is not those differences between us that are separating us. It is rather our refusal to recognize those differences, and to examine the distortions which result from our misnaming them and their effects upon human behavior and expectation. . . . Too often, we pour the energy needed for recognizing and exploring difference into pretending those differences are insurmountable barriers, or that they do not exist at all. . . . Either way, we do not develop tools for using human difference as a springboard for creative change within our lives. We speak not of human difference, but of human deviance.[8]

With this goal in mind, I redefine "difference" beyond the body, beyond group identity, and toward human dignity and community. Such a standpoint does not focus on "I/dentity" politics and essentialist projects of selfhood in relation to the "Other" of the subject of study (in this case, Baartman). Instead, it forces us to question what we might bring to the table as we address systems of power and domination. How do we start from a position of privilege or disadvantage to a place of social change, cultural diversity, and global justice? If women, especially black women throughout the African diaspora, identify with the historical figure of Baartman, what can her story tell us about our own positions of racial and sexual disadvantage (or privilege) in a world shaped by global white masculinist imperialism? More important, as Lorde reminds us, how can resurrecting her story or her image reshape our focus from "human deviance" to "human difference" in a way that takes her humanity as a given?

Such questions call to mind my own encounters with Baartman's story. I first learned about her in a women's studies graduate seminar titled "The Black Female Body in American Culture."[9] Although the course focused primarily on African American women's history and the body politic,[10] we began with Baartman's South African (or, to use a historic derogatory term, her "Hottentot") body. On paper, the horrors suggested by her display as an African "savage," a human "freak," and, later, a posthumous scientific specimen were implicit as we read various literature on the subject. It was, however, the image of her disembodied and dissected genitalia—preserved in a jar filled with formaldehyde fluid and shown to us in a slide show—that stunned the class into silence. In the long and awkward pause that ensued, we (all women, primarily of color) had to acknowledge that there was no effective language to emote or even intellectualize the body politic, as it relates to Baartman's legacy.

Later, when I embarked on a research trip to Paris in 1999, to visit the Musée de l'Homme, where Baartman's remains were housed at the time—in the midst of a broiling conflict between France and South

Africa, the latter government agitating for Baartman's return—I again found myself stunned silent. Both Namita Goswami, my research partner,[11] and I wandered into the basement corridor of the museum and literally bumped into a crate that held the plaster cast that Georges Cuvier formed from Baartman's cadaver in 1816 (Figure 1.1). Contained in box 33, Baartman's life-size cast reminded us of her ultimate powerlessness in death, when she could no longer refuse the persistent curiosity of those scientists who wanted to unveil her interior body. Later, her four-foot-eleven-inch skeleton was pointed out to us, hanging from a rack and marked number 1603, blending in, as it did, with

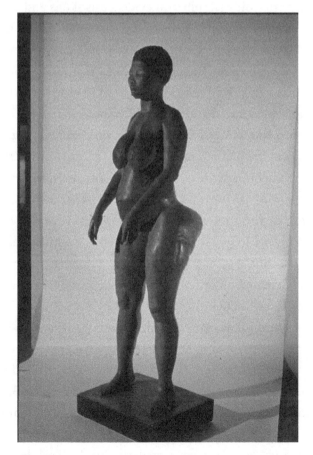

**Figure 1.1**   Plaster cast of Sara Baartman, 1816. Part of the collection of the Musée de l'Homme, Paris, 1999.

numerous other skeletons from the colonial past. The encounter suggested, through such ghoulish display, that little contrast can be drawn between the gothic horror of finding skeletons in a cellar and the educational display of bones marked for scientific study in the laboratory basement of a museum. This room of bones also tells an important story of how Baartman, who is often singled out for the abuses that she suffered, indeed was not alone.

Standing face to face with an actual skeleton and body cast of a nineteenth-century icon, this experience reinforced for us the paradoxes inherent in scientific institutions like anatomy and anthropology. These fields of study rely on such physical evidence as skulls and sex organs, while they simultaneously create myths, stereotypes, and lies based on bodily "facts." For an interpretation of Baartman's body—preserved, as it were, in a jar, or molded from a cast, or hanging from a rack—requires that we "read" this "hard" evidence through an accepted ideology of racial and sexual difference.

From what I had witnessed at the Musée de l'Homme, gazing at her skeleton or even the plaster cast, Baartman is not a woman "suffering" from an overwhelming case of steatopygia. She does, however, suffer under the dominant cultural gaze that defines her as an anomaly, a freak, oversexed and subhuman. As black feminist scholar T. Denean Sharpley-Whiting, in her study of Black Venus, summarizes: "Under the ever so watchful eyes and the pen of the naturalist, the master text on the black female body is created; the light of white maleness illumines the dark continent."[12]

Days after this visit at the Musée de l'Homme, when wandering the neighborhoods surrounding Montmartre, we encountered numerous black sex workers lining the streets, perhaps trafficked from the African continent or the Caribbean. Their presence recalled for us Baartman's story, as she too followed in a similar trajectory of international sex trafficking. It is fitting, then, that I extend my focus beyond Baartman to examine visual legacies constructed around the black body politic. Subsequently, I assert a project for women's studies, which recognizes the tenuous links between a specific black woman's past and transatlantic black women's collective present. In other words, Baartman's history is one of "migration" and "transnational" crossings, between South Africa, England, and France, and, in contemporary discourse, between Africa, Europe, and North America. Within my cultural studies focus, I utilize such "area studies" terms to illuminate that current global concerns have their roots in the past, and that cultural productions of images follow similar paths.

### Is the Black Female Body Beautiful?

Ever since nineteenth-century popular exhibitions in Europe of South African women with so-called steatopygia, black female bodies have been fetishized by this feature and identified with heightened sexuality and deviance. They have also been widely excluded from dominant culture's celebration of beauty and femininity. As a result, beauty becomes a significant site for political resistance and aesthetic transformation in which black women, whose beauty has been contested in dominant culture, strive to redefine their bodies by means of reasserting their womanhood and, possibly, their humanity.

This is significant for black women, more so than for black men, because in male-dominated culture, all women are judged by their physical attractiveness and evaluated in comparison to particular standards of beauty based on white supremacy.[13] As former fashion model Barbara Summers states: "Make no mistake about it. Beauty is a power. And the struggle to have the entire range of Black beauty recognized and respected is a serious one."[14] Although Summers defines beauty in relation to power, we may well have to question the kind of power that it promises. After all, what power do women access when they are recognized as beautiful? Is this power symbolized by finances, fame, and love interests, which characterize the "success" of supermodels and celebrity women who are defined in terms of their beauty? Moreover, can "beautiful" women elevate the status of all women once they achieve these things? Or, as is more likely, are they restricted because they are not subjective agents of change but merely sex objects? How, finally, can women change their status from object to subject, and what exactly do black women have to gain if their status is changed from "freakery" to "beauty"?

Certainly, in the arena of personal relationships, being physically attractive is the most valued quality, especially in our consumer culture, which places considerable emphasis on our bodies. If we add to this the cultural perception of whiteness as a marker of beauty and power, along with wealth as a means by which to maintain the body beautiful, then we may recognize those women who are nonwhite and poor as extremely disadvantaged. Patricia Hill Collins reminds us of a popular childhood game in African American culture, in which this hierarchical system of racialized beauty can be summed up in the following lines:

> If you're white, you're all right.
> If you're yellow, you're mellow.
> If you're brown, stick around.
> But if you're black, git back!

In other words, "no matter how intelligent, educated, or 'beautiful' a Black woman may be, those . . . whose features and skin color are most African must 'git back'" (1990, 79).

If women with the "most African" features are considered antitheses to beauty, then the emergence of supermodel Alek Wek onto the fashion scene in the late twentieth century, for example, might indicate a complex rendering of beauty and racial difference. This Sudanese model, with short hair, dark ebony skin, a broad nose, and full lips, may have personified a shift in representations of beauty once she made her debut on the November 1997 cover of *Elle* magazine. However, she might simply be regarded as a "new look" that can disrupt the beauty scene in late-twentieth-century appropriations and consumerism of cultural diversity, or what bell hooks describes as "the commodification of Otherness" (hooks 1992, 21).

Without altering dominant culture's beauty paradigm, which privileges white skin and Euro-based facial features, Wek can be cast as an exotic figure, whose racial "difference" signals the obsession of popular culture to market from a "new angle" a different body that has historically been associated with freakery and deviance. Wek can thus become an exemplar of ultimate difference. As Ben Arogundade comments in his collection of images of black beauty:

> Arguments raged about whether Wek—voted MTV's 1997 model of the year—was beauty or bad taste. Of course fashion sporadically promotes those it considers 'freaks' in order to satisfy its insatiable demand for self-renewal and to generate new focal points within the aesthetic homogeneity of looks, and Wek's features, taken out of the context of Africa, were suddenly jarring to Western sensibilities weaned on Euro-centric beauty values and Nordic blue-eyed blonds.[15]

That Wek's attractiveness was even an issue for debate attests to the power and privilege of whiteness in defining the body beautiful. Nonetheless, Alek Wek's appearance as a fashion model frames her in a discourse of beauty, even as she is removed from Sudanese aesthetic values. And although her "beauty" is recognized in terms of exoticism and racial difference, she still has the ability to convey that black female bodies are sensual and desirable. Television personality Oprah Winfrey confirmed this point when she stated to Wek, who appeared on Winfrey's talk show, that she would have had a different concept of herself had someone like Wek appeared on the cover of a beauty magazine while she was growing up as a young black girl in the United States (Arogundade, 144).

This "different concept" would have entailed a belief that beauty also encompasses black women, especially those who are most removed from Euro-based features. It also suggests a transatlantic connection between women of African descent and a shared sense of and need for a new aesthetic. This gets reiterated in 2014 when dark-skinned Kenyan actress Lupita Nyong'o, in an acceptance speech for Essence's Breakthrough Award, testified to the power of glimpsing Wek on the world stage, allowing her to feel "more seen by the faraway gatekeepers of beauty." I thus analyze in this study the connection that beauty has to black female bodies and examine how constructions of female beauty and sexuality reflect racial hierarchies of white supremacy and black subjugation. In particular, discourses of racial difference shape concepts of beauty, and transatlantic black women writers and artists utilize the site of the black female body to contest white supremacy in representations of their beauty and character.

### Disabling Bodies

When Foucault argues, "our society is one not of spectacle, but of surveillance . . . the hierarchical, permanent exercise of indefinite discipline,"[16] he rightly locates visual culture as a space for regulation and installment of "disciplinary regime" and the body as a site for contested power (Foucault, 193). Perceptions of "visual" difference, based on spectacle and surveillance, are thus assigned social and cultural values, mapped onto the body, and given political meaning. Thus, the spectacle of black bodies exists as a "deviation" in comparison with the "normative" white body. As Toni Morrison remarks in her critical race theory posited in *Playing in the Dark*, blackness could "be found with the dramatic polarity created by skin color, the projection of the not-me . . . an Africanism—a fabricated brew of darkness, otherness, alarm."[17]

Such alarm and fabricated otherness extends itself to a racialized sense of aesthetics that position blackness in terms of grotesquerie, whereas whiteness serves as an emblem of beauty. In considering Kant's definition of beauty as perfect realization, philosopher Noël Carroll notes that the opposite also occurs, in which nonbeauty, or ugliness, is the ultimate in imperfection. Thus, he suggests, "the moral credentials of [an ethnic or racial] group . . . can be endorsed by means of an association with beauty, or it can be demeaned by being represented as . . . ugly."[18] Although Carroll identifies the grotesque figure with denigration, Bakhtin, on the other hand, recognizes this figure as carnivalesque, which has "the right to be 'other' in this world, the right not to make common cause with any single one of the existing categories that life makes available."[19] For Bakhtin, the grotesque, carnivalesque body subverts social hierarchies and normalcy; however, such "subversions" can only occur within systems of power that "allow" the carnivalesque body to coexist with normalized bodies insofar as the grotesque supports—indeed, *enhances*—the status quo.

Rosemarie Garland Thomson reinterprets this carnivalesque body as a disabled body that "flies in the face of [an] ideal . . . presenting the ultimate challenge to perfection and progress."[20] In this Kantian summation, perfection and progress define the body beautiful, and the aesthetic project of altering female bodies, through cosmetics, surgery, or dietary exercises, renders unmodified female bodies much like disabled bodies unfixed, or "unhealed," by medicine—"unnatural and abnormal." Subsequently, Thomson pairs female bodies and disabled bodies within a feminist disability theory, which recognizes how these bodies are similarly "cast as deviant and inferior" (Thomson, 19). This particular representation is not unlike earlier racialized depictions of black bodies as "diseased." As Sander Gilman states:

> There is a long history of perceiving [black people's] skin color as the result of some pathology. The favorite theory, which reappears with some frequency in the early nineteenth century is that the skin color and physiognomy of the black are the result of congenital leprosy.[21]

Contained in this framework of freakery, the female body can be linked to the "disabled" or deviant body. Feminist philosopher Iris Marion Young observes in a similar analysis that "women in sexist society are physically handicapped. Insofar as we learn to live out our existence in accordance with the definition that patriarchal culture assigns to us, we are physically inhibited, confined, positioned, and objectified."[22] Within this definition, however, black female bodies complicate notions of "physical handicap." In their initial function in dominant society as enslaved laborers, black female bodies were described as anything *but* disabled, and their abilities for production and reproduction were categorized as far above those of white women.[23] As historian Jennifer L. Morgan notes in her study of English travel writings about Africa and the Americas from the sixteenth to eighteenth centuries, "Descriptions of African women in the Americas almost always highlighted their fecundity along with their capacity for manual labor" (Morgan, 184–85). However, the locus for "disability" lies more in their deviance and grotesquerie as dark-skinned, anatomically excessive, and sometimes even as physically strong in a Europeanized context that equated femininity with weakness.

If such a weakened state classifies the normative female body, then strength in a woman construes abnormality. This is most evident in presentations of "strong woman" shows that existed in sideshow circuits throughout the nineteenth and mid twentieth centuries and that exhibited women's muscles and physical strength.[24] A similar gaze would be applied to another black female figure, Sojourner Truth, this time by nineteenth-century white feminist Frances Dana Gage, who supplied us with one of the most inspiring accounts of the great black woman preacher and speaker.[25] As Nell Painter argues in her biography of Truth, Gage's narrative presents Truth's body within this context of unusual strength while it remains the most popular depiction of Truth's delivery of her famous "A'r'n't I a Woman?" speech. Delivered in 1851 at a women's rights convention in Akron, Ohio, Truth's speech posits her body in terms of masculinity and maternity. Gage, who presided over the affair, emphasizes Truth's physical presence and prowess in stark contrast to the white women present at the convention.

Writing on Truth's deliverance of "A'r'n't I a Woman?" in New York's 1863 *Independent*, Gage describes Truth as an "Amazon form, which stood nearly six feet high, head erect, and eyes piercing the upper air like one in a dream. . . . She spoke in deep tones" (Painter, 167). Such a narrative recasts Truth as a "superwoman," masculine though feminine in her refrain of "A'r'n't I a Woman?" In addition, Gage posits Truth as one who commanded the public gaze, as she demands, "Look at me. Look at my arm," while baring her arm to show "its tremendous muscular power" (Painter, 167). Additionally, while Truth lists the number of tasks her black female body could perform, from plowing to planting to "bearing the lash" to bearing "thirteen" children,[26] she redefines able-bodied womanhood while castigating her society for creating a double standard that argues for women's fragility yet demands these burdensome duties be executed by enslaved women.

More telling, however, is Gage's emphasis on Truth's strength as she rescues the weak and fragile white women at the convention who were overwhelmed and left speechless by the vicious attacks made by male ministers against their sex. Their "ladylike" incompetence made them unable to demand their women's rights, and, ironically, they relied on Truth's strength and Amazonian appearance to command authority on the platform and argue their case for equality. As Gage victoriously remembers, "She had taken us up in her great strong arms and carried us safely over the slough of difficulty, turning the whole tide in our favor" (Painter, 168).

Not only does this narrative depict Truth as a mammy figure cradling white womanhood in her arms, but it also reiterates a racial ideology of difference, which posits white women as feminine and black women as masculine or freakish. Within this context, Truth is subsequently framed, as Jacqueline E. Brady asserts, "as the 'primitive other' whose body . . . stands in stark contrast to the 'civilized' man of the marketplace and his preciously domestic Victorian lady."[27]

This presentation of the unfeminine black female body as grotesque links back to the spectacle of the Hottentot Venus, whose body is presented not in terms of this hyper-muscularity but in terms of hyper-sexuality, or excessive femininity through the emphasis on her supposedly prominent buttocks. As such, both figures deviate from the norms of femininity and, in the same vein, beauty. Such views of black femininity have led to my focus on Baartman's history, which exists alongside a larger representational history of black female beauty and sexuality. Because her exhibition has contributed to prevalent readings of black female bodies in terms of deviance and heightened sexuality, I seek to examine how black women in the ensuing decades and century attempt a redefinition of black femininity that frees it from such associations, or at least complicates such associations. These responses could be interpreted as revisions to dominant iconography, or as "signifying" discourses, in which, as Henry Louis Gates Jr. suggests, "all [black] texts signify upon other texts, in motivated or unmotivated ways" that lead to "repetition and revision, or repetition with a signal difference."[28] However, such signifying will be referred to, in this study, as re-presentations since the black women artists studied here are all concerned with a revision in public representations of black female bodies.

### Mis/Seen

Discourses of normalcy and dominance have long perpetuated black women's "outsider" and "disabled" status. Thus, their "disruptive" bodies provide further justification for their devaluation and discrimination; however, these carnivalesque bodies reflect not necessarily subversive representations, but instead distorted images, such as the ones found in a "carnival" fun house mirror. Utilizing the mirror as metaphor, we may come to understand how black women's representational history is thus one of "un-mirroring," to borrow a phrase from black feminist artist and theorist Lorraine O'Grady. As O'Grady writes: "To name ourselves rather than be named we must first see ourselves. For some of us, this will not be easy. So long unmirrored, we may have forgotten how we look."[29]

O'Grady specifically refers to an iconography of black female sexuality that casts black women as simplistic stereotypes, such as the "Hottentot Venus," "Jezebel," "mammy," "Sapphire," "welfare queen," and, more recently, "quota queen" and "baby mama." Subsequently, these stereotypes, manufactured as "controlling images" in systems of power (Collins, 1990, 72), distort the ways black women see themselves and each other. They also create the process of "un-mirroring," in which struggles for black female subjectivity constantly grate against the distorted images of the dominant culture. Thus, black women artists, in particular, who wish to gesture toward an aesthetic of the black female body find themselves in need of an oppositional stance. Somehow, the creation of a black feminist aesthetic must challenge dominant culture's discourse of the black body grotesque and articulate a black liberation discourse on the black body beautiful.

Can a black woman hold up a mirror that reveals a different image divorced from this iconographic history in dominant culture? This question echoes the concerns of black feminist theorist Evelynn Hammonds, who challenges in the following:

> Mirroring as a way of negating a legacy of silence needs to be explored in much greater depth than it has been to date by Black feminist theorists. An appeal to the visual is not uncomplicated or innocent. As theorists we have to ask how vision is structured and, following that, we have to explore how difference is established. . . . This we must apply to the ways in which Black women are seen and not seen by the dominant society and to how they see themselves in a different landscape.[30]

Likening black female sexuality to a metaphorical "black hole" in a "sexual universe," a term borrowed from Hortense Spillers' rumination on black women's status as "beached whales" in this universe—"unvoiced, misseen"[31]—Hammonds reminds us that the black hole is not a "void," as earlier black feminists, such as Michele Wallace, have argued, but instead "a dense and full place in space . . . detected by its effects on the region of space where it is located" (Hammonds, 140).[32] Within this metaphorical context, the discourse on black female sexuality is less about the unseen presence of blackness and more about its impact on its surroundings, or what Morrison calls the "Africanist presence" (Morrison, 1992, 6). Nonetheless, this full and dense "void" must be visualized in some way.

Otherwise, black women's self-representation cannot be realized in an "alternative sexual universe."

A different cosmos, in which the black body can be visualized, impacts this study on beauty and blackness. For, as mentioned earlier, some contemporary scholars and artists still have problems "seeing" or "mis/seeing" the body beyond the stigmas identified with it. As such, visual representations become problematic when reproduced, even within my own narrative here; however, I have chosen to include some of the images of Baartman and other black women that are deconstructed for their racialized depictions of female sexuality. Contrary to previous scholars writing on this subject[33] who chose not to re-present Baartman for fear of further objectifying her body, my inclusion of these images calls attention not to visual "differences" of Baartman's body but to actual visualization efforts in the representation of difference.

Whereas Anne Fausto-Sterling, for example, excludes such images with the idea that "such visual material would continue to state the question as a matter of science and to focus us visually on Baartman as a deviant" (Fausto-Sterling, 19), I provide these illustrations with the intent that readers not view them as "evidence" but instead as "cultural products." Certainly, Fausto-Sterling's argument is situated within her scientific discipline, as opposed to an art historian's or cultural theorist's perspective, which usually treats the visual as a site for analysis. Nonetheless, other scholars, such as Karla Holloway, warn about the possibilities of re-objectifying Baartman and, subsequently, reinforcing racial and sexual hierarchies that were in place during her exhibition (Holloway, 62–63). Yet we must keep in mind that such images need to be confronted, not only to recognize these hierarchies in place, but also to consciously subvert them.

Chapter 2 situates the Hottentot Venus exhibition within its historical context. Set against the backdrop of the transatlantic slave trade, European colonial expansion, the abolitionist movement, and social revolutions, this show managed to combine two existing tropes of black female sexuality: the Black Venus and the Savage Hottentot. The figure of Black Venus contrasts with the "wild savage" of the African continent, who is more repulsive than its erotic counterpart. Yet, these two figures are brought together in the figure of the Hottentot Venus, whose exhibition in early-nineteenth-century England and France dramatizes social anxieties and conflicting emotions that audiences held toward the black female body, which simultaneously elicits feelings of desire and disgust. Moreover, the representation of black female sexuality in both colonialist and abolitionist discourse cemented stereotypes that equated blackness with sexual savagery. The chapter concludes with a consideration of how the figure of the Hottentot Venus has shaped these lingering views in dominant culture.

Chapter 3 explores the resurgence of interest in Sara Baartman in present-day literature and art, as well as in post-apartheid South African nationalism. With the 2002 return and burial of Baartman's remains from the Musée de l'Homme in Paris to Cape Town, South Africa, which attracted thousands to her centuries-delayed funeral, I examine this renewed interest in Baartman's history, not just in terms of national politics, but also in terms of transnational discourse on race and gender difference. This is especially significant because the Hottentot Venus resurfaced as a figure in literary works by African American poet Elizabeth Alexander, playwright Suzan-Lori Parks, and novelist Barbara Chase-Riboud, or alluded to underneath the surface of Toni Morrison's *Beloved* (1987). She is also featured or referenced in late-twentieth-century artworks by African American artists Renee Cox, Carla Williams, and Renée Green, Latina artist Coco Fusco, South African artists Penny Siopis and Willie Bester, and French-Canadian artist Mara Verna. Specifically, I explore ways in which these projects seek to reclaim Baartman as both a historical and relevant figure in our own times.

Chapter 4 analyzes the fetishism of the black female posterior, popularized ever since the Hottentot Venus shows. Specifically, this chapter examines how this part of the anatomy has been ridiculed, celebrated, and pathologized, from the performances of Josephine Baker to contemporary popular culture, including art, film, and hip-hop music; yet it has been recognized as an aesthetic value in such arenas as dance-hall reggae and other African-based dance performances. Investigating these attitudes, the New York City–based dance troupe Urban Bush Women signify on the "batty"—Jamaican slang for the derrière—in their work as they create a black feminist aesthetic of the body beautiful. This aesthetic treatment parallels similar efforts by such black feminist artists as Ntozake Shange and Julie Dash.

Chapter 5 assesses configurations of black female bodies in both photography and film and examines black feminist aesthetic interventions in visual culture. To this analysis, I add black women's artistic re-presentations as they contrast with mainstream representations of deviance, such as the scandal of Janet Jackson's performance at the 2004 Super Bowl, or beauty, such as the arena of the beauty pageant. Chapter 6 updates this study by exploring the "bootylicious" body in millennial popular culture, in contexts of size and edibility, specifically examining the role of pop star Beyoncé in popularizing this aesthetic for black feminist practice. Finally, I end on a note of hope that such projects of re-presentation will move us forward in imagining our bodies differently, and, by extension, envisioning social change. I also suggest that the process of re-presentation can only come about once the gateways that lead to representational power, including access to media production and cultural managerial positions, are opened to underrepresented groups.

---

# VENUS AND THE HOTTENTOT:
# THE EMERGENCE OF AN ICON

In 1818, Mary Shelley first published her celebrated novel, *Franken-stein*, a cautionary tale of scientist Victor Frankenstein's "fervent longing to penetrate the secrets of nature." Her language highlights the sexual politics that equated science with masculine power and "nature" with victimized femininity. Significantly, just one year before this enduring fiction debuted on the cultural scene, Georges Cuvier—himself a celebrated scientist, baron, and Napoleon's surgeon general—published his own influential work on the developing science of anatomy. Whereas Shelley only hints in her novel at the ghoulish horror enacted by a scientist who experiments on the dead in his quest for supreme knowledge, Cuvier actualized such a feat, literally "penetrating the secrets of nature" with his tools of science as he acquired in 1816 the cadaver of the once-living and -famous Sara Baartman—performing as the "Hottentot Venus"—who died of an unknown illness by late December or early January of that year. Placing her corpse on his table, Cuvier proceeded to dissect her, unveiling the great mysteries of her genital organs, which he had "the honor of presenting to the Académie, prepared in a manner so as not to leave any doubt about the nature of her apron."[1]

Baartman's body, exhibited in London and Paris and framed as "freakish" in early-nineteenth-century sideshows, was presented to the public in such a way that emphasized both her racial and sexual alterity. She was displayed alongside European "freaks" of varying physical differences, and her particular body shape—her protruding buttocks—became the center of attention in the shows. Moreover, Baartman's genitalia, dissected and preserved in a jar for public viewing after her death, became the subject of scientific inquiry because the nature of her private parts—the subject of rumors from European travelers to the African continent who observed that women from Baartman's ethnic group possessed an "apron," or extra flap of skin covering the labia—dramatized this ultimate "difference" in race and gender. That this show capitalized on the sexual objectification of a black woman "freak" and cemented scientific debates, begun centuries earlier, about the human status of South Africans—later to impact all Africans and their descendants—underscores the role of racial ideology in framing sexual oppression.

I draw this analogy between Frankenstein and Cuvier, not so much to suggest the links between science fiction and scientific racism, but to remind us of the formations of monstrosity and freakery projected onto foreign bodies, which become sites of instability during an era of destabilization. Indeed, as Foucault argues about the modern, disciplined body during this time period, the Hottentot Venus throws the "modern" body in stark relief. While Shelley and her romantic colleagues bemoaned the passing of a dying world of nature—succumbing as it did to the industrial revolution and thus transforming into an "unnatural" state—Cuvier and his scientific cohorts sought to "order" the natural world in the midst of this changing landscape, assigning to diverse plants, animals, and people a hierarchical position that supported the supremacy of European masculinity. Considering that the industrial revolution taking place at the time emerged from the global economies of the African slave trade and European colonial expansion, Baartman's body—much like Frankenstein's monster—formed the basis for a new body politic. In part, she becomes the locus for various anxieties of racial and sexual encounters during an unsettling period of economic, political, and social revolutions.

In this chapter, I examine how Baartman's exhibition as the famed Hottentot Venus conjoined two existing tropes of black femininity in that era—the "Hottentot" and the "Venus"—that "made explicit the connection between bestiality and unbridled sexuality" (Abraham, 226). Whereas the Black Venus is an enticing representation of sexualized, exotic black femininity, the Savage Hottentot is a repulsive icon of wildness and monstrosity. Yet both representations elicit fear and attraction, which are combined and reflected in grotesque images of the Hottentot Venus.

Moreover, the preexisting imagery, which laid the foundations on which the exhibition was mounted, helped build a lasting legacy in visual representations of black female sexuality. As such, we may come to understand the Venus and the Hottentot, not just as the nexus forming an icon made famous in the exhibition of Baartman and subsequent displays of others who followed in her trajectory, but as the critical theories of race and gender differences that enhanced global white masculinist imperialism. In exploring these twin figures, I not only assess how these representations supported existing power structures, but also how countercultural components—namely, the abolitionist movement—utilized such representations and magnified the hypersexuality connected to black female bodies, which led to increased racialism despite the calls for slavery's demise. As a result, while slavery ends, the racist structures that supported this institution continue, especially with the circulation of sexualized representations of black female bodies.

### Slavery, Empire, and the Presence of Black Venus

Perhaps no other figure epitomizes the connections between grotesquerie, animalism, and hypersexuality than the "Hottentot Venus." The very appellation suggests competing claims of savagery and ultimate feminine sex appeal, thus eliciting both the repulsion and the allure that has shaped dominant cultural representations of black female bodies. Because of this, it is often interpreted that Baartman's nickname, "Hottentot Venus," reflects a contradiction in beauty and freakery. In her study of socially constructed disabled bodies in freak shows, Rosemarie Garland Thomson suggests that this title served to create a "frightening paradox": "one term perverts the other: the 'Hottentot,' which signified to the Western mind savagery and irredeemable physiological inferiority, is paired with 'Venus,' the West's apotheosis of femininity" (Thomson, 71). In another study, this time focusing on the traditional iconography of Hottentots, Z. S. Strother corroborates Thomson's view by proposing that the image of the Hottentot Venus can be understood as an anti-Venus, thus a "comfortingly anti-erotic" figure (Strother, 40). The archetypal Venus, an ancient Greco-Roman goddess of love, beauty, and sexuality, could not possibly be linked to savagery and sub-human status, Strother further argues.

Nonetheless, both scholars fail to comment on what has already been in existence long before Baartman set foot on European soil: the presence of *Black* Venus, who has been invoked since the era of the transatlantic slave trade and even earlier. Thus, such constructions of black female sexuality are less about incongruity and more about the double bind of lure and loathing, in the Fanonian sense,[2] for the foreign woman in the white masculinist imagination. Such cultural imagery, as Sander Gilman argues, has remained pretty linear throughout Western history in its equation between blackness and hypersexuality, from medieval descriptions of Africa to Darwin's appraisal of black female bodies as comic signs of inferiority to Freud's analogy between female sexuality in general and the "dark continent."[3]

While certain black feminist scholars have more or less taken issue with Gilman's reproduction of the offensive imagery of black female bodies in his publications, other scholars, such as Zine Magubane and Z. S. Strother, problematize his non-differentiation between blackness and "Khoisan-ness."[4] Both have argued against Gilman's reading of the "Hottentot" as the "essence" of black female sexuality (Magubane, 824; Strother, 39) because some European travelers regarded "Hottentots" separately from the "black race," who were viewed as more "lascivious" than reserved "Hottentot" women; however, to critique Gilman on this detail is to miss the point entirely with regard to constructions of racial difference.[5] Considering the social construction of "race," this historical attention to distinguishable groups of African ethnicities is misguided, especially with the increasing racialism of scientific and popular discourse that developed in the nineteenth century, which eventually collapsed race into the binary categories of "white" and "black."

We may argue, then, that the "erotic" is not at all missing from the show—contrary to the arguments of Strother—and that the Hottentot Venus is not a "frightening paradox," as Thomson suggests. The Hottentot Venus show more than emphasized sexualized savagery and the "erotic" nature of black femininity, which was also the focus in scientific investigation. Cuvier's own writings of Baartman employ this erotic perspective. Even as he found her face "hideous" and as he used the most formal scientific language when comparing her sex organs with primates, he detected no other deformities, thus commencing to find "the top of her chest graceful," "sa main charmante" (her hand charming), and her foot "alluring."[6] Moreover, Baartman's body was constantly depicted in the nude in various caricatures and sketches, which invited a pornographic gaze (Abraham, 226). Finally, the appellation Venus had already sexualized Baartman, even if this title served as a mockery, suggesting that the "joke" behind the show is that this figure could *not* be a Venus. The popular and scientific gaze fell on Baartman's buttocks and, later, her apron precisely because the Hottentot Venus show re-inscribed Baartman within the existing trope of hypersexed black womanhood. If nothing else, this show was about sex; and subsequent shows, even in our own times, borrow from this "T & A" spectacle.

Nonetheless, the conventional historical reading of the Hottentot Venus as an antierotic figure is shaped mostly by an imperialist ideology. As one Victorian English historian, Robert Chambers, records in his 1864 account of Baartman's exhibition: "With an intensely ugly figure, distorted beyond all European notions of beauty, she was said to . . . possess the kind of shape which is most admired among her countrymen, the Hottentots."[7] Chambers' comment on Baartman's "intensely ugly" figure reflects an increasing but consistent hostility that whites often held toward black bodies. This time, in the mid to late nineteenth century, such negative attitudes reflect the fears of encounters with black bodies during imperialist expansions on the African continent, as well as the fears of black emancipation in the Americas. Thus, although Chambers correctly reads the function of the exhibition—to draw distinct differences between African and European bodies, which supposedly erased interracial sexual desires—his Victorian moralism nonetheless misrepresents the complexities of such desires.

With regard to the debut of Black Venus in the European imagination, we may be able to trace her origins back to the first century when the Egyptian astronomer Ptolemy viewed the hot climate of Africa as evidence of its rule by the planet Venus—worshipped by the ancients as the love goddess—thus creating a perpetual link between African people and sensuality (Jordan, 34). As a result, any body that emerges from the continent is constituted as an oversexed body. During the medieval period, Black Venus later found her embodiment in the "beloved" figure of the biblical scripture of Song of Songs, one who is sometimes associated with the Queen of Sheba and who is known for proclaiming, "I am black and beautiful". This Ethiopian figure was heralded at a time when the distant Church of Ethiopia stood in the midst of an alien and impenetrable Islamic empire, which also created the view of the Queen of Sheba as an exotic and mysterious feminine figure.[8] Indeed, European medieval art began depicting this queen with darkened skin, which was initially viewed in positive terms. Later, however, she became demonized and was imagined as a corrupting force that lured King Solomon away from his Hebrew God.

As European countries, such as Portugal, initiated explorations on the African continent and interacted with North African slave traders who imported darker-skinned Africans into Europe, reports of Portuguese attempting to "wash off" the blackness of these captives led to such ubiquitous phrases as "washing the Ethiope white" (Pieterse, 192; Hall, 114). Such an expression captures an impulse to erase or subjugate visual difference—in this case, skin color—in response to the racial encounter. Although Kim F. Hall, black feminist scholar of Renaissance literature, recognizes this impulse in Renaissance poetry in which black female figures are in effect "whitened"—as in the case of the whitened "beloved" figure of Song of Songs—she nonetheless argues:

> These whitened Ethiopian females serve a dual function in that they allow poets to praise 'fair' European women while simultaneously reminding their audience of the disguised, potentially unruly sexuality and destructiveness of these potentially 'dark' women. . . . The whitening of the dark lady becomes crucial for the exercise of male poetic power. (Hall, 114–15)

Similarly, Sharpley-Whiting, in her study of *La Vénus Noire* in French literature and culture, argues that the Black Beloved figure was viewed in carnal terms because her flesh was considered "less agreeable to the gaze . . . [but] softer to touch," in comparison to European women, thus rendering her more suitable for "hidden pleasures" (Sharpley-Whiting, 1).

Out of this iconography, the trope of heightened sexuality framed conversations about African women. In the seventeenth century, with the development of the Atlantic slave trade, English traders customarily viewed their African female captives as "hot constitutioned ladies" with "lascivious" appetites,[9] thus projecting their own sexual exploits onto black female desire. This is in keeping with similar portrayals by European explorers of indigenous American women, whose bodies were viewed as "inviting" both sexual and colonial conquest, much like the land itself.[10] Subsequently, a gendered analysis of conquest necessitates that we constantly view the colonial narrative as one exerting sexual power and dominance. Whereas native female sexuality implicates the red female body in the physical and cultural destruction of the indigenous population—because of Native women's interracial liaisons with white explorers, which presumably led to genocide[11]—black female sexuality, in contrast, shaped the commerce and trade in African bodies through constructions of their ample, fertile, and agile bodies as "fitted . . . for both productive and reproductive labor" (Morgan, 184–85). A belief in black female hypersexuality virtually ensured that a steady supply of slaves would replace the dwindling numbers of indigenous Americans.

Furthermore, slave laws in the American colonies created gender and racial entrapments for enslaved black women. As historian Paula Giddings reminds us in her critique of seventeenth-century Virginia laws that stipulated all offspring of enslaved women would follow in their status: "Such legislation laid women open to the most vicious exploitation. For a master could save the cost of buying new slaves by impregnating his own slave, or for that matter having anyone impregnate her" (Giddings, 1984, 37). While the social structures in Latin America and the Caribbean offered slightly more mobility for enslaved women's children who were fathered by European men and thus able to achieve free status, we may be able to ascertain how such systems forced black women to use their sexuality for whatever possible gains were available in such restrictive systems.

Needless to say, slave systems in the Americas spawned a diverse class of "gens du coleur" (people of color)—often categorized in such scientific terms as "mulattos," "quadroons," or "octoroons," reflecting the degree of blackness with each successive and "whitened" generation. European perspectives on this emerging class of women of color, in particular, shifted notions of Black Venus to reflect this browning or whitening of African shades. Bryan Edwards, in his 1794 history of the West Indies, for instance, characterizes the mixed Jamaican woman as "Sable Venus." He remarks in the following:

The loveliest limbs her form compose,

Such as her sister Venus chose,

In Florence where she's seen;

Both just alike, except the white,

No difference, no—none at night—

The beauteous dames between.[12]

The poem refers to the form and limbs of the Sable Venus as "just alike" the white Venus, thus reflecting on the mixed-race possibility of Europeanized beauty in the black female body while also suggesting that color is insignificant to beauty if the physique is the same. German philosopher Johann Joachim Winckelmann writes similarly in 1764: "Color attributes to beauty, but is not beauty itself, and in general may be deemed insubordinate to form. . . . A black may be called beautiful if his features are beautiful. Travelers declare that daily contact with blacks removes the repugnance of the color, and their beauty is revealed."[13] Moreover, eighteenth-century scientists, including Buffon and Blumenbach, debated whether there existed distinct differences between Africans and Europeans apart from skin color.[14]

If black women's skin coloring was previously seen as the detraction, especially when compared to the fairer women of Europe, then the site for racial difference shifts from skin coloring to anatomy (Jordan, 501–2). As such, we find in the illustration, *The Voyage of the Sable Venus, from Angola to the West Indies* (Figure 2.1), a dark-skinned, as opposed to brown or "sable," figure who, contrary to what Edwards writes, is not "just alike" the Florentine Venus. Although the painting references Botticelli's Venus, the Sable Venus appears more muscular and indelicate than the white Venus figure. Subsequently, the image reminds us of the satirical tone Edwards uses to mock the interracial relationships of white men who were supposedly "enslaved" by their conquering black Venuses or, as historian Jenny Sharpe argues, to suggest a "narrative of the anticonquest . . . [that] eliminates the violence of slavery from the picture"[15] with its triumphant Sable Venus

**Figure 2.1** *The Voyage of the Sable Venus, from Angola to the West Indies*, in Bryan Edwards, *The History, Civil and Commerce, of the British Colonies of the West Indies* (London, 1794), vol. 2, facing p. 27. © National Maritime Museum, Greenwich, London.

holding the reins to her own "voyage" across the Atlantic, instead of journeying in the cargo hold of a slave ship.

Moreover, these constructs of racial difference that erased the possible beauty and desirability of black female bodies, despite the obvious sexual market for black women in the Americas, paralleled other accounts of travelers on the African continent, which turned to African women as the conduit between sexual grotesquerie and savagery (Morgan, 184–85). Other narratives, such as Peter Kolb's 1731 *The Present State of the Cape of Good Hope,* challenged prevailing stereotypes of "Hottentot" women—whose ethnic group was derogatorily labeled by Dutch settlers as "stammerers" (translation of the word

"Hottentot"), or as people who were presumed to have no language (due to the click sounds that the Dutch could not emulate) and thus no culture.[16] Acknowledging the rumors that suggested Hottentots were the most beastly and promiscuous of all Africans, Kolb attempts to "redeem" this group by reporting on their modest behavior. Nonetheless, Kolb corroborates in the beastly view of the group by including a grotesque image of a Khoikhoi woman whose breast is slung over her shoulder to suckle her young (Kolb, 162–63).

These visual exaggerations of African women's bodies, as recorded by European naturalist voyagers, create a monstrous hyper-woman in a sense. That is, the African woman seems to function as overly female compared with the European woman, and overly in abundance with regard to her femaleness: in this case, the stupendous size of her breasts. Moreover, because of the specificity of the female breast as a sign of sexual difference, the black female breast, highlighting race and gender differences, serves as an extreme deviation from the white male body.

Consequently, in their constructions of the "Other," European men would form connections between land, femaleness, animals, and blackness—all designed to distance white explorers, who remain in the equation civilized, reasonable, and highly evolved in human form—from identification with these beings who are defined as "nature" or as "savage." In short, a fabrication of Aristotle's Great Chain of Being is perpetuated in colonialism. This Great Chain, a hierarchical ordering of all living beings, from the "lowest" insect to the "highest" gods, implicated a "transitional zone" and thus "a missing link" between humans and apes. As Jan Nederveen Pieterse asserts, "Speculation among naturalists about the missing link dated from the beginning of the eighteenth century. . . . And it was the Hottentot . . . [whom many scientists] considered to be the missing link between apes and humans" (Pieterse, 41).

The idea of the "Hottentot" as a "missing link" was a major theme in scientific inquiry into Baartman's body. The curiosity that drove

scientists like Georges Cuvier to scrutinize Baartman and, in effect, deci-
pher any signs that might betray her "ape-like" qualities were most
likely stimulated by earlier descriptions in the eighteenth century.
Edward Long, a British planter and administrator in Jamaica in the late
eighteenth century, for example, had declared, "Ludicrous as it may
seem I do not think that an orang-outang husband would be any dis-
honor to an Hottentot female" (Cited in Pieterse, 41). This does seem
ludicrous indeed, but when one considers that in his statement Long is
essentially linking an orangutan (considered to be the highest order of
apes) with a Hottentot female (the lowest order of humans), we may
come to understand why, in white masculinist thought, this can seem
like a "reasonable" occurrence.[17]

Why the Hottentot female in particular, as the ultimate "wild
woman," would come to represent the essential *savage* may well have to
do with a view of the female body as somehow existing "closer to
nature." Moreover, the female body (black or white) is a "monstrous
error of nature . . . studied [by scientists] for her deviation from the
norm" (Schiebinger, 147).[18] In this line of argument, the black female
body *is* the "wild woman" or the "savage Hottentot." As Londa Schiebinger suggests, "African women shared with European women and
female apes the incommodious condition of being female in a male
world, and thus the scientific gaze fell upon their private parts—breast
and genitalia" (161).

Genitalia as another sign of savagery and animalism is illustrated in a
drawing by French traveler François Le Vaillant, who depicts the so-
called "Hottentot apron," the *tablier* (Figure 2.2), which was included in
his 1790 *Voyage de François Le Vaillant dans l'intérieur de l'Afrique*. The
image presents a "Hottentot" woman's elongated vaginal lips in the form
of a phallus, thus suggesting that overdeveloped labia functions much
like the male organ. The fact that Le Vaillant depicts the woman with a
beard supports this intention. Subsequently, black female bodies are
feared and found fascinating not only because of their so-called excessive
female traits but also due to their possible masculine characteristics.

**Figure 2.2** *Hottentote à Tablier,* in François Le Vaillant, *Voyage de François Le Vaillant dans l'intérieur de l'Afrique* (Paris, 1790), vol. 2, facing p. 350. (Courtesy of the M. E. Grenander Special Collections Department of the State University of New York at Albany.)

Such portraits of black female sexuality unfolded at a time when intense scrutiny of African bodies and scientific classification, through exploration and expansion, gave rise to a new ideology of race, class, and gender that witnessed the creation of class mobility, industrial work that soon replaced agrarian labor, and republican idealism and individuality—spawned earlier during the Age of Reformation and, later, the Great Religious Awakening of 1730, perhaps influenced by encounters with Native American egalitarian societies (Allen). As such enslaved African writers as Phillis Wheatley and Olaudah Equiano proved to dominant culture at the time that they could "write" and "join th'angelic chain"—in contrast to the derogatory image of the "Hottentots," presumed to have no language, much less a literary tradition—they invariably joined in the existing debates of African inferiority, formed primarily through representations of the black female body. Moreover, the Haitian slave rebellion of 1791 was allied with the revolutionary initiatives begun by the Americans and the French, while abolitionism intensified as a righteous movement espousing ideas of liberty and "natural rights." Even Thomas Jefferson's initial draft of the 1776 Declaration of Independence included a statement to abolish slavery, although lack of support led to his exclusion of this sentiment. Interestingly, as a result of abolitionist rhetoric, science was called upon to provide arguments for inherent African inferiority, as Jefferson later posits in his 1784 *Notes on the State of Virginia*, to de-legitimize such unfolding projects as the independent nation of Haiti, later forming in 1804; to continue in the expansion of slavery in the newly formed United States of America; and to begin the imperialist endeavor in Africa as a result of the ban on the transatlantic slave trade in 1807.

Abolitionism thus provided a moral argument for the refocus away from slavery toward other imperialist projects. Because of the revolutionary impulse that found European allies supporting slave rebellions in Haiti and other parts of the Americas, abolitionist employment of graphic imagery revealed slavery's horrors and thus rationalized the need for slave uprisings. We should not ignore, however, that arguments against slavery exacerbated racist thinking, with the help of scientific discourse. Interestingly, as Saidiya V. Hartman has argued, abolitionist discourse also employed scenes of horror for the vicarious thrill of readers.[19] In particular, it also turned the paradigm of the Sable Venus/Black Venus on its head—this time imagining the powerful, enslaving, hypersexed goddess as an abject victim of her sex, subjugated by the evil enforcers of the slave system.

William Blake's 1796 engraving, *Flagellation of a Female Samboe Slave* (Figure 2.3), included in John Gabriel Stedman's narrative based in Suriname, foregrounds a naked and flogged enslaved woman, whose

**Figure 2.3** William Blake, *Flagellation of a Female Samboe Slave*, in John Gabriel Stedman, *Narrative of a Five Years' Expedition against the Revolted Negroes of Surinam* (London, 1796), 265. © Victoria and Albert Museum, London.

"only Crime had consisted in her firmly refusing to submit to the loath-some Embraces of her despisable Executioner."[20] This motif of sexual abuse also shapes another abolitionist image of the period (Figure 2.4), in which a similarly nude and flogged young African captive aboard a slave ship (this time, hanging upside down from a hook) is punished for "her virgin modesty," as the caption reads. The text within the print comments on the irony of such punishment, were it to have been met on the young women of their own country. Interestingly, in a different but similar cultural context, Brazilian slave icon, Anastácia—revered as a saint and martyr of slavery—is routinely depicted in a torturous iron mask, also earned for her refusal of her enslaver's sexual advances.[21] Whether or not such imagery accelerated the ban on the Atlantic slave trade and, later, the abolition of slavery itself, we must recognize how this visual trope perpetuated similar representations of black female

**Figure 2.4** "The abolition of the slave trade, or the inhumanity of dealers in human flesh exemplified in Captn. Kimber's treatment of a young Negro girl of 15 for her virjen (sic) modesty." (London: S. W. Fores, 1792). (Courtesy of the Library of Congress.)

bodies. Nudity and illicit sexuality thus cling to the victimized black female slave in the same way that they cling to Black Venus.

With such representations amid revolutionary changes, is it any wonder that the Hottentot Venus emerged in 1810, three years after the slave trade ban and six years after Haiti formed as the first independent black nation, to calm the anxieties of both the populace and the institution of science? Placed on her sideshow pedestal, Baartman's body—re-presented to heighten her "missing link" status and sexual savagery—justified the ensuing colonial expansion into Africa; with the reduction of the labor force stemming from the continent, plantation capital relied on the reproductive abilities of enslaved women in the Americas. Such practices depended upon a theory of real and imagined Venus Hottentots. Out of the chaos of revolutions came the order of science and "civilization."

### *Exhibiting the Hottentot Venus*

From the little that we know of her history, Baartman was a Khoisan captive from the colonial Cape of South Africa.[22] She may have been separated from her family, including her parents and husband, during warfare between the Dutch and the indigenous population, and forced to labor as a servant for a Boer farmer named Peter Cezar. What we do know for sure is that, during her labor at Cezar's farm, Baartman caught the attention of Cezar's brother Hendrik, who entered her into a contract in which she would share in the profits made on her exhibition in Europe (Edwards & Walvin, 182). New research continues to reveal and rewrite this accepted history of Baartman.[23]

The existence of this contract might suggest that Baartman acted as a free agent when she left for England, perhaps at age 20 or much older, with Hendrik Cezar and Alexander Dunlop, the latter a ship surgeon.[24] Because no records have been found that provide Baartman's story from her own point of view, however, we can only speculate about what choices she may have had, especially considering that she died penniless in Paris five years later.[25] What we also know is that her colonized body—namely, her buttocks, which were stigmatized in Europe as a condition of "steatopygia"—was first exhibited in September 1810 in London at 225 Piccadilly Circus at the Egyptian Hall, perhaps named after Napoleon's scientific expedition into Egypt. She thus served as an important symbol of racial alterity both in her exhibition in London and French sideshows and her later dissection by French anatomists.

The popularity of the Hottentot Venus exhibition gave rise to numerous cartoons featuring Baartman's prominent behind, grossly exaggerated for comical effect. She was even featured on the five of clubs in a special deck of playing cards in 1811 (Willis & Williams, 62). The lesson that audiences in London and Paris learned from attending these shows was not only that Baartman's body was "ugly" and "freakish," but also that this "ugliness" was considered "beautiful" and "normal" in Africa, as one sketch dramatizes in its foregrounding of Baartman against a background that imagines similarly shaped "Hottentot" women in their "natural" habitat (Figure 2.5). This is further emphasized in the broadsides and advertisements of the show, which described Baartman as a "most correct and perfect specimen of her race" (Lindfors, 133; Strother, 25). The appellation of "Hottentot" also invoked in the minds of her audience travelogues of this period, which described in mythic tales "strange" encounters with these most mysterious of Africans—the "Hottentots."

The perceived "differences" between African and European men would suggest that the latter group would "obviously" not find Baartman an appealing figure and could thus attend the Hottentot Venus show in a spirit of light-hearted mockery and bawdy curiosity for pornographic deviance. However, such a reading depends on an ideology that upholds racial segregation and that imagines that interracial sexual encounters could not take place. In other words, only men of African descent—specifically the group known as "Hottentots," who were

**Figure 2.5** "La Vénus Hottentote. Sara, a woman of the Hottentot race, 25 years old, observed, drawn, and painted in the Natural History Museum in March, 1815." 42 × 29.7 cm. Engraved by Louis-Jean Allais from the painting by J. B. Berré. Part of the collection of the Musée de l'Homme, Paris, 1999.

already perceived as existing on the "lowest rung" of humanity—could find the figure of a "Hottentot" woman attractive, whereas European men could look upon such a figure and not respond sexually. Moreover, such a reading of the show also imagines that Europeans' increasing contact with foreign cultures, including the aesthetic values of such cultures, would not hold any influence over European culture. Yet, for all the refinement and civilization of European men, Baartman's exhibition was so popular that satirists often called into question the fascination that European men *did* have for this African woman on display, as in one French cartoon, titled "Les curieux en extase ou les cordons de souliers (The Curious in Ecstasy or Shoelaces)" (Figure 2.6).

In this satire, Baartman is centered in the illustration, standing on a pedestal engraved, "La Belle Hottentote" (The Hottentot Beauty), while others examine her private parts. The white characters' gazes focus our attention toward her buttocks. One soldier remarks upon this view: "Oh, goddamn, what roast beef!" Another soldier, attempting to get a better view of her covered genitalia, comments, "Ah, how amusing is nature!" Still another male in plainclothes proclaims, "What strange beauty!"

The only other woman in the cartoon is also the most obvious in her voyeuristic position, commenting, "Sometimes misfortune can be a good thing," which refers to her particular location, as she bends down to tie her shoelaces—thus the subtitle for the cartoon—to get a better view up Baartman's "skirt." However, we may deduce that she can see

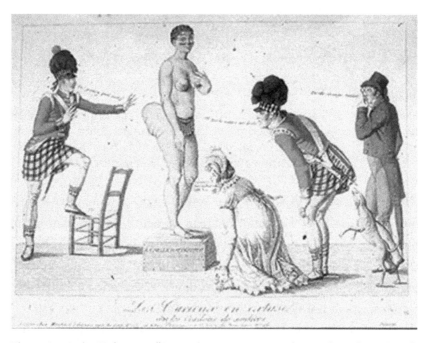

**Figure 2.6** Artist Unknown, "Les curieux en extase, ou les cordons de souliers." French cartoon, 1814. (Courtesy of Bibliothèque Nationale de France.)

underneath the kilt of the Scottish soldier who stands behind Baartman, which may also reference black female genitalia, especially the infamous apron, as "phallic" and thus similar to the genitalia of the Scotsman. What is apparent is that this white woman views Baartman as sexually deviant, which suggests that white women in general are also encouraged to view Baartman's body as inherently different from theirs. In addition, this white woman is given a "male" gaze as she views Baartman in a manner similar to the white male subjects in the cartoon. Her *white* gaze serves as a *masculine* gaze because she enacts power and dominance over Baartman through objectification.

Even as this gaze is dominant, the act of gazing, especially at private parts, is demeaning and shameful. Considering that the cartoon is sympathetic to the "belle Hottentot"—and we know this by the Europeanized depiction of Baartman's facial features—it castigates the viewers and links them to the dog, who also participates in the act of looking underneath a Scotsman's kilt, as this particular ethnic group is deliberately utilized because of their kilts to draw attention to the voyeuristic nature of Baartman's exhibition.[26] The addition of a dog in this visual piece suggests that the behavior of the onlookers is base and animalistic. That this view is described as "curious ecstasy" raises a significant theme of Baartman's exhibition: The show capitalized on the pleasure that whites gain from objectifying racial and sexual Others, whether the gaze is located in popular culture or in science.

In these ways, white surveillance, incorporating both male and female gazes, of black bodies is sexualizing and dehumanizing. Subsequently, Baartman's body can only be recognized in fragmented parts (focusing almost exclusively on her buttocks) and viewed with pleasure when it is identified as freakish or exotic. On the one hand, she inspired the humorists in each locale to draw cartoons exaggerating her body and to satirize her image in popular ballads and vaudeville. On the other hand, events that followed the shows in London and Paris further objectified her in different contexts: legally in the former city and scientifically in the latter.

The impending courtroom debate that followed Baartman's show in London demonstrated the kind of sentiments that Londoners, particularly those with abolitionist beliefs, held toward those whom they viewed as racially and culturally "inferior." Having already created imagery that equated black female bodies with victimized nudity and sexual violence, the abolitionist response to Baartman's exhibit was one of horror and moral outrage, in contrast to a non-abolitionist stance that enjoyed and made a mockery of the sexual spectacle. As a result, Hendrik Cezar, who brought Baartman to England, came under attack for having kept her in a cage. That Cezar was probably Dutch—thus *not* English—reminded English citizens of a similar battle between the Dutch and the English that currently played out on the South African terrain, in which the English posited themselves as the better "civilizing" European force in this early "scramble for Africa."[27] One "Englishman," for instance, was compelled to write to the *Morning Post* in October 1810 to describe his outrage upon seeing "a wretched creature . . . who has been brought here as a subject for the curiosity of this country." He further remarks:

> This poor female is made to walk, to *dance,* to shew herself, not for her own advantage, but for the profit of her master, who, when she appeared tired, held up a *stick to her, like the wild beast keepers,* to intimidate her into obedience. . . . I am no advocate of these sights, on the contrary, I think it base in the extreme, that any human beings should be thus exposed. It is contrary to every principle of morality and good order, but this exhibition connects the same offence to public decency, with that most horrid of all situations, *Slavery* [emphasis in orginal].

This Englishman would further express his "shock" that such an incident could occur in his country, which posits itself as the great model for democracy and justice. This outrage at the ill treatment of Baartman reflected the morality of abolitionist sentimentalism, as well as similar outrage that some English settlers expressed toward Dutch settlers at the Cape of Good Hope in that era. There, missionaries from

England "felt an obligation to protect [the native South Africans] against the Dutch settlers, whom they accused of innumerable murders and acts of cruelty toward the Hottentots."[28] From this sociopolitical and cultural context, the drama of the Hottentot Venus in London paralleled the drama that unfolded on the African continent.

Like the abused and "wretched creatures" at the Cape under Dutch rule, Baartman represented the primitive under the cruel hands of a Dutch showman, Hendrik Cezar, and he, in turn, represented a non-Englishman who knew nothing of being benevolent and kind toward his "inferiors." Finding himself under attack, Cezar felt compelled to vindicate himself in the popular press, as he wrote in the following:

> And pray, Mr. Editor, has she not as good a right to exhibit herself as an Irish Giant or a Dwarf. . . . However, as my mode of proceeding at the place of public exhibition seems to have given offence to the public, I have given the sole direction of it to an Englishman, who now attends. (Edwards & Walvin, 173)

Cezar grants Baartman more agency than she probably had. Some accounts of the exhibition described Baartman's "sullenness" at being exhibited and often her anger, which was expressed by her attempts at times to strike her watchers (Altick, 269). Moreover, Cezar grants agency to the European "freaks" also on display at Piccadilly Circus, where they were constantly featured in various human exhibitions. Interestingly, Cezar identifies the "giant" and "dwarf" on display at Piccadilly Circus, whom he compared to Baartman, as "Irish," thus locating them outside of English identity and rendering their bodies as strange and foreign, much like Baartman's.[29] In addition, Cezar's resolution to the controversy was not to stop the exhibition, which had "given offence to the public," but to turn it over to an Englishman, perhaps reasoning that such an operation would prove less offensive and more "benevolent" in the minds of the public.

The African Institution, an abolitionist group in England who conveyed this sentiment of paternalism and benevolence, thus brought

Cezar to trial on the grounds of practicing slavery and the use of obscenity in his exhibition of Baartman. This organization was willing to pay for Baartman's voyage back to South Africa if they could prove that she was being held against her will. Having achieved victory with the ban on the slave trade in 1807, the English abolitionists during Baartman's era may have felt that an exhibition that *suggested* slavery was reason enough to bring Cezar to trial. This suggestion was even more unbearable when some abhorred the idea of slavery practiced on English soil, but were fairly tolerant of this "practice" far away in the Caribbean colonies. Because of Baartman's prescribed racial difference, however, the issue of slavery was raised in ways that it would not have been in the exhibitions of "disabled" Europeans. In this way, she was recognized as black and, subsequently, as a "victim"—an African woman who could not speak or act on her own behalf.

After many witnesses, Baartman took the stand and told the courts that she was willingly exhibiting herself, although historians would debate her ability to speak for herself, seeing that Cezar, her exhibitor, could easily have primed her into saying what he wanted her to say.[30] Still, Baartman is on record as stating that she had a hand in her own exhibition. Moreover, the courts seemed to agree, because they dismissed the case but warned that the show could not continue in its "indecency."

Afterward, the show seemed to have gone underground, as some scholars believe the exhibition continued in the English countryside. Additionally, evidence reveals that Baartman was baptized in Manchester, England in December 1811.[31] Little is really known about those years in England, and more recent research suggests that Dunlop usurped Cezar's role in exerting more control over Baartman during this time (Crais and Scully, 97). However, she resurfaced in Paris in 1814 where her exhibition continued and where she was turned over to an animal trainer named Reaux. In Paris, she caused the same sensation as she did in London.

Such public spectacle formed the subject of a French vaudeville play *The Hottentot Venus, or Hatred of Frenchwomen,*[32] performed at the Theater of Vaudeville on November 29, 1814, the same year Baartman debuted in Paris. This play mocked French male attraction to Baartman and advocated the "superior" value of French women. It even accused those who "preferred" savage women of lacking patriotism and national fervor. That the play centered on the efforts of an aristocratic woman, Amelia, to "save" her betrothed cousin, Adolph, from the clutches of a "savage Hottentot"—indeed to bring him back to his senses—highlights the deep anxieties inherent in the public display of a foreign black woman, even through the guise of humor. The play further implies that any desire for a "Hottentot Venus" was truly "hatred of French women." Because the desire of one supposedly meant hatred of the other, the French popular press, like the vaudeville play, kept reassuring themselves that the "monstrous" form of Baartman provided such a contrast to the "pretty faces" of the women of their own country: Note the absence here of white women's bodies—and possibly an absence of sexuality—through emphasis on their facial features (Strother, 31).

Nonetheless, even while the play "offers a comforting view of the dangers of miscegenation" (Strother, 31), this anxiety does not altogether disappear: The final song of the performance repeatedly admonishes the French, "Do not abandon France!" Moreover, the fact that an aristocratic woman such as Amelia would have to don the Hottentot Venus look just to inspire male desire indicated that a "national fervor" for the preference of French women really was in jeopardy with the appearance of one "Hottentot" woman in town. This is especially telling when, in the same antimiscegenation message of the play, one of the men, upon learning that Amelia was not really the Venus Hottentot that she pretended to be, utters in an aside, "What a shame she is not a savage." As Fausto-Sterling suggests, "The soap opera dramas about Baartman that played in contemporary Paris suggested that French men, despite their 'civilization,' actually desired such women; civilization kept the European woman under control, decreasing the danger of rebellion, but thwarting male desire" (41).

On the other hand, another soap opera drama emerges in the midst of such bawdy tales and performances. One newspaper account, for instance, goes to great lengths to ridicule the "curious in ecstasy" and humanize Baartman's sufferings. In a January 1815 article that appeared in *Journal des dames et des modes*, the author describes a scene in which audience members attending one of Baartman's shows at a restaurant "entice her with bon bons" to sing, dance, and play on her musical instrument.[33] Baartman's audience has learned the performance well, as they rely on bribery and flattery—"She is told that she is the prettiest woman in all of society"—to encourage her to entertain them. But Baartman is presented as a "poor wretched creature"[34] when she realizes that the audience first reacts to her presence in fright, then with fascination. The author describes the following:

> The door opens and the Hottentot Venus enters. Upon seeing her, the ladies huddle and hide behind a curtain. This poor Venus notices and becomes sullen. Her head leans on her chest, tears fall from her eyes. She wears tight, skin-color clothes. Her face is flat and her nose is small. But she has big hips. This is a Callipyge[35] Venus. Her feet are small and her legs short, and her complexion is light green. In short, this is not an attractive Venus.[36]

The author begins his story by condemning his French readers for relying on entertainment that dehumanizes others. He further allows us to hear Baartman's own voice—interpreted, he admits, from his own limited knowledge of the languages in which Baartman spoke, including Dutch, English, French, and "Hottentot." Baartman lamented to the author about her condition:

> [The whites] separated me from my country. Then they settled on a land that was not their native land! Alas! I can no longer return to this sacred land. On each journey I take, I believe that I'm going to return to palm trees and sandy shores. . . . But no, no, never! Poor Sarah! Your husband, your father, your family, all are lost! You alone survived

to live in a troubled world, where nothing can soothe your sorrows, where *curious looks offend your suffering* [emphasis added].

This particular quote of Baartman reveals her despair and awareness that she must perform for white "curious looks." She also places blame on whites for her displacement, both in South Africa and in Europe. She bears witness to the transgressions of those who violate both the "sacred land," which is "not their native land," and the "curious" gaze upon her body that insults and makes light of her suffering.

Nonetheless, these words of Baartman are given to us by someone who wrote this piece as a "lesson" in the moral depravity of his fellow citizens who depend on the foreignness of their colonial subjects for their source of entertainment. Whether his audience learned this valuable lesson or not, their curiosity certainly did not lessen. In fact, a few scientists would probe further with their "curious looks" as they sought to learn the truth about the mythical tale of the *tablier*.

Unlike the abolitionists in London, who were uncomfortable with the suggested slavery and nudity in Baartman's exhibition, the audience in Paris seemed more concerned about such issues as desirability and whether or not the exhibition of the near-nude form of the Hottentot Venus could inspire sexual desire in their fellow countrymen. More important, they fixated on the *nature* of her sexuality as they questioned the existence of the Hottentot apron. It is through this sexual curiosity that Baartman was subjected to scientific inquiry into the status of her humanity.

Subsequently, a team of zoologists, anatomists, and naturalists, including Georges Cuvier, Henri de Blainville, and Geoffroy St. Hilaire, subjected Baartman to a three-day examination in March 1815 at the Jardin du Roi. During this time, they sketched Baartman in the nude, although she resisted full exposure by covering over her private parts with a handkerchief. They attempted to "observe" her genitalia and tried to entice her to disrobe through gifts of alcohol[37] and candy (much like her salon audiences), but Baartman refused to satisfy their curiosity. Nonetheless, they wrote disparaging remarks in which they compared her to a monkey.[38] However, in either December 1815 or early January 1816, Baartman died, and her body was given over to the Museum d'Histoire Naturelle, where Cuvier thoroughly examined her body and, at his will and leisure, dissected her "apron" and, in 1817, wrote a detailed description of it included in both the *Notes of the Museum d'Histoire Naturelle* and *Histoire naturelle des mammifères*, an exhaustive volume on the study of mammals, in which Baartman is the only human included in the study.[39]

By the time Cuvier preserved Baartman's genitalia in a jar of formaldehyde fluid, her immortality was ensured; her exhibition continued posthumously while the jar, alongside her skeleton, plaster cast, and another jar containing her brain, remained on display at the Musée de l'Homme in Paris until the late twentieth century. Not only did this treatment of Baartman's private parts usher in pseudo race science, which attempts to locate racial characteristics within the biological body, but it also shaped the ways in which black female bodies are viewed: with an emphasis on the rear end as a signifier of deviant sexuality. As a result, such associations of black female sexuality with animalistic characteristics emerge not just in pseudoscientific studies of human anatomy but also in popular culture.

### Darkest Africa, Whitened Slaves

While Baartman's genitalia—on exhibit at a natural history museum—shaped discourse on race science, other "Venus" shows continued in a similar trajectory. The next "Venus" to be exhibited in London was Tono Maria, the "Venus from South America." Tono Maria, an indigenous Brazilian, was exhibited in 1822 to display the nearly 100 scars on her body, presumably indicating the number of sexual transgressions she committed in her own tribe. The lesson learned through the exhibition of this body is that nonwhite women are openly licentious, debauched, and depraved. This time, the "mark" of Tono Maria's excessive sexuality was a social stigma instead of the biological sign embedded in Baartman's buttocks.

Nonetheless, both "Venuses" are recognized for their lasciviousness, as evidenced through their bodies. The lesson further draws a sharp contrast between the morally "depraved" black woman and the morally "pure" and "refined" white lady. An English journalist, upon seeing Tono Maria, declared that he would "pay the homage due to [white women,] the loveliest works of creation, *enhanced* [emphasis added] in value by so wonderful a contrast" (Altick, 272; Thomson, 55).

In addition, other "Hottentot Venus" exhibits existed. One such Venus entertained guests at a Parisian ball given by Duchess du Barry in 1829 (Gilman, 1985, 88). Still another appeared at a fair in Hyde Park on the Coronation Day of Queen Victoria in 1838. As an observer, T. E. Crispe, recalls in his "reminiscences":

> From a Hottentot point of view the beauty of the dusky goddess consisted in an abnormal development, and a strength which enabled her to carry a drayman round the arena without inconvenience. On this *steed* [emphasis added] of Africa, I, a featherweight, was placed a-straddle, and holding to a girdle round her waist—the almost sole article of her apparel—I plied a toy whip on the flanks of my beautiful jade, who, screaming with laughter, raced me round the circle. (Edwards & Walvin, 182)

This disturbing and probably fabricated scene of a white Englishman "riding" a nude "African" woman, if indeed she were (and this time, the Hottentot Venus "delights" in this performance as a "steed," unlike the often sullen Baartman who was described as resentful of her treatment on exhibition), carries with it all the sexual connotations of bestiality and female submission. This is also a powerful dramatization of Western imperialism, with the emergence of the Victorian era.

The scientific display of Baartman's fragmented body would further shape other acts committed against black female bodies. This is exemplified specifically in the founding of gynecology, as antebellum physician J. Marion Sims invented the speculum while practicing surgical experiments on enslaved black women in Alabama from 1845 to 1849. One named Anarcha would be operated on thirty times without anesthesia.[40] Such enslaved bodies, while representing racial differences, nonetheless conveyed a similarity embedded in all female bodies (Kapsalis, 42). Thus, Anarcha's body under surgical experiment can serve as both a valuable surrogate for the white female body and a disposable, unprotected body on which medical experimentation and cruel acts can be conducted. We may thus conclude that Baartman's treatment under Cezar, Dunlop, Reaux, and Cuvier set the stage for the dehumanizing treatments under which nonwhite female bodies, from Tono Maria to Anarcha, were subjected.

In these ways, the icon of the Hottentot Venus took on a posthumous life of its own, also appearing beyond the scientific realm in such literary works as William Makepeace Thackeray's *Vanity Fair* (1848), in which the character Rachel Swartz, a "mulatto" heiress from the Caribbean island of St. Kitts, is unfavorably compared to this image to discredit her as a suitable subject for desire and marriage.[41] In French literature, she emerges as Charles Baudelaire's Black Venus in *Flowers of Evil* (1857), appearing as the poet's "mulatto" mistress, Jeanne Duval, whose descriptions render her as a dangerous femme fatale and prostitute (Sharpley-Whiting, 62). Subsequently, the figure of Black Venus can be read more in pathological and grotesque terms, in the wake of Baartman's exhibition, compared to the pre-nineteenth-century imagery that emphasized sensuality.

Although both literary figures are far removed from Africa, their mixed-race bodies hint at traces of "darkest Africa"—the isolated "black" blood flowing through their veins and threatening the "purity" of the white body through acts of miscegenation and proliferation of a mulatto, or *gens du coleur*, class. At the same time, these tales of the interracial encounter, whether as warnings to the destabilization of white supremacy or as a fascination of race-mixing and subsequent whitening of a black race, continued to disguise the wholesale exploitation of numerous disempowered women of color under slavery and other systems of servitude, which more or less cemented their exposure to sexual assault and, thus, supported these sexualized representations.

Yet again, this time with abolitionist efforts focusing on antebellum America in the advent of British abolition of slavery in 1833 in the Caribbean colonies, the popular discourse can re-inscribe the trope of Black Venus to that of the abject sex victim. Even so, mid-nineteenth-century abolitionism—tied to a system of Victorian morality that refused to discuss in plain terms the sexual politics of slavery—still relied on the public's prurient interest in the subject of white men's sexual conquest of black women. Within slave narratives, former slave subjects, such as Mary Prince from Bermuda and Frederick Douglass in the United States, struggled to create agency and to voice their experiences to a white, voyeuristic audience. Yet, as Sharpe reminds us, narrators such as Prince remained silent on the subject of sexual assault that shaped her experience as a slave because "the slightest hint of sexual impropriety could have destroyed Prince's credibility" (Sharpe, 121). As such, her 1831 Caribbean narrative reiterates the motif of the flogged slave, rather than focus on rape, as she details the abuse and subsequent murder of a fellow slave woman called Hetty.

In the case of Frederick Douglass's 1845 narrative, he too magnifies the spectacle of the flogged and naked enslaved black woman; however, although the possibility of building solidarity between himself and fellow slaves exists, the focus on whipped slave women provides a gender contrast between female enslavement and male liberation.[42] Douglass prefaces his experience of being whipped by his overseer with a detailed description of the punishment of his Aunt Hester. Through this binary, captured in the written narrative, Frederick Douglass gives testimony to "slavery's horrors" through his authorial voice along with his body on display in abolitionist lecture halls. As is evident in Douglass's narrative, however, wounded black female bodies are reduced to sexual spectacle, often to raise the level of horror among mid-nineteenth-century readers, who would object to women so abused in a culture that emphasized the fragility and delicate nature of the female sex.[43] Douglass recounts Aunt Hester's flogging:

> Before [Mr. Plummer, the overseer] commenced whipping Aunt Hester, he took her into the kitchen, and stripped her from neck to waist, leaving her neck, shoulders, and back, entirely naked. He then told her to cross her hands. . . . After crossing her hands, he tied them with a strong rope, and led her to a stool, and tied her hands to the hook. She now stood fair for his infernal purpose. Her arms stretched up at their full length, so that she stood upon the ends of her toes.[44]

Douglass's details are quite graphic as he emphasizes Aunt Hester's exposed and vulnerable body prepared for a whipping and any other "infernal purpose." It also resembles the eighteenth-century engravings earlier mentioned. Such imagery not only associates the black body with victimization, but it also perpetuates the image of the black female body with savage and illicit sexuality—whether the "wild" and "uncontrollable" sexuality belongs to the enslaved woman or to her male violator.

Despite whatever truths were presented about the institution of slavery in terms of violations against black female bodies, these representations nonetheless reinforce black women's image with hypersexuality—as victim or as seducer. Subsequently, Douglass participates in this sexual objectification, reiterating in his text that women—more so than men—are subject to slavery's horrors, while he can "become a man." He becomes a man by seizing the overseer's whip and thus his phallic power, as he returns his oppressor's blows. That Aunt Hester's whipping precedes this scene emphasizes the masculine project of his narrative (Foster, 1979). In Mary Prince's narrative, she too provides graphic details of the flogging and eventual murder of fellow slave Hetty; however, unlike Douglass, she foreshadows her own sufferings with a description of Hetty not to offer a binary between the "not-free" and "soon-to-be-free," but to give testimony to her survival of a brutal and harsh system when others did not survive.

Because of the prevalent trope of the whipped and stripped black woman in slavery, black female narrators who wished to tell their own stories had to subvert this representation and recall a more empowering image that captured their resilience and courage. However, as with the case of the narrative of Louisa Picquet[45]—told in an interview with an abolitionist minister, H. Mattison—they had to contend with a voyeuristic gaze of the Other who wished to relegate their bodies to traditional associations of rape and overt sexuality. Consider Mattison's first question posed to Picquet: "Did your master ever whip you?" (Picquet, 7). Such a question may have served an abolitionist agenda to expose brutalities occurring under slavery; however, it reinforced Louisa Picquet's status as a victim. Mattison further sexualizes her in his efforts to "disrobe" her before the viewing public, as he asks these other blunt questions: "Well, how did he whip you? . . . Around the shoulders, or how? . . . How were you dressed—with thin clothes, or how?" (Picquet, 12). These leading inquiries might suggest that Mattison had read Douglass's narrative and others like it and seems to already know the "trope" of black female slave experience, along with the types of abuses and experiences to embellish. Furthermore, the title of this narrative, "Louisa Picquet, the Octoroon: A Tale of Southern Slave Life," which emphasizes Picquet's "octoroon" color, also calls attention for his Northern readers—who wish to learn more about "Southern life"—to her body, which is already coded as illicit. Her very color gives evidence to the interracial unions taking place, most often between white enslavers and enslaved black women. Nonetheless, Picquet endeavors to maintain her own subjectivity as she maneuvers through Mattison's invasive questioning.

Interestingly, while male narratives emphasized enslaved black women's victimization, black female narrators who wrote their own stories—including Harriet Jacobs and Elizabeth Keckley, to name two—often presented themselves with more agency and control. Harriet Jacobs, in her 1861 *Incidents in the Life of a Slave Girl*, rejoins the slave narrative trope with her body cast as a fugitive slave who gains her freedom not by "seizing the master's whip" but by outwitting him and finding safety among her community of enslaved and freed persons who help her journey to freedom.[46] Her narrative also hints that sexual oppression did not affect enslaved women alone, as attested by her account of the experience of an enslaved man called Luke, whose invalid master subjected him to the "strangest freaks of despotism" (Jacobs, 192).

However, Jacobs includes Luke's story, not to emasculate him but to underscore the communal experience of both black women and men's physical and sexual oppressions instead of emphasizing sexual differences that cast slavery as a female domain and freedom as a male prerogative. Through such a narrative, Jacobs manages to subvert traditional imagery of black female bodies as abject victims and to complicate the heterosexist discourse of slave oppression. She also enters into a public setting to reshape representations of black female sexuality and embrace emancipation.

### Conclusion

Against the backdrop of African American emancipation struggles, the specter of the Hottentot Venus exhibition lingers. Perhaps the strongest evidence of this legacy resides in the mounting of various world fairs, with one of the first mounted in London at the Crystal Palace in 1851, celebrating the British empire, and exhibiting displays of non-Western people from Britain's colonies. One of the most impressive world fairs in American history followed in this trajectory with the 1893 World's Columbian Exposition in Chicago, set against Southern U.S. lynchings and the "scramble for Africa" that ensued between the European imperialist powers.

Not surprisingly, exhibits at this fair, which resembled the Hottentot Venus show, displayed "primitive" African "savages," including a Dahomey village featuring bare-breasted women (described in "full dress"), in sharp contrast to the advancements of technologies and "progress" that defined the "White City" representing American culture. Subsequently, the irony of the fair's nickname was not lost on people of color, nor was the obvious goal of promoting white supremacy. Moreover, the fair marked the 400th anniversary of Columbus's "discovery" of America, a bitter reminder of Native American defeat, which was made evident by the recent massacre of the Sioux tribe at Wounded Knee in 1890. When we consider that Sitting Bull, one of the heroes associated with this battle, had previously performed in such ethnographic exhibitions as Buffalo Bill's Wild West show, we are reminded of the power of social representation to reinforce social reality. The "White City" further dramatized the exclusion of most people of color. In response, noted African Americans, including Frederick Douglass and Ida B. Wells, prepared a pamphlet in protest titled, *The Reason Why the Colored American Is Not at the World's Columbian Exposition*, and staged a boycott against an organized "Colored People's Day," which was parodied in a derogatory newspaper cartoon, "Darkies' Day at the Fair," collapsing as it did stereotypical images of "watermelon-eating" African Americans with the various tribes of "darkest Africa."[47]

While black radicals organized and raised the political consciousness of their communities—which linked such representations with the realities of oppression enacted against African Americans—the deeper, entrenched iconography of "wild African savages," subjugated yet absent Haitians, and a vestige from the "old days" of slavery (e.g., the debut of Aunt Jemima) intermingled in the fair space that simultaneously heralded white "progress" and "civilization." In essence, this imagery formed a lasting legacy of visual representations that undermined struggles of African descendants and people of color everywhere to participate on an equal level in public arenas, as well as in the democratic process. It also necessitated their diligent efforts to dismantle white supremacy.

Like Shelley's intelligent, exiled monster, whose cinematic transformation into a criminalized and inarticulate Other shifts the cautionary tale from the dangers of "progress" and "civilization" to one of fears of uncontrollable savagery, Baartman's humanity, which shaped the humanity of her fellow Africans, is never taken for granted. She is reduced to her body, indeed her disembodied parts—once pickled and housed in a scientific museum. The grotesquerie, then, lies not in her embodiment but in the acts committed against her, as the European conquest of the African continent and the scientific unveiling of "nature's secrets" are mapped onto the female body. The challenge for postcolonial and black feminist discourse in the face of such cruel history subsequently remains in the continued struggle for restoration of the human dignity of Baartman and others who preceded her or followed in her path.

3

---

# THE HOTTENTOT VENUS
# REVISITED: THE POLITICS OF
# RECLAMATION

The Hottentot Venus is being resurrected as a *cause célèbre* and bestowed with a Frida Kahlo-like martyrdom.

**Lisa Jones**[1]

The question must be asked why this woman has been made to function in contemporary academic debates as the preeminent example of racial and sexual alterity.

**Zine Magubane**

The Hottentot Venus lives on, surpassing even the women who embodied her in entertainment shows, art, and literature. The image would remain popular today since it is often invoked in academic discussions of black diasporic women's sexual histories or their representations in visual culture. Yet, for all this renewed present-day interest in the figure, relatively little is known about the woman who first brought the icon to life: Sara Baartman.

Apart from inspiring African American women writers and artists to confront such an ugly history of racism and misogyny that clarifies black women's collective devaluation in dominant Western culture, Baartman has also energized a nation to reclaim an oppressive symbol in the midst of such postcolonial projects as ending South Africa's racial apartheid system and envisioning peaceful approaches to social injustices of the past, as dramatized in the Truth and Reconciliation Commission. What is a more powerful act of "truth and reconciliation" than that of confronting Baartman's history, locating her physical remains at the Musée de l'Homme in Paris, and demanding her return to South Africa? When a choir of 100 women sang out to welcome Baartman home, and the state buried her bones on National Women's Day on August 9, 2002, we witnessed the redemption of history.

Such actions have nonetheless prompted some to caution against re-objectifying Baartman. After all, if the woman behind the icon of the Hottentot Venus was eclipsed in nineteenth-century popular culture, she stands to be erased once again as her mythic roles as "Mother of the Nation" and "Martyr of all Black Female Martyrs" are magnified in collective narratives. Whereas writer Lisa Jones views such reclamation projects as celebratory pride and resistance against dominant culture's devaluation of black female bodies, historian Zine Magubane cautions that Baartman, the historical woman, is flattened and lost in rhetorical debates. In the process, such an uncomplicated image has raised her status, perhaps inappropriately, to that of an "icon." Magubane correctly asserts that:

> Baartman was one of thousands of people exhibited and transformed into medical spectacles during the course of the nineteenth century . . . Examples abound of women [in 'freak shows' and circuses] . . . believed to be the 'missing links' between the human and animal worlds . . . However, none of these women . . . have been made to stand as 'icons' of racial or sexual difference. (Magubane, 830)

Although Magubane raises an astute point, she underestimates Baartman's importance by presenting her as just another "freak show" personality. I do not want to minimize the tragedies of other historical personalities who followed in a similar trajectory, but I cannot emphasize enough that Baartman was neither atypical nor was she another statistic. She deserves all of our present-day attention and accolades because she was made to represent the African race in its entirety. Baartman functions as "the preeminent example of racial and sexual alterity" *because* her ridiculed and pathologized buttocks take on a life of their own, not just in the continuation of "Hottentot Venus" shows after her death but in the stereotyping of black female sexuality perpetuated by popular culture and science. Neither should we forget that her genitalia—until recently left to float, embalmed, alongside other jarred specimens such as a white man's brain and a Chinese woman's bound foot[2]—cast an *entire* race in terms of its sexuality.

Who else but Baartman would be forced to represent all of humanity in a voluminous scientific study of mammals, as in Frederic Cuvier and Geoffroy St. Hilaire's 1824–27 *Histoire naturelle des mammifères*? Who else but Baartman served as the quintessential black woman—cutting across continents and cultures—subjugated under slavery and colonialism? Finally, who else but Baartman could inspire a wholesale stereotype in which black women, en masse, are "known" to have big behinds? Because of this complex function, we must carefully assess the present-day claims of the woman and the icon. For I can call into question only whether these various reclamation projects successfully assert Baartman's full humanity or merely perpetuate her objectification.

I analyze in this chapter the literary and visual works of varying contemporary artists—mostly African American, some South African, others of different ethnicities—who invoke the Hottentot Venus to revisit painful histories of colonial conquest and sexual racism, as well as to reflect on ways that such legacies mirror contemporary political scenarios. I then juxtapose these creative productions with contexts of contemporary global politics of race and gender. Finally, I question the role of science in treatments of Baartman's remains and consider what, if any, should be reconciliation efforts in the realm of twenty-first-century scientific developments.

### Who Speaks for Sara Baartman?

Sara Baartman can best be described as a subaltern figure. Forever elusive in the historical record and fragmented as a scientific specimen, Baartman becomes what Gayatri Spivak has characterized: "The subaltern as female cannot be heard . . . [therefore] the subaltern cannot speak."[3] Despite this inability to speak, others have actually tried to speak *for* her. Yet, how can one honestly reclaim Baartman's voice and subjectivity without reproducing what historian Mark Reinhardt describes as the "propensity to ventriloquize," thus creating the problem of "subaltern discourse" in which "voices appear to issue from elsewhere than their source."[4]

The poet Elizabeth Alexander comes to mind because her poem, "The Venus Hottentot," serves as a counterpoint to Georges Cuvier's scientific thesis.[5] First parodying Cuvier's voice as he lauds the mastery of science and its superb ability to order the natural world, Alexander later invokes the Venus Hottentot who comes to voice; however, this "voice" seems to parrot the historical words that have been used to describe her. Nonetheless, this Venus Hottentot proclaims, "Since my own genitals are public/I have made other parts private"(6), thus reinforcing her elusive status as a subaltern figure whose story parallels the gaps of African women's written histories. Because of these "silences," we might recognize Alexander's poem as a narrativization of what historian Darlene Clark Hine calls the "culture of dissemblance."[6] This term is used to describe a seemingly prevalent mandate for African American women's silence about their intimate lives in response to historical overexposure of black female bodies in public spaces (e.g., the sideshow stage and auction block). This practice of "dissemblance" also encouraged black women to create masks and façades of openness while concealing their own sexuality. Hine thus states: "By dissemblance, I mean the behavior and attitudes of black women that create the appearance of openness and disclosure, but actually shielded the truth of their inner lives and selves from their oppressors" (380). Paula Giddings adds to this: "even from ourselves."[7]

Because of these imposed silences, contemporary writers and artists who wish to articulate sexual histories, especially as they relate to Baartman's story, perhaps have the best success when they mirror in artistic form the silences and ellipses that construct the difficult subject of black female sexuality. Indeed, as Reinhardt comments, using Toni Morrison's 1987 novel *Beloved* as an example, such writing:

> is as much about withholding as unveiling. [Morrison] confronts readers with their will to possess or master her characters through the acquisition of intimate knowledge . . . [she] repeatedly underscores slavery's silences by replaying them, calling attention to what has not been said and what, in the world of this novel, *cannot* be said. (Reinhardt, 117, emphasis in original)

If we examine *Beloved* even more closely, we may recognize that such ambiguities and elliptical renderings of "slavery's silences" encompass a wider, diasporic narrative on black female sexuality. Quiet as it's kept, the Hottentot Venus lurks in the shadows of this novel, thus inviting a double entendre reading in which "Beloved" is not just the ghost of the "disremembered and unaccounted for" among African descended slaves; nor is she just a young, lost, and deranged soul who doubles for Sethe's murdered baby. She is the African Venus herself. One of the first materializations of the titular character, appearing after Paul D exorcises the baby ghost from 124, concerns Denver's witnessing of a ghostly dress appearing alongside her mother Sethe:

> 'I saw a white dress holding on to you,' Denver said.
> '. . . Describe it to me.'

'Had a high neck. Whole mess of buttons coming down the back.'

'. . . What else?'

'A bunch at the back. On the sit-down part.'

'A bustle? It had a bustle?'

'I don't know what it's called.'

'Sort of gathered? Below the waist in the back?'

'Um hm.'

'A rich lady's dress . . .'[8]

This scene seems to add an element of the supernatural in a novel that has too often been reduced to a ghost story. Unfortunately, this is reinforced with the 1998 movie adaptation—produced by Oprah Winfrey and directed by Jonathan Demme—which failed to recognize that the "horrors" of the story lie not in ghostly hauntings but in the legacies of slavery upheld by white supremacy. As a result, the scene, quoted previously, can be read less in terms of "magical realism" and more so as a metaphorical device to force us to connect this dress with Sethe's description of "rememory" that follows suit. According to Sethe, *rememory* is a trace or remains of things past, an actualized "real" in the Lacanian sense because the lingering presence, the palimpsest, retains a stronger sense than the original item or event. As she describes, "If a house burns down, it's gone, but the place—the picture of it—stays. . . . A thought picture" (Morrison, 1987, 44–45). Here, Morrison emphasizes visual language and signs, suggesting that pictures encode deeper layers of the trauma of racial and sexual oppression in ways that the word cannot. For Morrison's venture into slave history, upon her discovery of a nineteenth-century newspaper clipping detailing the murder of a child by its mother, Margaret Garner, suggested to her a complex story of enslaved women's love, possession, and suffering. With so much of the written African American slave experience suppressed in the historical record, however, the visual (mis)representation of black bodies loomed large in its place. As Beloved queries in her "unspeakable" thoughts: "how can I say things that are pictures?" (Morrison, 1987, 259).

This brings us to the dress with the bustle. Much has been written to connect the nineteenth-century bustle—an extra padding at the back of a dress that gave the appearance of a large behind, worn by middle-class Victorian women—with the Hottentot Venus (most obviously in the expression "Hottentot bustle"). In this regard, we may presume that Morrison uses the "thought picture" of the bustle—an appropriation or simulation of the "Hottentot Venus" shape in high fashion—to tell the difficult story of Baartman and her links to the enslaved woman's experience. Shortly after Denver describes the ethereal dress, Sethe launches into a description of schoolteacher, the brother-in-law of their former enslaver, Mr. Garner, whose death prompts his arrival at Sweet Home. Schoolteacher, unlike the seemingly permissive Mr. Garner, brings to Sethe and the Sweet Home men enough troubles to outlast the system of slavery—the institution that "burns down" but is "still there." He thus becomes the embodiment of Georges Cuvier and his later pupils, such as antebellum anatomist Louis Agassiz, who used science to justify racial inequality. And it is science, which Thomas Jefferson had called on to prove the racial inferiority of his slave subjects at Monticello in his *Notes,* that eventually cements in visual documentation—from Baartman's frontal and profile sketches to her floating organs to other African subjects under slavery and colonialism—the subordinated positions of African Americans, instead of their actual status as slaves. Subsequently, if the image of the Hottentot Venus functions as theory, then slavery—or imperialism, segregation, apartheid, genocide, and racial profiling that follow in its trajectory—becomes the practice.

In many ways, by evoking "pictures" to speak the unspeakable, Morrison attempts to explore what would drive someone like Margaret Garner to kill her own child. To then rely on racist iconography to provide clues requires what bell hooks has described as an "oppositional gaze." Such a gaze refuses to look away from dominant culture's gaze; however, in its resistance, hooks asserts, "Not only will I stare. I want my look to change reality" (hooks, 1992, 116). To change this "reality,"

Morrison's characters speak in clues and code words that are quite reminiscent of the musical tradition of spirituals and blues. They provide doublespeak, as suggested in Gates' theory of the signifying monkey, and bespeak a multitude of evils conveyed in terms like "schoolteacher," "stolen milk," and "whitefolks' jungle." They reverse dominant culture's values of "enlightenment education" to suggest that such learning promotes cultural ignorance and that schoolteacher's "measuring strings," notebooks, and descriptions of their "human" and "animal" characteristics are worthy of their derision.

Additionally, in projecting the violence of the "Wild African Savage," caricatured by a white performer in blackface at a carnival scene in the novel, the "whitefolks" became what they most feared through their participation in lynchings and mob violence.[9] However, while Paul D and others in the black community project an oppositional gaze by uncovering the masquerade of white "blackface" performance or by laughing at the "spectacle of whitefolks making a spectacle of themselves" (Morrison, 1987, 60), the materialization of white savagery is enough to exhaust the marrow in the bones of the diligent and stoic community leaders Baby Suggs and Stamp Paid. As Morrison writes:

> Whitepeople believed that whatever the manners, under every dark skin was a jungle. Swift unnavigable waters, swinging screaming baboons, sleeping snakes, red gums ready for their sweet white blood. . . . But it wasn't the jungle blacks brought with them to this place from the other (livable) place. It was the jungle whitefolks planted in them. And it grew. It spread. In, through and after life, it spread, until it invaded the whites who had made it. . . . The screaming baboons lived under their own white skin; the red gums were their own. (244)

Blending historical imagery of both scientific and popular stereotypes of "Africans in the wild jungle" with photojournalistic depictions of lynchings, Morrison invites her readers to recall a visual legacy of racism and to imagine the psychological onslaught that leads black subjects either to the brink of insanity or to rigorous pursuits of black nationalist endeavors to "love black flesh," as Baby Suggs sermonizes to the community. And, even she gives up, as the battle against white supremacy "ain't a battle but a rout."

Such resistance results in the devastating act of infanticide, which Sethe reasons to her imagined daughter's ghost, "[Should I have let] schoolteacher haul us away, I guess, to measure your behind before he tore it up?" (Morrison, 1987, 250). Each of these words encode and recode visual meanings and "thought pictures." We may thus imagine Sethe's statement as not just the indignity of slavery's reduction of enslaved women to scientific measurements but also in the institution-alized rape suggested in the image of a "torn-up behind." Far more entrenched is the image of Baartman's behind being measured and dissected by the likes of Cuvier.

By the time Beloved appears in the flesh, our titular charac-ter becomes a walking signifier, doubling as both African Venus and Hottentot Venus. She emerges "fully dressed" from a stream—perhaps alluding to Yoruba cosmology, in which the love goddess, Oshun, appears from her dwelling place at the bottom of the river, or even to Botticelli's Venus, or perhaps the Sable Venus, herself having crossed the Atlantic voyage—as Beloved's fragmented first-person narrative suggests her own crossing aboard a slave ship. Still, she could be the "Black Beloved" of Song of Songs—"black but comely" and longing to be loved, as indicated in her refrain, "I am Beloved, and she is mine." Moreover, her elaborate dress with the bustle, reappearing in black this time against her "midnight skin," suggests that Beloved doubles expo-nentially in her Venus roles (perhaps alluded to in the house number 124). She thus embodies both the sexual pleasure and pain of the novel's characters.

Then again, she may simply be a lost young woman who happened upon Sethe's family, her elaborate dress indicating that, in 1873, she may have been a "kept" woman or prostitute, her "smile" mirroring those of the "Saturday girls" who "smiled" for their customers, creating the rememory of the smile of Sethe's mother, caused by the bit used on the mouths of slaves as an instrument of torture (Morrison, 1987, 250–51). Either way, her role befits her Venus status, as would the sexual oppression that she alludes to when asked about her name, "In the dark my name is Beloved" (92). This imagery is later repeated in another haunting line: "Ghosts without skin stuck their fingers in her and said beloved in the dark and bitch in the light" (Morrison, 1987, 296). A surface reading encourages us to imagine Beloved as a victim of slave rape. When the rapist/enslaver is reimagined as a race scientist invading the insides of a black female body, later projecting "animal characteristics" onto her body, we can more readily comprehend the legacy of the Hottentot Venus.

Playwright Suzan-Lori Parks utilizes similar elements in her recreation of the Hottentot Venus in her play, *Venus,* first performed on Broadway in 1996. Like Morrison, Parks signifies on the "beloved who was not loved," as captured in her refrain of the "Unloved" Venus in reference to Baartman's first time on display.[10] The play also ends eerily with the spirit of Venus, after she has long died from "overexposure," beseeching her audience: "Kiss me Kiss me Kiss me Kiss" (162). Again, Parks signifies on Morrison's end in *Beloved,* with all traces gone of the titular character, while Morrison suggests that there is "[c]ertainly no clamor for a kiss" (338) in the wind or the weather; however, Parks insists that the Venus lives on, longing for what has been denied her: the right to be adored like her namesake. Both novel and play underscore the impossible discourse of the subaltern who cannot speak because what we hear raises more questions than they answer and heightens the mystery of our subject. Because of this, subaltern discourse quite often leads to frustration and misinterpretations since the ambivalence that shrouds these narratives prevent our firm grasp of the subject matter. This is especially dramatized in the following literalist interpretation of Parks's play, which has yielded accusations of reobjectification. Critic Jean Young writes of the New York City premier production in 1996:

Parks's play *Venus* feeds the audience a steady stream of domination and eroticized humiliation, as the seminude Venus is kicked in her greatly exaggerated padded buttocks amid the laughter of the Chorus of Human Wonders. She is sexually accosted by The Brother, and later by The Mother Showman, yet seems unaware of her victimization. Venus's 'love interest,' The Baron Docteur [representing Cuvier], is ironically played by a Black actor. This attempt at multicultural casting by director Richard Foreman suggests that Black men are the primary exploiters of Black women, further distancing white males from a recognition of Baartman's (i.e., the Black woman's) exploitation and dehumanization.[11]

Young assumes that Parks is not fully aware of the history and what, in actuality, she may be attempting to redress since, as Morrison herself recognizes in her own literary work, Parks speaks "the unspeakable." Or, in this case, she performs the unperformable. A symbolic reading of such a performance reveals that Cuvier the "lover" is exceedingly ironic, as is the portrayal of him by a "Black actor." Moreover, for our reviewer to assume that Parks presents Venus as "seeming unaware of her victimization" is to miss a crucial scene, Scene 24, announcing, "The things they noticed were quite various/but no one ever noticed that her face was streamed with tears," masked by Venus's insane burst of laughter in mimicry of her spectators. Finally, Parks's device of listing the scenes in reverse suggests that we also invert the meanings and the representation. She calls for a "reversal" of what we imagine has occurred in Baartman's history to highlight the spectacle of performance, the absurdity of theater, and the acceptance of what we, the spectators, witness as the real thing.

Parks does not engage in a simple act of "ventriloquism"; instead, when she attempts to speak for Baartman, she speaks in absurdity. Venus invites the audience to look at her "oddity"; she encourages the Baron Docteur to "touch me down there" (Parks, 104), when historical records, which the play highlights in its script, indicate that Baartman refused to have scientists examine her, and it wasn't until her death that

Cuvier even had access to her body. However, this fictive Venus suggests to Cuvier: "You could be whatshisname: Columbus. . . . You could discover *me*" (Parks, 104, 108). Such lines parody the quest of science and the legacy of racism. Though one could argue that such humor, in light of the real effects of this lingering history, is much too sophisticated and perhaps even irresponsible considering that there *are* audience members who invest in such ideologies, we should allow Parks the space to conjecture creatively in experimental forms the suggested horror of Baartman's exhibition. Such projects are especially significant in light of critics who are too invested in realistic, documentarian presentations of African lives when the ethnographic display of Baartman's cage and pedestal should caution them otherwise.

Nonetheless, I do take issue—as Young does—with the play's representation of Venus in padded breasts and buttocks. This is further exaggerated in the carnivalesque off-Broadway revival of *Venus* at the Signature Theatre in 2017, in which actress Zainab Jah portrays Baartman in butt-padded brown-skinned costuming that heightens the racial and sexual spectacle of the Hottentot Venus. Indeed, this production inspired a *New York Times* critic to compare the titular figure to reality star Kim Kardashian, known for her curvaceous backside, thus prompting backlash and accusations of racial insensitivity to Baartman's history.[12] Such costuming, while emphasizing the caricatured nature of the Hottentot Venus in nineteenth-century iconography, nonetheless fails to imagine Baartman's body as one belonging to a normal African woman.

The problem of seeing Baartman in fact mars the attempts of novelist Barbara Chase-Riboud to retell her story in her 2003 novel, *The Hottentot Venus.* Whereas Parks's play reminds us that the Venus Hottentot is a fabrication, a literal cartoon character, Chase-Riboud unwittingly recreates the caricature in the first chapter. Envisioning Baartman's death scene, she describes our titular character, who has become stuck while soaking in a tub, in the following: "My huge hips and buttocks were held fast, wedged against the sides of the tub. My shape held me prisoner."[13] One could argue that, like Young, I am rendering this scene in too literalist an interpretation; we may, in fact, analyze these words as an apt metaphor for Baartman's imprisonment within the caricature of the Hottentot Venus to which she was reduced. However, other scenes in the novel fail to move us pointedly beyond the subject of Baartman's buttocks and apron. Subsequently, Baartman's subaltern voice is submerged through dominant discourse, which silences alternative narratives.

Perhaps this results from Chase-Riboud's framing of each chapter with epigraphs from the words of Cuvier, much like Alexander's poem. Thus, she invites us to read her novel as a counterpoint to his scientific thesis on Baartman. Because of this, when Baartman—named Ssehura in the novel—speaks in the first person voice, we hear Cuvier's words: "I had beautiful small hands and feet and a tight cap of black curls that glistened with cocoa butter" (Chase-Riboud, 20). Moreover, in scientific or ethnographic detail, she narrates a procedure that an aunt of hers conducts on her body to create the rumored "Hottentot apron." Without exploring the possible fears, excitement, anticipation, anxiety, or even the intense pain that Ssehura might experience while undergoing this procedure, our protagonist chooses instead to "educate" the presumed Western reader about this practice. Ssehura thus gushes, though it seems a bit heavy-handed in its didacticism: "For my husband, I could procure rapturous levels with this apron of pulsing flesh filled with racing blood, fluttering like the burning wings of a butterfly or the fiery folds of a medusa" (22). Unlike Morrison and Parks, Chase-Riboud resists elliptical renderings of Baartman's "unspeakable" history and so relies, not on imagination, but on the colonialist narrative to refurbish her revisionist history.

The detailed account of Aunt Auni's surgical procedure on Ssehura, which elongates her vaginal lips, is strangely reminiscent of anthropological narratives of African female circumcision. Interestingly, this very procedure is later alluded to when the wife of Peter Cezar, for whom Baartman is forced to serve, accidentally witnesses Ssehura's nude form and reacts with horror at the sight of her apron. As Mistress Alya tells Baartman, "I have heard of the Abyssinians and the Egyptians cutting girls, but never the contrary" (Chase-Riboud, 51). Chase-Riboud thus encourages readers to view Ssehura's body ethnographically and in a similar context of deviance. As Nigerian scholar Oyeronke Oyewumi queries, in her critique of African American women writers who attempt to "speak for African women" through fiction, "How and why does female circumcision, which is not practiced by many African cultures, become the defining characteristic of Africanness?"[14] Oyewumi ties this prurient interest in African female genitalia to the Hottentot Venus exhibition, which has led, she argues, to a "somatocentric" preoccupation with the body: "It must be remarked that though [Baartman] was displayed for European consumption because her parts were *hyper-sexual* from a Western perspective, the African woman today is displayed for the *hypo-sexuality* caused by her presumed missing parts" (Oyewumi). Oyewumi further remarks, angrily it seems, that African American women collude in such colonial gazes. She thus suggests: "Feminist purveyors of global sisterhood—a sisterhood based on common genitalia—would do well to note that even apparently similar body parts have different histories and locations."

Although Oyewumi rightly concludes that those of us in the West are preoccupied with the body, she seems to want to end all conversations that invite transnational discourse on black diasporic women's bodily experiences, which have been shaped by violent apartheid and colonialist histories. The cultures and contexts may be different, but the themes are relatively similar. Perhaps a goal for global feminism should not be the creation of "vagina monologues,"[15] but instead *dialogues*, for what good can come from turning the gaze inward while staring into the speculum's mirror, which divorces us from other conversations or erases the histories of women like Baartman or Anarcha? Re-envisioning one's body can lead to self-empowerment, but it also poses the danger of narcissistic self-absorption that fails to engage in collective actions that move us forward. Reproducing the objectifying and fetishizing male gaze merely renders the female body once again "un-mirrored," to invoke O'Grady again, and the black female body in particular remains visually elusive. Unfortunately, although Chase-Riboud humanizes Baartman's tragic story by recreating the settings of conquest and colonial displacement that force someone like Ssehura to leave home to exhibit herself, she nonetheless "un-mirrors" the very body she attempts to redress and thus reproduces the dominant cultural gaze.

### The Venus Pose

The difficulties posed in reimagining Baartman's body outside of dominant cultural discourse necessitate a counter-aesthetic in the creation of a global black body politic. I would like to explore possibilities for developing such an aesthetic. To that end, I will consider the work of South African, African American, and other artists who have signified or alluded to the Hottentot Venus exhibit in their works. They strike what I call a "Venus pose" to suggest ways in which historical imagery of the body lingers in the present and in which an alternative aesthetic might disrupt such imagery.

Against the backdrop of violent crackdowns in 1980s South Africa on antiapartheid activists, Penny Siopis, a white South African artist, resurrects the figure of Baartman in a series of artworks that intersect race with female sexuality. Within a highly charged climate that classified diverse ethnic groups in a complex system of race and power, Siopis's art especially alludes to the constructed binaries of "black" and "white" and to the creation of master narratives. Her 1988 painting, *Dora and the Other Woman,* provides a curious rendering of these racial and gendered politics (Figure 3.1). Because blackness often works in tandem with white sexuality—indeed, its presence, as Gilman (1985) and Morrison (1992) have both argued, signals white sexual deviance or destabilization—this work ironically reproduces historical meanings. Emulating the style of dramatic painting, with its emotional mise-en-scène rendered in bold red, black, and gold colors, the problematic silences around female sexuality unfold. Siopis utilizes nineteenth-century caricatures of the Hottentot Venus to comment on Freud's psychoanalysis of one of his white female patients, Dora—the subject of this painting—whose sexuality he regarded, like that of all other women, as

**Figure 3.1**  Penny Siopis, *Dora and the Other Woman,* 1988. (Courtesy of the artist.)

a mysterious "dark continent." Through this phrase, Freud links female sexuality with the African continent and thus renders the black, or "blackened," female body as an unknowable, incomprehensible site of danger and chaos—dramatically represented by the disheveled room and pictures of the Hottentot Venus scattered on the floor and pinned against Dora's white sheet (perhaps to "sully" the purity of whiteness). Although a victim of rape, or because of this, Freud deems Dora's sexuality as "hysterical" and deviant. And, in this labeling, the white female subject is darkened in appearance—her face averted and hidden in the white sheet that is used for cover. The shadowy background and the heavy curtains that hang over our subject's head equate female sexuality with blackness and the unknown. Certainly, the curtains dramatically unveil the subject to suggest that Dora, as scientific study for Freud, and Baartman, as scientific study for Cuvier, are mirror images—white and black female sexuality doubling for each other and complicating the racial narrative.

Renee Cox, a Jamaican-American photographer based in New York City, strikes a different Venus pose with her 1994 black-and-white self-portrait, *Hot-En-Tot* (Figure 3.2). She also collaborated with fellow artist Lyle Ashton Harris in a similar photograph, this time in color, titled, *Venus Hottentot 2000*. Through these photographic depictions, Cox's body appropriates the "image" of Baartman and plays with false

**Figure 3.2** Renee Cox, *Hot-En-Tot*, 1994. (© Renee Cox. Courtesy of the artist.)

notions of racial and sexual difference, as Europeans of the nineteenth century sought to falsify with Baartman's body. Whereas Cuvier and his scientific cohorts attempted to prove that Baartman's "protuberant" breasts, buttocks, and genitalia represent inherent differences between the races, Cox modernizes this concept through her donning of prosthetic breasts and buttocks, tied with strings that visibly hang near her pubic area (perhaps alluding to the "Hottentot apron" that Cuvier and others were desperate to observe in their examination of Baartman). She constructs fictions of the black female body, similar to Parks's play, by illustrating false and "caricatured" depictions of black female sexuality prevalent in the dominant culture's imagination.

However, as art critic B. E. Meyers comments on this piece:

> Even though the more modern Cox [in comparison to her nineteenth-century Hottentot Venus counterpart] photographs with the knowledge that she controls the conditions under which the picture is taken, she also operates with the understanding that she has very little control over what or how the image she produces finally 'means.' She or her predecessors may wish to be taken seriously, but so much history conditions their reception that when they appear in print, their nakedness and vulnerability are readily met with disbelief: eyes and glances have already figured them out and assigned to them a type.[16]

Cox's photograph may exist uncomfortably under the colonizing gaze, as Meyers argues, which can still render the image as "hypersexual" and "deviant," but we might also contend that her artwork nonetheless creates a counter-aesthetic. By posturing her body to re-figure and re-member the "Hottentot Venus," she also signifies on the historical body and empowers Baartman in the process. Cox also confronts the viewer with her arresting gaze and, through this gesture, allows Baartman to "gaze back" at her audience. She is not just putting herself out there and risking vulnerability and judgment, but she is also attempting to recreate the site of memory that Baartman's body represents. To place her body within the space of Baartman's, she repositions black female bodies within the context of a corrective historical narrative.

African American photographer, Carla Williams, also uses her body to confront this problematic history with regards to the Hottentot Venus. She thus specializes in photographing, like Cox, nude self-portraits. While deliberately avoiding what she views as the capitalist, exploitative space of the gallery, Williams produces these intimate images for her own private consumption, although she shares her work occasionally and mostly through her website, which she feels provides her some control over their presentation. Williams's self-portraits allow her to envision a vibrant and self-defined sensuality, such as in her black-and-white photograph, *Venus* (Figure 3.3). Although the title of this portrait seems to evoke the "Hottentot Venus," we might recognize the older archetype of

**Figure 3.3**  Carla Williams, *Venus*, 1994. (Courtesy of the artist.)

the Greco-Roman Venus, or perhaps Black Venus, the "callipygous" figure known for her beautiful backside who also possesses the power to gaze from behind at her own buttocks and, thus, to reclaim her body as an erotic site of beauty and desirability. In *Venus*, Williams does not literally "look from behind"; instead, she captures her image for her own gaze and, subsequently, replicates this posture through her camera. She seems to reproduce an image of sensual female nudity commonly found in the work of male artists, and Williams admits as much when she states, "My self-portraits were initially informed by the history of portraits made by male photographers of their wives, lovers, and muses. . . . Turning the camera on myself, I sought to capture the intimacy of those unguarded moments."[17] However, she reveals her need to recapture a self-portrait of black nudity that transforms the black female body from comical and derisive spectacle to a serious contemplation of beauty and sensuality.

It is when she selects her portraits for exhibition that Williams finds her body subjected to "un-mirroring" because, as she observes, "I realized that my body could never be simply formal, or emotional, or personal. Most viewers would always see a black body regardless of my intent" (Williams, September 2002). This recognition led to her development of a series of photographs titled, *How to Read Character*. This photo–text installation presented six large, gilt-framed, black-and-white photographs of the artist's fragmented body, accompanied by historical texts and images. Borrowing its title from a late-nineteenth-century book on phrenology and physiology, Williams provides commentary on how science framed the body in a language that "reads" racial and sexual characteristics onto the flesh.

One of these photographs depicts her derrière, which is paired with an image and written description of Baartman (Figure 3.4). By creating this bridge between history and the present, between her body and Baartman's, Williams calls into question her self-representation, as it negotiates the gaze of her viewers, who cannot quite escape the historical meanings inscribed on her body. As she explains, "I hope to suggest to the viewer that such precedents, while seemingly absurd and

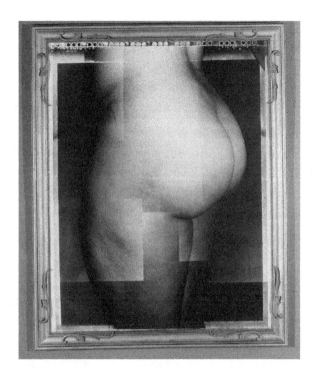

**Figure 3.4** Carla Williams, "Untitled," from *How to Read Character*, 1990–91, University Art Museum, University of New Mexico, Albuquerque. (Courtesy of the artist.)

outdated, still contain a great deal of resonance and power with respect to the way that we read and respond to contemporary images of African American women" (Williams, September 2002). Despite this response, Williams frames her body—literally in gold through her utility of gilt frames—as a gesture toward an aesthetic appreciation.

Unlike Cox and Williams, artist Renée Green chooses to pose the Venus without the body present. Instead, she invites viewers to reposition their own bodies in the site of memory that Green re-creates to highlight exhibitions and exhibitionism. Within this framework, Green presents her 1989 installation, *Sa Main Charmante*, which was included in an exhibit, *Anatomies of Escape*, in 1990 at the Clocktower Gallery in New York City. Through this work, Green comments on the body of the Hottentot Venus through absence as she chooses not to include a visual representation of Baartman. While expressing concern about the aesthetics of depicting black female bodies, she comments on our dependence on the visual.

The title for this art, *Sa Main Charmante*, borrows from Cuvier's written report on Baartman, during which he described her face as "hideous" but "her hand charming." In addition, Green signifies on the nineteenth-century cartoon, "Les curieux en extase." This cartoon, as analyzed in chapter 2, exaggerates Baartman's derrière like all the others, but the cartoonist seems to exhibit some sympathy toward the Hottentot Venus, represented by Baartman, standing on a box titled, "La Belle Hottentote," as he mocks the European audience who cannot escape the joy and "ecstasy" of staring at the private parts of a black woman. The installation includes the platform represented in this caricature, "La Belle Hottentote," but there is no Hottentot Venus standing on it, thus signifying on Baartman's absence, even as the viewers are invited to stand on the box and be displayed themselves. She also includes written texts that describe Baartman and a camera lens, which shoots blinding light into the pupil of a viewer who attempts to view the caricature, on which this installation is based, placed on the opposite end of the lens.

In this way, Green effectively raises for the viewer her or his position as a voyeur and denies the viewer sight. She subverts dominant culture's visual orientation by denying us visual access to Baartman's body. This depiction is thus complicated as Green signifies on the hypervisible black female body by making it invisible. However, because the black female body, particularly the fragmented black female rear end, has received overexposure in visual culture in the latter half of the twentieth century through popular culture, especially in the genres of hip-hop and dancehall reggae music, Green revisits Baartman's history and disrupts what film theorist Laura Mulvey has termed "visual pleasures,"[18] which have framed much of our visual culture from art to advertising to cinema and now Internet. Green invites viewers to place themselves not only in the role of Baartman's audience but also in Baartman's position as they strike this Venus pose on the platform.

Coco Fusco, a Latina performing artist and scholar, addresses similar themes of exhibitionism through critical re-presentations of the ethnographic exhibitions of the past. In response to the quincentennial celebrations of Christopher Columbus, who began this racialized practice of exhibiting nonwhite people, Fusco collaborated with fellow artist Guillermo Gómez-Peña to perform their controversial 1992 piece, *Two Undiscovered Amerindians*.[19] This performance included exhibiting themselves in a cage and passing themselves off as fictitious "undiscovered" natives of a tribe of Amerindians from an equally fictitious island in Latin America called Guatinaui. They also engaged in a hybrid of tasks blending the contemporary with the "primitive," such as watching television, working on laptop computers, and sewing voodoo dolls. As Fusco connects the performance of the nonwhite on exhibit in earlier centuries with her own performance as a late-twentieth-century nonwhite reenacting cultural identity, she comments, "Our cage became the metaphor for our condition, linking the racism implicit in ethnographic paradigms of discovery with the exoticizing rhetoric of 'world beat' multiculturalism" in the nineties (Fusco, 1995, 39).

While their cage performance traveled the exhibition circuit in Spain, Australia, the United States, and Latin America, various audiences misinterpreted their performance as the "real" thing, thus suggesting that such displays, in history and in the present, authenticated the myths of racial and sexual difference that these ethnographic "studies" highlighted. Despite the obvious "absurdity" of their performance of the "primitive" (i.e., Gómez-Peña's use of a nonsensical language, Fusco's improvisational dance to hip-hop music, and their elaborate costume and makeup), the fact that their "cage" existed within the museum space (thus an "educational" setting) prevented audiences from recognizing pastiche and stereotype. Worse, it numbed viewers to the horror that this cage should have evoked. As a result, Fusco's "Venus pose," in the sense of recreating Baartman's caged position on display, recreated the power of the ethnographic viewer who is invited to gaze and objectify—to actually "read" the nonwhite body on display as existing within her "natural" setting and subordinated status.

Despite the "absurdity" of this caged performance, Fusco and Gómez-Peña remind us of the complexities of cultural identity. From the moment of contact, shared exchanges between cultural groups have challenged notions of "ethnic purity" and "authenticity." Thus, their performed transition between sewing voodoo dolls (to guard against what?) and typing on a laptop computer (a hypermodern version of "voodoo" simulation?) reenact in our own times cultural attempts at syncretizing the old with the new—actions that our ancestors most likely negotiated. They thus assemble in their metaphoric cage the "debris" of the modern to reassemble the ethnographic "primitive" (Fusco, 1995, 59).

A similar act of "assemblage" occurs in the work of South African artist Willie Bester. Through the 2000 debut of his sculpture, *Sara Baartman*—on permanent exhibit at the University of Cape Town library—Bester "reassembles" the body of Baartman. Having grown up in the townships of Cape Town, where he struggled like many other black and colored South Africans against apartheid policies, Bester routinely utilized scrap metal parts, found in the rubbish heaps in these segregated neighborhoods, to create art.

Unlike Cuvier's plaster cast, designed to document anatomical evidence of inferiority, Bester instead refashions in his sculptural work a new-millennium Sara Baartman, composed out of recycled metal materials, to suggest a symbolic body and national womanhood. Such an industrialized hybrid reflects in our postmodern age of fluid identities, overconsumption, and information overload the reassemblage of our technologies, not unlike the remix of such music styles as hip-hop and techno-pop. The Baartman sculpture appears robotic, refueling the industrial wastes of class and racial inequity. Her arms hang in the same position as her plaster cast; however, the sculpture appears alert and intent in her gaze. Her mechanical breast is erect and pointed. The steel "apron" veils the very parts that science disrobed, and her behind, upright and taut, counters depictions of Baartman's caricatured and grotesque body. Out of rubbish, beauty emerges and, with it, a counter-aesthetic that affirms the black body politic.

### The Return and What Remains

Bester's sculpture functions in a global context in which late-twentieth-century and early-twenty-first-century art increasingly highlight the materials of our scientific and hypermodern information age—video installations, digital technology such as cyberspace, and industrial waste materials in mixed media. As a result, racial discourse is often eclipsed in such technological assertions that our digital information is somehow "race free." As Fusco quips, in "the age of digital technology 'we' don't need to be concerned with the violent exercise of power on bodies and territories anymore because 'we' don't have to carry all that meat and dirt along to the virtual promised land."[20]

While sardonically recreating the discourse of information society, Fusco critiques the problematic binary between futuristic representations of race transcended and historical depictions of race entrenched. Perhaps this dichotomy has contained much of the artistic narratives on race and racism during the late twentieth century within a setting from the past, most notably the nineteenth century with references to the Hottentot Venus or to African American antebellum slavery, as in the cut-out silhouette drawings of Kara Walker, which invite us to imagine racial and gender stereotyping as a "Victorian" dilemma and not a problem for our information age. This is especially troubling because our constructions of "race" and sexual racism are often seen as a problem of another time instead of as current, fluid, and rapidly changing constructs that call for our immediate response and outrage. Although some of the art pieces that I have analyzed, which reference Baartman's story, utilize such early technologies as photography, they nonetheless situate the Hottentot Venus, whose iconographic meanings have managed to materialize and mutate throughout cyberspace in various porn sites that fetishize black women, within an outdated and antiquated visual system of reading race and gender onto the body. Regardless of their assertions that the image still functions in our subconscious renderings of black female bodies, the "historical" presentation reminds us that the "Hottentot Venus" is a product of history and *not* of our present time. What is particularly suggestive about Bester's piece, on the other hand, is its manifestation of Baartman in the present juncture of our twenty-first-century lives as raced and gendered subjects.

Mara Verna, a French-Canadian artist, has contributed to Baartman's narrative through digital technology in her website performance, *www.hottentotvenus.com*, launched in 2002.[21] Instead of re-presenting Baartman's history, however, she focuses on the present-day politics surrounding the repatriation of Baartman's remains to South Africa. Verna's gesture toward cyberspace as a fitting genre to document this narrative suggests that she, like Fusco, hopes to redress assertions of digital technology as sites transcending race, especially in highlighting the oppressive roles that science and technology have played in history.

Contrary to the dream of transcending our bodies and, by extension, our race and gender, which Donna Haraway describes as the "cyborg manifesto,"[22] cyberspace manages to recreate power differentials that still leave in place the un-demarcated category of whiteness, the assumed gender of maleness, or the expected familiarity with dominant Western culture that confronts any nonwhite, nonmale, and non-Western surfer of the Internet. Or, it maintains emphasis on the computer inter*face* while conveniently invisibilizing the hands of countless U.S.

immigrant and "Third World" women laborers, such as the maquila-
dora workers on the U.S./Mexican border, who assemble our computer
chips. Although such artists as Fusco, Keith Piper, and Prema Murthy
and scholars such as Evelynn Hammonds, Lisa Nakamura, Alondra
Nelson, and Jennifer Gonzales have routinely challenged these erasures,
we nonetheless encounter discourses on information society, which still
pin futuristic hopes in the abilities of science and technology to elimi-
nate race and gender difference. Considering the damage inflicted on
someone like Baartman, it would be foolhardy to imagine science
advancing us in this arena. What is more likely is that science will
once again emerge with all its disciplinary authority to order our
natural and social events, and its public institutions—namely scientific
museums and universities—will uphold its laudatory stature.

Set against this milieu, Verna's website complicates scientific and
technological discourse through its confrontation with the *confrontation* of Baartman's history. Designed against a white backdrop, Verna
presents three virtual wooden crates, on top of which are placed small
brown boxes. Virtually evoking history as a setting that one needs to
"unpack" and repackage, this metaphor also references the packing and
shipment of Baartman's remains from the Musée de l'Homme in Paris
back to South Africa more than a century later. We might also imagine
Baartman's spirit packing all of her belongings—her jars containing her
brain and genitalia and her skeletal remains—for the trip home. The
crate on the left side of the website homepage contains seven boxes
with caricatured labels; each serves as an internal link to a page that
features an enlarged image of the caricature—all drawn by Khurran, a
Parisian street caricature artist. The cartoon image, appearing as if it
had been reassembled after having been torn, is accompanied by an
audio interview with the artist of the person caricatured, as well as a
JavaScript crawl of the written transcript on the bottom of the screen.
Such jagged caricatures remind us of their constructedness, much like
Baartman in nineteenth-century cartoons, and the multimedia format
suggests the flexible, nonlinear flow of information that Internet surfers

can select or overlook. Similarly, Baartman's history, constructed within present-day politics, is told and retold depending on the teller.

The cartoon images depict different personalities involved—directly or indirectly—with the events unfolding as the Parisian museum prepares to hand over Baartman's remains to South African delegates. South African poet, Diana Ferrus, for instance, is featured performing her poem, "Tribute to Sara Baartman," with the refrain: "I've come to take you home." Other personalities include Phillip Tobias, a professor of science, who publicly addresses the French Senate on Baartman's legacy, and Basil Coetzee, a Khoisan chief who expresses his outrage that Baartman's plaster cast will not be returned along with her physical remains. As he expresses to Verna: "They [the French scientists] created it, they could destroy it . . . they should destroy it."

Perhaps a far more revealing interview concerns the Parisian pedestrian, a bystander who shares with Verna his objectifying gaze of African people. Not fully understanding the political climate unfolding between France and South Africa, he instead proclaims that he is "not a racist" since "I'm coming back from Senegal. I've come from Mali . . . I want to see Black people [walking the streets of Paris]. I embrace Black people." Convinced that his positivist "adoration" of African people frees him from the racist label, this narrative highlights his Western ethnographic gaze and his "fascination" for racial difference as exhibited on the streets of Paris, not unlike the French fascination for Baartman's exhibition in Europe. His ultimate failure to problematize his sentiments prompts Verna (whose comments are parenthesized in the written transcript) to exclaim in disbelief that such attitudes prevail and follow in a fairly linear pattern that stems back to nineteenth-century ideology.

At the center of the main web page is another crate, upon which is placed a single box labeled "2002." It links to an image of the now infamous Musée de l'Homme, with three red dots overlaid on the image. The top dot links to a close-up of a frontispiece on the building, which reads in French: "Rare things or beautiful things here learnedly assembled to educate the eye of the beholder like never before seen all things that are in the world." With its emphasis on spectacle, the museum characterizes what Foucault has described as the "disciplinary regime" of surveillance. Because of this visual realm of power, Verna thus denies us an image of Baartman's plaster cast, presented as a link from the middle red dot. The image (Figure 3.5) depicts a digitally erased photograph—technologically altered but with enough visual markers remaining to suggest its original imagery—as the lower part of the image reveals the cast of Baartman's feet. Below the image reads the following: "Claiming that the painted full plaster body cast made by Georges Cuvier upon her death in 1816 is too fragile for transport, the

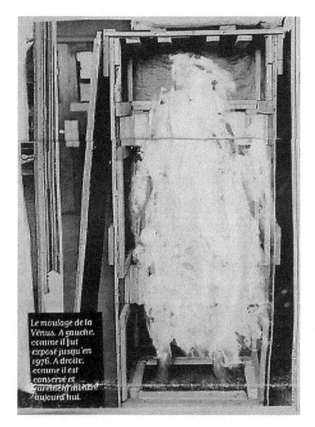

**Figure 3.5**    Mara Verna, *Plastered in Paris,* 2002. (www.hottentotvenus.com.)

Musée de l'Homme decided they will keep it, where it remains to this day, stored in a crate on the third floor." Expanding on Chief Coetzee's outrage, Verna questions why the museum is adamant in holding on to this object and what the dangers might be in preserving it for future scientific studies. Her digital erasure of the cast, then, is similar to Green's installation in that both recognize the potential for reproducing scientific inquiry and re-objectifying Baartman's body. They also call into question my own conscious use of the image in my first chapter. As I have mentioned earlier, however, I hope my inclusion reframes the visual, encouraging a reeducated eye that reads the photograph not in terms of scientific evidence, but as historical witness to the imperialist and genocidal onslaught on the black body.[23]

It is in this vein that Verna adds to her critique a reprinted article, featured on a page titled "Nothing Has Been Lost" (or "rien n'a ete perdu"), from the February 2002 issue of the French newspaper, *Libéra-tion*. The article, linked from the bottom red dot, details the ways in which the museum had lied to scholars and interested parties about its holdings—most notably Baartman's genital organs—thus calling into question the scientific institution's claims to truth and fact-findings. It also documents the political moves of other countries, such as Uruguay, to agitate for the remains of their own historical expatriates who followed in Baartman's tragic path as scientific specimens. Finally, by providing another virtual crate, to the right of the main page, which links to a variety of websites concerning the Hottentot Venus, Verna creates a gateway to alternative information and, through her bilingual report-age—English and French—encourages transnational information flow. She criticizes the spheres of science and technology and documents politically contested spaces of history and of black female bodies.

Interestingly, the writers and artists surveyed in this chapter share similar struggles with the Grinqua, descendants of the Khoisan indige-nous groups of South Africa once called "Hottentots" (Khoikhoi) and "Bushmen" (San), who began demanding the return of Baartman's remains in 1995 in South Africa's post-apartheid government. They have built an intriguing response to Baartman's history in the past decade. For both artistic and interest groups, Baartman's body is a site of healing, which can mend a break in the traumatic history of our own collective bodies. For the Khoisan, in particular, this requires confronting the painful period of cultural genocide against their people by the Dutch or Afrikaans, and the lingering legacy of this, as reflected in the apartheid and post-apartheid policies of South Africa. They recognize in Baartman's exhibition and scientific examination how her body is *their* body: scrutinized, objectified, ridiculed, spurned upon, and, ultimately, annihilated. Similarly, for black women on both sides of the Atlantic, Baartman's body is a reminder of how black female bodies are vulnerable and labeled as oversexed, primitive, savage, and beastly. Worse, her body is rendered silent and passive—a mere "object" and "specimen." Within the national movement to reclaim Baartman's remains, however, her body can once again be restored to dignity.

### Conclusion

Since Baartman has been returned to South Africa, buried along the banks of the Gamtoos River, different representative groups have reportedly been interested in conducting DNA tests on her remains to determine if she is an ancestor to different Khoisan descendants. Such claims easily blur the lines between reclamation efforts and re-objectification. The tools of science had already subjected Baartman to despicable labeling as subhuman and bestial. How would such insistence thus pose a different threat? Twenty-first-century science has shifted its focus to genetic strands and mixing. Subsequently, we must ask how this new information will be used to impact ideologies of race and gender.

These scientific shifts have led activists such as M. A. Jaimes Guerrero to label this new focus as the "New Order Eugenics."[24] Referring specifically to the Human Genome Diversity Project, which targets indigenous people for their DNA samples in efforts to preserve knowledge about "first peoples," Guerrero warns, "Given the genocidal history toward the indigenous people of the Americas, it is difficult not to discern within this project a hidden demographic agenda, especially in terms of how such data will be used in the long run" (Guerrero, 428). Current scientific projects, which have already utilized genetic technologies to alter our ecosystems (as documented by such ecofeminists as Vandana Shiva), remind us of the need for vigilance against scientific tools that double as weapons.

At the same time, we do witness the same tools used for social justice, as forensic anthropologist Clea Koff demonstrates in her 2004 memoir, *The Bone Woman*.[25] With roots in colonial genocide—as various scientific institutions and museums in Europe and its colonies amassed skulls and bones from the battlefields for further study—Koff redefines the epistemology and methodology of anthropology by recounting the ways in which forensic science similarly amasses bones to gather evidence, this time *against* perpetrators of recent genocides in Rwanda and Bosnia. This turnabout of the discipline, especially with technological advances, such as DNA evidence, complicates earlier assertions that "the master's tools will never dismantle the master's house."

In a different setting but with a similar goal of reconciling the past, DNA was used to settle the question of Thomas Jefferson's paternity of his slave Sally Hemings's children in 1998 here in the United States. Although the agency and limited choices for Hemings are rarely considered in debates of Jefferson's "guilt" or "innocence" in his involvement with a young enslaved teenager, at least for her descendants, the full truth of their heritage can be publicly acknowledged. Yet, as scholar Ann DuCille so astutely observes, "How ironic it is that the 'Sage of Monticello,' who described black women as the preferred mates of orangutans and called on genetic science to prove their inferiority, should be exposed . . . by that very same science."[26] And how ironic would it be if Baartman is actually exonerated by the very same science that debased her. May her bones, which once hung indelicately on a rack in a scientific museum, finally find rest in the earth.

4

---

# THE "BATTY" POLITIC: TOWARD
# AN AESTHETIC OF THE BLACK
# FEMALE BODY*

When tennis champion Serena Williams, days before winning the 2002 U.S. Open, appeared on the courts in a black spandex outfit, media frenzy ensued. Her body, adorned in all its "ghetto" glamour—bleached-blonde braids and tight-fitting suit, outlining the contours of her curves, among other things—managed to disrupt, literally and figuratively, the elitist game of tennis. Williams, who defended herself by stating that she wanted to wear something "comfortable" as she moved around the tennis court, was nonetheless attacked in the press for her "tackiness" and "inappropriate" display of sexuality.

This seemingly exaggerated response to Williams' choice of sportswear belies an anxiety that is best understood within a larger historical context of attitudes toward the exhibition of the black female body.

---

*An earlier version of this essay appears in *Hypatia* 18: 4 (2003): 87–105. Reprinted by permission of Indiana University Press.

This history—a history of enslavement, colonial conquest, and ethnographic exhibition—variously labeled the black female body "grotesque," "strange," "unfeminine," "lascivious," and "obscene." Such negative attitudes toward the black female body target one aspect of the body in particular: the buttocks. As I have already discussed, these responses are rooted in popular nineteenth-century exhibitions of the Hottentot Venus. Similarly, the attention to and criticisms of Serena Williams's body, alluded to previously, call unabashed attention to her generous-sized backside, highlighted by her outfit, thus inviting comments of such sexiness as "lewd" and "obscene."

As this brief discussion of Williams suggests, the meaning assigned to this aspect of the black female body has a long and complex history, a history worthy of further investigation. Subsequently, this chapter analyzes the prevalent treatment of black female bodies as grotesque figures, due to the problematic fetishism of their rear ends, and considers how an aesthetic based on a black feminist praxis might offer a different way of treating the representation of black female sexuality. In the following, I first provide an historical overview of black women's performances that resist dominant culture's problematic views of their bodies and that run counter to an ideology of black female deviance and hypersexuality. Second, I examine discourses of sexual desire for the black female backside, in contemporary mainstream popular, hip-hop, and dancehall cultures, and how this desire frames the body in terms of humor or "vulgarity," which challenges aesthetic values but also reinforces the exclusion of black women from categories of beauty. Finally, I consider the role of dance and performance in repositioning the black female body—specifically the "batty," or rear end—as a site of beauty and of resistance.

### Decolonizing the Body

The title of this chapter is an obvious pun on the phrase, "body politic," yet the choice of "batty," the Jamaican vernacular term for the rear end, requires explanation. The "batty" in Jamaican culture, and to a larger extent West Indian culture, is taken rather seriously and given certain reverence in discourses of beauty and desire. Whether in working-class Jamaican dancehall settings or in carnival scenes in Trinidad and the Caribbean diaspora of Brooklyn, Toronto, or London, black female batties are let loose and uninhibited in glorious celebrations of flesh and sexual energy. Even though such displays have historically been characterized as "riotous and disorderly,"[1] such movements of the batty, in contexts of dancehall and carnival, invite a public discourse that challenges colonial constructs of "decency" and "white supremacy." Granted, the term "batty" has since taken on a more negative association in Jamaican culture, especially in homophobic expressions that describe gay men as "batty boys"—clearly emphasizing the queer sex act. Nonetheless, "batty," specifically its use by Urban Bush Women studied in this chapter, implies for me a more liberatory and unashamed view of the body.

The batty can thus function as a site of resistance, instead of reinforcing shame and self-deprecating humor. This is captured, for example, in the Jamaican legend of Nanny of the Maroons. The legend describes a fugitive slave in the eighteenth century, Nanny, who forged her own community in the Jamaican rainforests with other fugitives known as maroons; she is credited with defeating English armies by catching their bullets in her behind and hurling back their ammunition (Sharpe, 1–43). In this myth, Nanny's batty suggests possibilities for the black female body as a site for decolonization. Nanny also serves as a powerful contrast to the enslaved black woman, whose exploited sexuality fueled the economies of slavery and colonialism through forced reproduction and labor, and to the Hottentot Venus, whose powerful batty was diminished by freak show display and scientific dissection. Nanny existed within a larger cultural context of enslaved and fugitive women's resistance in Jamaica. They often countered oppression through embodied and encoded signs of disrespect.[2] Such behavior may have extended back to the African continent where different ethnic groups of women, from regions that we recognize as Nigeria, South Africa, or Kenya, have collectively disrobed in public to protest sexist and imperialist oppression in precolonial, colonial, and neocolonial settings. Indeed, archaeologist Carmel Schrire describes instances in the nineteenth century when South African women at the Cape, in the wake of scientific inquiry into the status of their "Hottentot aprons," flashed themselves to show their ultimate contempt at such "inquiry"—an act that European colonialists reinterpreted as signs of black women's "lascivious" behavior.[3]

Similar acts of defiance emerge in narratives about nineteenth-century African American women. One such story, as told to a black interviewer in the 1937 WPA narratives of Virginia by ex-slave Fannie Berry, describes a rebellious slave called Sukie, who defiantly disrobes on the auction block.[4] Sold as a direct result of physically defending herself from her master's sexual demands, Sukie sardonically remarks and warns about the threat of her "vagina dentata"[5] when she lifts her dress and proclaims, while traders and buyers examine the teeth in her mouth, that they had also better "see if dey could fin' any teef down dere" (Perdue, Barden, & Phillips, 49). Challenging the master's gaze, Sukie reclaims her body for subjectivity and signifies on master narratives of black female sexuality through this discursive battle.

In the example of the freed black female body, Sojourner Truth, having already signified on her rights to womanhood, performs a similar act of defiance and decolonization when her gender is called into question. This is captured in one of her more subversive speech acts in which she bares her breasts to a hostile audience, who questioned her female identity, in 1858. When asked to reveal herself aside to a few white ladies at the assembly, Truth chose instead to expose her body to the entire audience, to "shame" not herself but the few audience members who suggested this action. As *The Liberator* relates in the following:

> Sojourner told them that her breasts had suckled many a white babe,
> to the exclusion of her own offspring; that some of those white babies

had grown to man's estate; that, although they had suckled her colored
breasts, they were, in her estimation, far more manly than they (her
persecutors) appeared to be; and she quietly asked them, as she disrobed her bosom, if they, too, wished to suck![6]

Truth invokes both images of the mammy/wet nurse and Jezebel/
Venus in the baring of her breasts and reinterprets both tropes by hon-
oring the function of this part of her body. Her breasts are not shameful; only those who expect her to exhibit them for biological proof of
her womanhood. Breasts themselves are publicly displayed to "prove"
the sanctity and dignity of the work many enslaved and free black
women perform in their nourishment of the future generation, rather
than prove that they merely serve as "erotic" or animalistic spectacle.
Nonetheless, one of the men in the audience sought to "animalize" her
when he comments that her breasts resembled "an old sow's teat"
(Painter, 141). As much as the legendary story of Sojourner Truth's
breast-baring incident expresses resistance, the exchange between her
exposed self and the immature white man in her audience dramatizes
the risks involved in black women disrobing themselves in public defiance, especially in a context of ubiquitous antebellum imagery of black
nudity and savagery.

Such interracial encounters subverted black women's attempts at
decolonizing the body, although we might recognize an empowering
aspect in which these women provided a discursive space for reclamation and a defiant challenge to the male/ethnographic gaze. Moreover,
these early actions provide a blueprint for black feminist resistance in
black women's performances. Nonetheless, such actions are also subject
to reinterpretation and derision; at the same time, these interactions
reveal a contention between two distinct aesthetic values: one emphasizing the language of the body and one emphasizing the form of the body.
This is a distinction that dance scholar Kariamu Welsh Asante recognizes in terms of an "African" aesthetic versus a "Western" aesthetic.[7]
While Asante realizes that she makes sweeping generalizations in these

distinctions, she nonetheless maintains that one can "speak of an African culture [or Western culture] if one is talking about commonalities and points of convergence" (Asante, 16–19). She thus draws cultural divisions in the following argument:

> Western male's obsession with [the body] . . . leads to the objectification of the female body. . . . [Function] actually becomes an inconvenience. Breast feeding, while functional, is viewed as a detriment to the aesthetic beauty of the breast. So function is devalued and form is overvalued and the dichotomy is played out on the woman's body . . . the real value of [an African woman's] beauty lies in its function. If she is perceived as dysfunctional then her beauty goes unacknowledged. (16–17)

Such differences in aesthetic values of the body have led, Asante believes, to misinterpretations of African female nudity in contexts of hypersexuality and lewdness, which shape prevalent ideas that associate civilization with dress and nudity with "eroticism, sin, and primitiveness" (16–17). She refers specifically to European explorers and missionaries who encountered women on the African continent and interpreted their bodies, when working or dancing bare-breasted, in terms of lasciviousness.

Ubiquitous images that equated black dance with sexual savagery thus threaten to undermine black women's defiant performances. In the anglophone Caribbean, such as Jamaica and Trinidad, their dances fell under constant imperialist and elitist surveillance. Set Girls in Jamaican slave carnivals, for example, danced and paraded in the most decorative high fashion—much to the amusement of colonialists and mixed-race elites—to challenge their impoverished state as enslaved women while also parodying notions of "European" ladylike behavior. Less "feminine" were the "disorderly" dances of the Jamettes in post-emancipation Trinidadian carnivals who engaged in "wild" dancing, *chantwell* singing (a precursor to male-identified calypso songs), and stick fighting. As scholar Belinda Edmondson comments, "These disreputable women, these thorns in the sides of lawmakers and the respectable classes . . . were habitually castigated as being lewd and erotic, and for allegedly instigating obscene dancing."[8]

Such "masculine" and "hypersexual" acts led black, mixed-race, and South Asian elites on the island to imagine a more feminine public persona that supported efforts toward Trinidadian national identity. Thus, as popular-culture scholar Natasha Barnes notes, carnival queen competitions emerged during the festivities in the decades before colonial independence (290). Through such feminine and decorous roles, brown or mixed-race women asserted a more respectable presence that countered the disruptive black female body.

The very essence of black women's dancing, as these examples suggest, threatened systems of class, gender, race, and nationality. Additionally, the black female body, defined as primitive and lewd, perpetuates this association between African dance and vulgarity. On the continent itself, as Asante asserts, colonialists "focused on the [bare] breasts [of African women] as if they were intrinsic icons of the African dance" (18). Not only did bare-breasted dancing meet with their disapproval but so did the movements in the dance themselves, which, as dance scholar Patience Abenaa Kwakwa describes, "exploit all the features of the female body in the total range of symbolism, natural functions and aesthetic values associated with them."[9] This symbolism refers to fertility and motherhood, which are emphasized through the movements of breasts, hips, and buttocks—body parts that were not emphasized in such European dance forms as folk jigs, ballet, or the waltz.

These distinctions between "Europe" and "Africa"—or "civility" and "primitivism"—thus compete in black women's re-presentations of the "batty." Within modern performances, African American entertainer Josephine Baker provides both a problematic re-inscription of colonial narratives and complex re-presentation of black women's dance by signifying on the "primitive." Baker's performance emerged during the period of primitivism, which opened the twentieth century, and Paris—the cultural center for this celebration of the "primitive"—allowed Baker, the Hottentot Venus reincarnate of the 1920s and 1930s, to catapult her way to success. Taking advantage of this interest in primitivism, combined with the long-existing trope of La Vénus Noire in the French popular imagination, Baker "hammed it up—pigeon-toed, knock-kneed, rump out, she wiggled, shimmied, slithered, and bumped her way to fame."[10]

This celebration of primitivism also coincided with a period of eugenics and scientific racism, spurred on by fears developed out of Europe's colonial rule and the "threat" of people of color and interracial unions. Along with exoticism and disillusionment over Europe's demise—represented by the First World War—came a fear of decadence and racial "degeneration," or a "regression" into black primitivism.[11] Josephine Baker's very body threatened Europe's "civilization," and her nudity and "wild" dancing elicited outrage in such cities as Berlin, Vienna, Prague, and Dresden, where she was denounced as a "black devil," quite similar to denouncements in America of jazz as "devil music."[12]

Baker expressed irreverence to those whose stiffness and prudery caused offense against her "vulgar" body—made so, apparently, through her emphasis in dance of her rear end. She declared, "The rear end exists. I see no reason to be ashamed of it. It's true that there are rear ends so stupid, so pretentious, so insignificant that they're good only for sitting on" (Rose, 1989, 24). Her statement mockingly reveals an attempt to redefine the erotic power and aesthetic value of black female derrières—long associated with primitivism, lewdness, and sexual pathology. Underlying her critique also is a rejection of the white dismissal of the beauty of the rear end and a reference to Europeans' supposed lack of endowment in that area. To be sure, Baker's performances emphasized this anatomical part as she played to and mocked her era's interests in jazz, black sexuality, and African "savage" dance; however, she revises an aesthetic of the body, which emphasizes the function and movements of her rear end, instead of its form, because her behind was good for more than "sitting on" it.

Signifying on the image of Black/Hottentot Venus, Baker embodied many of the stereotypes attributed to Baartman, particularly her energizing of the behind as more than spectacle. Through her *danse sauvage*, she recreated popular stereotypes of the black female savage, femme fatale, and wild animal but altered her performance of these stock types to mock European concepts of black female beauty and sexuality. In so doing, she parodied the West's obsession with the black female rear end, as represented by the earlier Hottentot Venus shows, and redefined it not just as an object and fetish but as an energized aspect of her sexuality.

Although her biographer, Phyllis Rose, argues that such fame derived from Baker's ability to redirect "the erotic gaze of a nation [as it] moved downward" toward the rear end, we may hardly refer to this sexual focus as "a new region for desire" (Rose, 1989, 24). Certainly, her Parisian audience—only a century earlier—had long noticed this particular region of the black female body. Indeed, the white gaze on black female "steatopygia" had made such bodies synonymous with sex. If anything, Baker's success indicates a significant shift in attitude toward the primitive versus the civilized and a new appreciation for things "wild" and "libidinous"—qualities still associated with "exotic" black bodies but viewed this time with admiration while still maintaining an air of mockery.

Such wild abandon, as whites could only suppose that black bodies can do this better than theirs, characterizes all that is associated with this celebration of the exotic primitive. Yet, Baker cannot quite escape the controlling gazes of her white audience. This is well exemplified through her interaction with artist Paul Colin, who studied her body in the nude for research on the "authentic" black body, but nonetheless reduced Baker's body to pure stereotype in his posters. That his sketch and design of her banana skirt remains a popular icon of Baker in our cultural memory reminds us of the power of stereotype and sexist and racist representations. This is also powerfully dramatized in the 2003 francophone animation feature *Triplets of Belleville*, in which a caricatured Baker in her banana skirt emerges onto a stage to delight her audience with one of her *danses sauvage*, thus exciting the male spectators who literally revert back to their "ape" origins and raid her bananas. Most telling in this portrayal is the decidedly prominent feature Baker's behind receives in an animation that visually parodies the breasts and buttocks of women in general.

As an icon, Baker played to fantasies of racial and sexual difference by performing the black savage, thus poking fun at white hegemonic discourses of beauty. Perhaps this self-conscious performance on her part helped make her a popular entertainer for black audiences as well as white, especially for African Americans.[13] Such audiences may have recognized Baker's signifying of black sexuality and thought it was a good joke, not to mention her overall ability in achieving fame and fortune. Not all audiences delighted in her performances, however, as evidenced by a protest in 1931, when Baker was crowned Queen of the Colonial Exposition. Protestors reminded organizers that Baker was neither French nor from the French colonies.[14] Baker's portrayal of Black Venus thoroughly erased her African American identity as her stage and film portrayals of African (North and sub-Saharan) and Antillean characters aligned her with blackness, Africanness, and Caribbean-ness.

More recent scholarship in African American and Diasporic Studies makes efforts to reclaim Baker as a modern artist, borrowing elements from African-based cultures to inform her art, in much the same way as such European and white American artists as Picasso and Martha Graham, respectively. Within a black feminist arts tradition, such scholars as Anthea Kraut align Baker with other dancers/choreographers and ethnographers, such as Katherine Dunham and Zora Neale Hurston.[15] As Kraut argues:

> [P]rimitivism's hegemonic grip on European and American spectators often overshadowed the nuances of a Black Atlantic. What is less certain is whether primitivism and the free associations between African American vernacular dance and Africa that it encouraged unwittingly laid the foundations for diasporic formulations. (Kraut, 450)

Such formulations are not always free from power differentials, as enacted through the ethnographic gaze that both Hurston and Dunham utilized when conducting their anthropological studies of Haiti in particular. Nonetheless, they have given us a black feminist consciousness that can bridge the Black Atlantic divides as they gesture toward possibilities for decolonization of black women's expressions in the Americas and on the African continent.

### Race, Gender, and Aesthetics

Black women performers often find it difficult to avoid the weight of racial difference, cemented in Baker's performances and challenged in the work of such dancers as African American Katherine Dunham and Trinidadian Pearl Primus.[16] Although both Dunham and Primus articulate, through their dancing bodies, an African-based aesthetic that honors fluid movements of the hips, they often find themselves defending against claims of "sexiness" in their dances, a defense that art historians Deborah Willis and Carla Williams would characterize as existing within representations of "noble" black female bodies, designed to refute the more common stereotypes of heightened sensuality (Willis & Williams, 88). Such defenses thus contribute to the difficulties in articulating fully rounded discourses on black women's sexual expression. As a result, primitivist images linger in contemporary visual culture.

Similar to Baker's performance of primitivism, the androgynous Jamaican provocateur/entertainer Grace Jones, in the 1970s and 1980s, played to and parodied such imagery. One of her more outrageous performances included appearing as an "animal in a cage," as designed in a performance art by her French ex-husband artist, Jean-Paul Goude. Whereas Fusco's cage performance, discussed in the previous chapter, served to reenact history by visibly reminding us of the troubled representation of cultural difference and ethnographic exhibition, Jones's "cage" (ungrounded in historical consciousness) created a sense of extreme pastiche in its stereotypical links between black female bodies and bestiality. This time, the "animal" that Grace represents is that of a tiger, as Goude collaborates with Jones in a 1976 stage performance in which Jones verbally combats with the roars of an actual caged tiger. For dramatic effect during such a "performance," the lights go off, and the audience is only able to hear a violent roaring of two "tigers" in battle. When the lights are on again, the tiger has disappeared, and Jones is in its place chewing on a piece of meat. Goude would later represent this performance in a publicity photograph for the show, which depicts a caged and nude Grace Jones with a fierce facial expression.[17]

Presenting Jones as a powerful tiger may at times seem subversive enough, were it not for that long tradition of visually representing black people as animals. At the same time, black female sexuality is rendered with the power and allure of a tiger, perhaps alluding to what art critic Miriam Kershaw calls the "power iconography [of tigers and leopards] among the royalty in certain parts of Africa prior to and during European trade and colonialism" (21). Nonetheless, whatever subversions are at play in the image, the representation is severely undermined. The cage, pieces of red meat in it, along with Jones's sleek, glistening black nude body, and a sign that reads "Do Not Feed the Animal" all add to this reinforced stereotype of black female animalism. This is further evidenced by Goude's own admission of exoticizing racial "Others" from an early age in his 1981 *Jungle Fever*. Claiming that "Indians" had fascinated him before he discovered "Blacks," he recounts a memory of a carnival in France where he first encountered the black Other. He describes the following incident, which resembles the carnival scene in Morrison's *Beloved* (1987):

> I must tell you about the Foire du Trone. Every year all the carnivals of France move up to Paris. . . . This is where I saw the fire-eaters. They were chained inside a cage. I remember there were four or five black wild men. But there was one who was my favorite—one with a bone in his nose. He would hold the bars and shake them like a gorilla. There

was a rattling of chains and the savage would spit out enormous flames
over our heads. . . . I think I was six when my father told me that these
were not real savages. He said they were white people painted black.
Boy, was I disappointed! (Goude, 4)

This narrative in Goude's introduction ends with a confrontation between himself and his father, who admonishes him for persist-
ing in fantasy and who demands that he "grow up" and face "reality";
however, Goude's art allows him to imagine the reality of stereotype
and racially and sexually constructed differences. Through a performance of racially constructed fantasies, Goude utilizes the black female
body in his art—via Grace Jones—to recreate racial and sexual myths,
in much the same way that the Foire du Trone recreates theirs. Whether
or not the encounter with the "wild savage" at the carnival ever occurred
for Goude, or if the narrative attempts irony in its description of dominant culture's fantasy of the "jungle," his "black woman in a cage," a la
Hottentot Venus, reinforces black women's sexual savagery. What is just
as significant is the way in which black female performance corroborates
this representation. Perhaps it will take much more than white masculinist artistic vision—and black female performative collusion—to free
the black female body from this representation. Such limited visions,
divorced from political consciousness of race and gender issues, would
only perpetuate familiar stereotypes.

Goude's *Jungle Fever* further reveals his fascination and desire for
black female derrières—likening them, in one instance, to a "race-
horse." Goude refers specifically to his creation of a doll, recast from a
life-size replica of an African American fashion model, Toukie Smith,
who is given a horse's behind in the miniature figure—an idealized
"girl horse" of Goude's primitivist desires (Goude, 41). His photographs often refashion such bodies through doctored images that
attempt to "improve on a masterpiece" (Goude, 40). Such an
"improvement" renders the black female backside highly exaggerated,
grotesque, and comical, as in the 1976 example, *Carolina*. In this

image, Goude portrays the rear end as a virtual table, on which a champagne glass is balanced as it fills with the beverage, gushing forth from a bottle that our nude model holds in her hands. This subject wears an "exotic" hairstyle and "smiles" for the camera in the pose of a "happy savage pleased to serve," which suggests her complicity in having her body depicted as a literal object, a "primitive" vision to provide pornographic pleasure and intoxication presumably for a white male spectator.

Goude functions in a French culture that has a long tradition of celebrating black female sensuality, as popularly portrayed by Josephine Baker. American culture, on the other hand, does not have a similar celebration of black femininity. The more popular icon of black femininity in this context, the mammy, is often interpreted as devoid of sexuality. This may point to certain stereotypes of Americans seeming more "prudish" or "puritanical" while the French are "sexy," thus resulting in their particular distinctions between celebrated black womanhood. Goude, however, is playful and comical in his treatment of black female bodies. This comical representation, mimicking similar "humor" in depictions of the Hottentot Venus, renders black female sexuality as too deviant, too bizarre to take seriously.

Subsequently, black female bodies rarely receive serious aesthetic treatment in visual culture. With the focus on their infamous behinds, black women's bodies are typically ridiculed, not revered. Because of this, it is worth noting that black male bodies are less stigmatized by the label of "deviant sexuality." The locus for black male deviance is presumed to lie not in the anatomy, but instead in black male libidos. Recall that the body of the Hottentot Venus, while serving as a symbol for the grotesque, was thought more so by the desire for her body held by her "fellow countrymen." Even then—in the nineteenth century as now—this difference between black and white male sexual desires is only one of degree instead of inherent racial difference.

This would suggest that white men are considered "deviant" insofar as they desire black women or white women with large posteriors, who themselves were regarded as "prostitutes" in the late nineteenth century if they exhibited this feature (Gilman, 1985, 94–101). Thus, white men and women both, when labeled "deviant," were paralleled with "black" sexuality. Such associations, however, did not prevent middle-class white women of the period from donning bustles. This appropriation of a "big behind"—a sign of grotesquerie, later connoting a sign of luxurious beauty in the bustle—illustrates the complexities of white responses to racial and sexual difference, which elicit both repulsion and desire.

In light of this iconographic history of deviant black sexuality, we find contemporary black male performance corroborating myths of black male hypersexual desire, especially desire for rear ends, in the music of hip-hop. SirMixaLot's controversial 1992 rap, "Baby Got Back," frames black male desire as more base and raw than white male desire. He declares that he "likes big butts" yet challenges that "even white boys have to shout," a dichotomous construction in which black men are less inhibited in their sexual expression while white men, who—in stereotypical fashion, because they are too wired, stiff, and mechanical to express their "base" desires—require the raw and hypersexual black female body to enable them to "shout." The music video provides humorous reenactment of this desire, in which an uptight white-collar, white male struggles to make this "shout," as he pulls on his tie when confronted with the black female backside. Thus, as a response to dominant culture's view of sexual deviance, SirMixaLot challenges that black male libidos are not necessarily "more deviant" than white male libidos, only "less pretentious" and more connected to "real" masculinity.

This so-called "appreciation" for black women's bodies does not necessarily challenge ideas of grotesque and deviant black female sexuality. Interestingly, both the song and video uphold and celebrate the black body precisely because it differs from the standard models of beauty in white culture. The white female body, a "legitimate" emblem of beauty in white dominant culture, is exposed by SirMixaLot for its inauthentic beauty, a product of a technical world that disables white men, making it impossible for them to "shout." SirMixaLot castigates the beautiful white body as a "silicone toy," an unreal and unnatural Barbie doll. In contrast, the black female body, with its well-proportioned "back," serves as the "real" thing, unpretentious and "in the flesh."

On the one hand, this rap performance could be viewed as subversive in its critique of white beauty standards; on the other hand, it reinforces the binary opposition between whiteness and blackness, while reducing black women to one essential body part. Black women are still viewed in the music lyrics and video as inherently "more sexual" than their "envious" and "inhibited" white female counterparts, and black men, through their desire for rear ends, are stereotyped as "more real" and more expressive of their libidos than their white male counterparts. Significantly, although the black male sexual expression of hip-hop made it more acceptable for members of the dominant white culture to desire black women openly, it left the "hypersexual" and comical nature of this representation unchallenged. The emphasis on the black female rear end—with its historic and cultural tropes of rawness, lasciviousness, and "nastiness"—led, as captured in 2 Live Crew's 1989 album cover, *As Nasty as They Wanna Be*, to charges of "obscenity" in the mainstream media.

That the popular single from this album, "Me So Horny," is taken from an infamous line spoken by a cough-ridden Vietnamese sex worker in Stanley Kubrick's 1987 *Full Metal Jacket*, in which the first shot of this character is of her derrière, further frames this reading of black and nonwhite female bodies within a context of disease, danger, lewdness, hypersexuality, and contamination. Indeed, the controversy over the obscenity of 2 Live Crew's performances, as covered in the North American media, often centered on the backsides of black women performers gyrating in thong bikinis onstage. Yet, Luke, lead M.C. of the group, and his 2 Live Crew helped usher in the pornographic practice of overexposing black female rear ends in music videos, concerts, and spring break crowds in the 1990s. With mainstream culture's acceptance of hip-hop culture, black male rappers and other music artists—via MTV and BET's music videos—have redirected America's gaze onto the butt in a similar but different way than Josephine Baker did in 1920s Paris. Thus, if MTV's early 1980s music videos objectified white women's "legs" and those who "know how to use them,"[18] SirMixaLot and his successors focused on black women's behinds.

Emerging from this cultural milieu of hip-hop, the body of performer Jennifer Lopez offered a slightly different take on rear-end aesthetics. Her Latina body, already colored as "exotic" in a so-called changing American racial landscape,[19] bridges the desires of black and white men, both for whom she can serve as the "racial Other." More important, Lopez's derrière does not carry the burden of Baartman's legacy. Whereas Baartman and most other black women's rear ends tend to be viewed in terms of pathological "steatopygia," Lopez can instead function in dominant culture as "callipygous," or having a beautiful backside. Her appearance as "the galaxy's most beautiful woman" on the cover of the September 2001 issue of *Stuff for Men*, while looking over her shoulder in the style of Venus Kallipygos, confirms this point.

Interestingly, it was hip-hop culture, which routinely documents black and Latino male desire for derrières, that first called attention to Lopez's body. Dominant culture later came to celebrate Lopez's behind as part of a recognition of "exotic" and "hot" Latinas, women perceived as "more sexual" than white women but "less obscene" than black women. In this way, Lopez's body avoids the specific racial stigma that clings to black women's bodies. Despite the widespread appreciation of her endowed anatomy, Lopez, it is worth noting, has slimmed down considerably, at the height of her career, to conform to white beauty standards.

Whether this fetishism of Lopez's rear end has transformed anything significant in the beauty paradigm of American culture, since the discourse is done so in seemingly favorable tones, what has not changed is the racism and sexism underlying her popularity. Above all, her objectification parallels similar sexual objectification efforts in hip-hop culture. Subsequently, prevalent images of black and brown beauty offer little means for radical subjectivity and liberation. With regard to the popular portrayals of black and Latina women in hip-hop music videos—more regularly infusing the rhythms of Jamaican dance-hall music—we now witness what hip-hop scholar Imani Perry has labeled the "signal of cultural destruction" of African diasporic dance. As she argues:

> Black . . . dance is 'discursive' (in that sexuality is usually combined with humor and the body is used to converse with other moving bodies). The women who appear in these videos are usually dancing in a two-dimensional fashion, a derivative but unintellectual version of black dance, more reminiscent of symbols of pornographic male sexual fantasy than of the ritual, conversational, and sexual traditions of black dance. Despite all the gyrations of the video models, their uninterested [dance moves fail to elicit] . . . polyrhythmic rear end movement, innuendo, and sexual bravado.[20]

Here, Perry rightly observes the flattened, commodified image of black women's dance—no longer existing to signify on black women's beauty and sexuality or to engage in discursive challenges of the male/ethnographic gaze or even of the dance floor space. Such expressive and vibrant performances are lost in the hubris of mainstream, hegemonic depictions of "black culture" mass marketed to a global audience.

Isaac Julien's 1994 documentary, *The Darker Side of Black*, however, provides a counter-narrative on dancehall reggae and hip-hop when it depicts in one segment the raucous and aggressive moves of "the body vulgar"[21] with working-class black Jamaican dancehall performers. Any viewer of this film might be taken aback by the women's dance movements, or what ragga DJ Lady Saw describes as "dirty reality," despite having been weaned on a diet of pornographic music videos. The difference between the dancehall performers of the film and music video models is simply one in which the Jamaican dancers refused a comforting voyeuristic gaze.

Similarly, women rappers in hip-hop have resisted this dominant gaze. Using the example of Salt-n-Pepa, from the late eighties, hip-hop feminist scholar, Tricia Rose, observes of their 1989 music video, *Shake Your Thang*, that it "speaks to black women, calls for open, public displays of female expression, assumes a community-based support for their freedom, and focuses directly on the sexual desirability and beauty of black women's bodies."[22] Nevertheless, the proliferation of black women's behinds in hip-hop music videos, movies, even porn videos and websites, has become so widespread that any act of subversion on the part of hip-hop performers, following in the wake of Salt-n-Pepa, is severely undermined, not unlike the actions of the eighteenth- and nineteenth-century black women discussed earlier.

We now witness, not the decolonization of the black female body, but its commodification and appropriation, as evidenced in the performances of such contemporary rappers as Lil' Kim and Foxy Brown—the latter figure alluding, with no historical irony, to an earlier blaxploitation image of Black Venus in the seventies, courtesy of actress Pam Grier. While some might view their highly sexualized performances as discursive responses to the prevalent misogyny in the genre of hip-hop and a rewriting of the black body vulgar—not unlike Nanny and Sukie's "vulgar" responses to their enslavers—we must question the possibilities and the limits in locating liberation discourse within familiar tropes of black female hypersexuality. Indeed, when hip-hop and spoken-word artist Sarah Jones attempts reclamation of black female sexuality through her poem, "Your Revolution," which signifies on poet Gil Scott-Heron's "Your Revolution Will not Be Televised," she received a fine from the FCC for obscenity.[23] As she rhymes, "The real revolution ain't about bootie size/the Versaces you buys/or the Lexus you drives," Jones targets both the misogyny in male hip-hop lyrics, with their fetishistic treatment of the rear end, and the commodified performer, alluding to Lil' Kim, who was once approached by Versace, the elite clothing company, to appear in their ads since she had already "dropped" their brand name in her lyrics. Yet, Jones's censorship by

the FCC indicates that struggles for black female sexual agency and articulations of this subjectivity become mired in the same pornographic
discourse.

The performances of Lil' Kim and Foxy Brown encompass what
Gwendolyn Pough describes as conflicting sexual images that "men
rappers rapped about. . .with no real constructive conversations going
on about sex, Black female identity, and the shaping of public gendered
subjects outside of the academy."[24] However, the black female pop stars
following in their wake—including Trinidadian rapper Nicki Minaj, Barbadian singer Rihanna, and African American singer Beyoncé (analyzed
further in Chapter 6)—would base their own images of black womanhood on their pop, R&B, and hip-hop predecessors while also reframing
their sexual expressions through a feminist lens. This new generation of
performers has benefitted from a feminist discourse that has traveled
outside the academy, making its way to the Internet.

We see this when Nicki Minaj literally attacks the "male gaze" in her
music video, "Looking-Ass Nigga" from 2014, even as she plays to this
gaze while showing off her curves, or when Beyoncé samples Nigerian
author Chimamanda Ngozi Adichie's "We Should All Be Feminists"
TED Talk on YouTube for her 2013 song "Flawless" while also mimicking a stripper-pole-dance just before standing in front of a neon-lit
FEMINIST sign at the 2014 MTV Video Music Awards show. This popularization of a feminist speech via pop music further led to the creation
of a tee-shirt logo, "We Should All Be Feminists," which Rihanna then
wore in promotion of a political idea and sales that would benefit her
different charities.[25] Indeed, Beyoncé's sister and music artist Solange
Knowles revealed how important it was for her, as a non-college graduate, to learn black feminist theory on the blogs Crunk Feminist Collective and Black Women's Blueprint, which subsequently led to her own
feminist consciousness-raising.[26]

It is not just that the latest crop of pop stars is exposed to feminist
discourse, but they also now utilize that language to challenge as well as
embrace the pornographic through a discourse of sexual empowerment.
To that end, transnational fusions often insert their way into the music

and performances of Beyoncé and Rihanna, such as their incorporation of the Jamaican dancehall "dutty wine," which asserts an aggressive
"batty" politic that simultaneously disrupts both national and respectable borders: from Beyoncé's Super Bowl performance in 2013 and her
subsequent concerts to Rihanna's 2016 "Work" music video with pop
star Drake. Such performances reposition their bodies beyond mere sexual objectification, thereby inviting discourses on the complex meanings of sexual agency.

In the next section, I explore possibilities for black feminist performance as a subversive site for resistance and aesthetic reclamations.
Because of perceived racial and sexual difference, which, as we have seen,
has historical and cultural associations with grotesque and deviant sexuality, black women, who have attempted an aesthetic of the body, still
struggle to articulate an affirming discourse of black female beauty. This
struggle involves not only recovering the "un-mirrored" body but also
reclaiming agency and subjectivity.

### *The "Batty" as Site of Resistance*

Part of the struggle in redefining historic images requires black women
to resist the defensive "policing" of each other's bodies and sexualities.
Among North American black women, this strategy perhaps dates back
to the era of "club women" during the late nineteenth and early twentieth centuries, who often defended themselves from the prevalent depictions of lascivious black female sexuality in the dominant culture by
adhering to rigorous, highly moral values. Similar steps were also taken
among black middle-class and religious working poor women in the
Caribbean, who struggled in both nineteenth-century post-emancipation and twentieth-century colonial independence periods to affirm a
respectable black national identity. Such values often pitted bourgeois
and church-going black women against their working-class counterparts. One way that black middle-class women transformed their bodies within the confines of respectability (apart from hair straightening

and skin lightening) was in the "quieting," rigid presentation of their "too large" behinds, which needed to be tucked in and made as invisible as possible. When black women failed to adhere to this behavior, and indeed called deliberate attention to this part of their anatomy, they were seen as encouraging dominant culture's labeling of their bodies as deviant and grotesque.

These tensions have been dramatized in certain African American and Caribbean films. In 1997, the popular African American film *Soul Food*, directed by George Tillman Jr., celebrated Southern roots maintained in a Northern city by "Big Mama," the black matriarch of a contentious family, whose luscious meals, inspiring the movie title, unite everyone at her dinner table. However, if Mama (or Mammy, as the case may be) is a force of black solidarity and familial unity, then her counterpart—Jezebel or Black Venus—is the queen of discord. This is made evident in an early scene in which a rather "steatopygic" black vixen threatens the recent union of bride and groom at a wedding reception. Her "vulgar" gyrations, while dancing with the groom, prompt the women of the family to action as they warn the bride of the immediate danger imposed by this sexualized dancer. In a film celebrating black motherhood, the wholesome intervention of Big Mama saves the day. She simply replaces the vixen on the dance floor as she cuts in to dance with her son-in-law.

Similarly, in a more complex film, Kasi Lemmons' *Eve's Bayou*, which debuted shortly after *Soul Food*, the threat of the black vixen reemerges—again in the midst of a family-oriented setting, such as the party thrown by the Batistes, a prominent black Creole middle-class family in Louisiana. Within this context, the butt-enhancing dance of the adulterous Matty Mereaux foreshadows the destructive force that she eventually unleashes on the Batistes as we later learn of her illicit affair with Louis, the Batiste patriarch. Interestingly, at the same party, Cisely, the older sister of our titular character, sashays before her father in obvious flirtation and competition with the "other woman" for his affections. This dance seems to mark her for later molestation at the hands of her father.

Unfortunately, despite efforts to reclaim African American cinematic subjectivity and to film black vernacular dance, the presentation of sensual dancing in these films reinforces both dominant and black bourgeois cultures' condemnation of black female bodies and their sensual expressions. In the Jamaican film, *Dancehall Queen*, also debuting in 1997 and directed by Rick Elgood and Don Letts, there is more of an effort to affirm the working-class aesthetic of the "batty" in dancehall culture, as it follows the story of Marcia, a street vendor who enters a dance contest with the promise of class mobility. Our protagonist embraces the sensual dances that emphasize rear-end movements, which eventually propel her to victory as she topples the reigning dancehall queen; however, while the film celebrates such "saucy" and daring moves, it nonetheless casts Marcia as morally suspect when she willingly "prostitutes" her daughter to a family member, who is in a position to pay for her children's education. We are expected to share her daughter's outrage when, in demanding of her mother a reason why she herself did not succumb to these sexual demands, Marcia flippantly replies, "It's you him want." Marcia's dance moves thus mirror, it seems, her disreputable choices. As a result, these films fail to move us pointedly toward a black aesthetic that affirms women's physicality, sensuality, and overall sense of character.

Such a move requires us to consider the transformative possibilities of art versus popular culture. The black diasporic and New York City–based dance troupe, Urban Bush Women, is one contemporary example that can best move us forward in a path of resistance. Perhaps drawing significance from black women's embodied histories, the troupe provides an important discourse on the "batty" that attempts an aesthetic of the black female body, as well as establishes this part of the anatomy as a site of resistance, through the 1995 dance piece *Batty Moves*. Choreographed by the group's founder, Jawole Willa Jo Zollar, this performance captures the sensibilities of a ballet and modern dance–trained performer who "got tired of tucking and holding and apologizing" for the movements of her buttocks in these Western-based dance forms. As such, the performance constantly fluctuates between the gestures of ballet—such as pliés and arabesques, which require the strict, rigid, and disciplined nonmovement of the derrière—and the butt-accentuated moves in Afro-based and Caribbean dances.

*Batty Moves* begins with a line of dancers, dressed in form-fitting leotards, positioning their backs to the audience. As a result, they find themselves in the position of "object," in the stance of a Hottentot Venus on exhibit; however, this historical body undergoes transformation as each dancer moves and poses in ways that suggest that their batties will no longer function as fetishes but as expressive extensions of their mobile, energetic bodies. Indeed, this point of transformation occurs when one dancer, reflecting on this performance, decided, upon hearing an audience member "gasp" at the site of her body: "I'm going to shove it in your face, so you can just take it!"[27]

The resolve of this dancer reflects her need to resist disapproval of her rear end—to, in fact, "shove it" all the more as a defiant gesture that dares to claim the black female batty as visible, pronounced, sexy, and beautiful. This resistance is not just an individual protest. Instead, she expresses defiance at a historical tradition that degrades black women's bodies. One by one, each dancer performs and defines for herself, through spoken-word language and dance moves, the body beautiful, finally culminating in a group dance—positioning their backs toward the audience for the entire performance—that reclaims the powers of the batty in communal affirmation and confrontation of dominant culture. Borrowing Jamaican slang for the title of this piece, Urban Bush Women not only signify on the sexual impulses of black women's rear-end shaking dances in Jamaican dancehall settings, but they also create an African diasporic discourse in which black women, across the Atlantic divides, can begin a cultural exchange in which their behinds figure prominently in arenas of hip-hop, reggae, soca, and calypso. Although these male-centered music forms objectify black women's backsides, often in extreme, misogynistic language, black women, through their dance moves, negotiate dance spaces to assert their sensuality. In response to Urban Bush Women's performance of *Batty Moves*, dance critic Eva Yaa Asantewaa notes, "They took back, from men on the street and society in general, the power to name, direct, praise, or critique their buttocks."[28]

Urban Bush Women may have found inspiration from the earlier example of poet and dancer Ntozake Shange, who successfully staged her celebrated choreopoem, *For Colored Girls Who Have Considered Suicide/When the Rainbow Is Enuf*, on Broadway in 1976. As Shange describes, this performance combined poetry and dance in an effort to learn "the wealth of our bodies, if we worked, if we opened up, if we made the dance our own."[29] She further contends that:

> With the acceptance of the ethnicity of my thighs & backside, came a
> clearer understanding of my voice as a woman & as a poet. The free-
> dom to move in space, to demand of my own sweat a perfection that
> could continually be approached, though never known, waz poem to
> me, my body & mind ellipsing, probably for the first time in my life. . . .
> Everything African, everything halfway colloquial, a grimace, a strut,
> an arched back over a yawn, waz mine. I moved what waz my uncon-
> scious knowledge of being in a colored woman's body to my known
> everydayness. (xi)

Significantly, in pursuing dance through poetry, Shange follows the first poem, which beseeches the audience to "sing a black girl's song," with both a lullaby and ring game. As our performers dance to the chorus of "Mama's little baby likes shortnin bread," they immediately transition into the ring game/dance of "Little Sally Walker." Both girlhood rhymes highlight the unselfconscious bodily pleasures and desires of young black girls, the communal affirmation that they promote, and the rootedness in black female cultural identity. They also serve as precursors to the sensuality and eventual pain of sexual assault and rejection that unfold in the choreopoem's narrative.

A far more unique presentation of the ring game resides in Julie Dash's 1992 *Daughters of the Dust*,[30] a film discussed in greater detail in the next chapter. Dash juxtaposes the young girls' play on a beach with a scene in which the family matriarch, Nana, implores her great-grandson, Eli, to "call on those old Africans . . . they come to you when you least expect 'em." The same old souls "unexpectedly" descend onto the ring game as the young women's vernacular dance opens itself to spirit possession. In that instant, the leisurely, youthful game of sashaying and hip shaking transforms into sacred space, a fluidity recognized in most African-based cultures. Moreover, this added spiritual component elevates black women's dance to a higher plane of aesthetic appreciation.

### *Conclusion*

Across the diaspora, black women often begin in girlhood to define their sensuality through their backsides. Whether in the African American ring game, "Little Sally Walker," where young girls are encouraged to "shake it to the east, shake it to the west," or in the similar Afro-Caribbean "Brown Girl in the Ring," who is urged to "show me your motion," these circles of black girls provide a female-centered space for affirmation and pleasure in their bodies, even as these scripts prepare them later for the male gaze. As adult women, this display becomes not only more sexualized but racialized as well, as black women find their bodies subject to misinterpretation and mislabeling by the dominant culture. Not only that, but these bodies no longer respond to self-motivated desires and expressions but to the requests of others—whether to black male desires in such hip-hop shouts as "shake what your mama gave ya" and such soca-calypso demands as "wine yuh waist," or to other black women's policing call to "tuck it in."

We may need to recreate that circle of women—first enacted in childhood—who reaffirm that our bodies are fine, normal, capable, and beautiful. We may also need to enlarge that circle to include men, who can challenge their own objectifying gazes, and nonblacks, who can overcome the equation of blackness with deviance. Most of all, black women, who have been un-mirrored for so long, must confront the prevailing imagery of grotesque derrières and black female hypersexuality to distinguish the myths and lies from our own truths and the ways we wish to represent ourselves. Only then will we be able to follow the lead of Serena Williams, proudly displaying our behinds while continuing our winning streak.

---

# MIRROR, MIRROR: FRAMING THE BLACK FEMALE BODY FOR STILL AND MOTION PICTURES

Would the mirror Black women hold up to themselves and to each other provide access to the alternative sexual universe within the metaphorical black hole?

**Evelynn Hammonds**

In just seconds, the flash of Janet Jackson's breast at the Super Bowl halftime show in February of 2004—exposed under a glistening black "dominatrix" outfit by the roving hands of music sensation Justin Timberlake—propelled her into Internet history. What could easily be described as a deliberately choreographed striptease, or a terribly humiliating gaffe to teach us of the dangers of performing live before millions of football stadium spectators and television viewers, we are nonetheless reminded of the effect of black nudity on the national psyche. While news coverage and Internet downloads circulated both the still and motion pictures of Janet's revealed body, public moral outrage at this "indecent exposure" disguised the public obsession with black female bodies. According to CNet News at the time, Janet's half-time performance became the most searched for event on the Internet since the September 11 tragedy and the most downloaded video offered by TiVo, a site that allows viewers to rewind and replay moving images.[1]

That Janet's body—and not Justin's undressing of her body—would take the brunt of this scandal also reminds us of the difficulty in women's self-representation, as well as the racial undercurrents that shape the public condemnation and fascination for her duplicated image. How, for instance, would the public discourse differ had the performance featured celebrated blonde singer Britney Spears and the black rapper 50 Cent? Would such terms as "disgusting," "shocking," and "inappropriate for a family show" (as if the Super Bowl's violent sporting event were ever about good family values) circulate around Britney's exposed body, or would these terms instead transfer onto the act of a black man unveiling her white flesh? Moreover, why was Janet immediately accused of performing a "publicity stunt" when one could easily freeze-frame her expression after the "wardrobe malfunction"[2] to observe her genuine shock at seeing her outfit come undone? Needless to say, of the countless images of Janet's body that traveled across cyberspace—including close-ups of her metal jewelry–enhanced nipple and animated images of the "moment"—most failed to capture a close-up of the dismay shown on her face.

I raise the spectacle of Janet Jackson in a chapter on framing the black female body for photographic imagery because the still and motion pictures of her body represent something larger than what the performer might have intended. Whether we believe Janet was deliberate in having her body exposed, or that her exposure was accidental, we should observe that the photographic representation transcended beyond her control of the self-image. To reiterate Hammonds's question in the epigraph opening this chapter, can a black woman hold up a mirror that reveals an alternative image of herself, free from the iconographic history in dominant culture that cast black female bodies as illicit, hypersexed, primitive, and obscene?

Perhaps this need for "mirroring" has led to confrontations with a literal mirror in much of black women's photography and film. We may consider, for example, Carrie Mae Weems' 1987 satirical photo-text, "Mirror, Mirror" (Figure 5.1), from her *Ain't Jokin'* series (1987–88). In this piece, a white spectral woman appears in a mirror and returns the gaze of a black woman. This specter responds to the question, "Who's the finest of them all?" with "Snow White, you black bitch, and don't you forget it!" The mirror image invoked is one of mistaken identity, and the ego engages in struggle for visual self-representation that is divorced from white aesthetics, as represented by "Snow White," the fairy tale in which those of us raised in white dominant culture learn of the hegemonic beauty of whiteness. The irony, of course, is that this "joke" of

LOOKING INTO THE MIRROR, THE BLACK WOMAN ASKED,
"MIRROR, MIRROR ON THE WALL, WHO'S THE FINEST OF THEM ALL?"
THE MIRROR SAYS, "SNOW WHITE, YOU BLACK BITCH,
AND DON'T YOU FORGET IT!!!"

**Figure 5.1** Carrie Mae Weems, "Mirror, Mirror," 1987–88. Silver gelatin print. © Carrie Mae Weems. Courtesy of the artist and Jack Shainman Gallery, New York.

seeking one's image in the mirror, only to find it un-mirrored by the dominant Other, "ain't no joke."

This sense of looking into a mirror negates Mary Ann Doane's assertion in feminist film theory that "the female spectator's desire can be described only in terms of . . . narcissism—the female look demands a becoming."[3] Instead, the gaze of our black female subject in this piece derives no "visual pleasure," nor can she demand a becoming. She experiences erasure, condemnation, and a reminder that, as Jane Gaines articulates: "While white feminists [theorize] the female image in terms of objectification, [fetishization], and symbolic absence, their black counterparts describe the body as . . . the 'paradox of being' . . . when black female did not signify 'woman.'"[4]

Weems and other black female visual artists self-reflexively insert literal and figurative mirrors in their works as a way of reminding viewers of the power of seeing and unseeing, of becoming and unbecoming. In what remains of this chapter, I will assess configurations of black female bodies in both photography and film and determine the effectiveness of black feminist interventions in the realm of visual–cultural production to trouble notions of seeing/unseeing. I will examine, specifically, photographic representations of the black body in terms of aesthetics (or lack of), sexuality, color, and size. I add to this analysis black women's artistic re-presentations as they contrast with national and international political representations of beauty in popular culture, namely, the impact of Vanessa Williams' historic win as the first black Miss America and the effect of Nigerian Agbani Darego's victory as the first black African Miss World. Moreover, I juxtapose black women visual artists across continents to create a transnational black feminist criticism that addresses global circulations of our photographed bodies.

### Picturing Evidence

The photograph captures perceived data and, so, is taken as a form of visual "truth-telling." It further substantiates what art historian Lisa

Gail Collins terms "visual evidence," in which "photography can be used to place people in contexts and tell stories of humanity, [but] it can also be used in endeavors to dehumanize and catalog difference."[5] Through light and mirrors, it reflects back to us an observable image, frozen in time or motioning through reel. Nonetheless, it colludes in an iconography of black female sexuality, shaping misrepresentations and misinformation through stereotypes that shortchange us on the lived experiences of black women. As such, what are we to make of this so-called evidence of pictures? Various art historians who study representations of race have been adept at reminding us that early photography, not long after its invention, was used to corroborate in pseudoscientific studies of race and ethnicity, thus providing observable "facts" of the human anatomy.[6] Interestingly, early stages of motion pictures developed with the same intent of providing such scientific evidence of the body. Whereas paintings, in the wake of photographic technologies, ventured into the realm of the suggestive and the symbolic respectively through impressionism and abstract art, still and motion pictures invariably became associated with "realism."[7]

Out of this "realistic" representation came early modes of reading race and gender onto the body. Consider, for example, the daguerreotypes of African American nude slaves from a South Carolina plantation, taken in 1850 by Joseph T. Zealy for the purposes of illustrating theories of black people's inferiority, as posited in the *Types of Mankind* research by Swiss anatomist Louis Agassiz. Following in the footsteps of his teacher, fellow Swiss naturalist Georges Cuvier, Agassiz further developed the race science that emerged from Cuvier's study of Baartman by projecting colonialist discourses of African subhumanity and hypersexuality onto enslaved African Americans. As Collins argues, this early use of photography in documenting race science and anatomical study establishes a visual reading, devoid of aesthetics, of nude black bodies in this peculiar context of education (Collins, 2002, 19).

In response to these daguerreotypes, Weems developed a series, from 1995 to 1996, titled *From Here I Saw What Happened and I Cried.*

Similar to her *Ain't Jokin'* series, Weems combines text with photography, as she enlarges the images, then tints most of them the color red. The red tone, perhaps suggesting the artist's anger at witnessing the images, contrasts with the more melancholic indigo tint applied to a photograph of an African woman in profile, which appears again in reverse. These two images—one captioned, "From here I saw what happened," while the other image bears the rest of the phrase in the installation's title—serve as bookends to a series of thirty red-tinted photographs, arranged in groups of four. Zealy's daguerreotypes appear in an arranged quartet that challenges, through Weems' reflective wordings, the scientific evidence that photography supposedly documents in visualizing the black body.

The two enslaved women from the group, photographed by Zealy, appear as if they had been undressed by the camera man, and they assume Baartman's pose: one called Delia (Figure 5.2a) stands in profile, while the other woman, Drana (Figure 5.2b), stands in a frontal position that crudely exposes her full breasts; however, Weems's narrative revises this "visual evidence" and demands that we identify with these slave subjects. She overlays on Delia's image the statement, "You became a scientific profile," while Drana's image bears the last part of the sentence: "& a photographic subject." In effect, Weems continues in the same vein of the African American writers and artists featured in previous chapters, who employ the "oppositional gaze" to confront the dominant cultural stare and reclaim black subjectivity. She also undermines the scientific authority of the daguerreotypes, literally positioning her words to disrupt the women's nudity and evoking a sympathetic voice, which encourages us to disrupt the "objective" facts of the black body and, instead, "cry" and emote over what we have seen.

The link between black nudity and anatomical education continued throughout the late nineteenth century, as evidenced by photographic displays of the National Geographic Society (founded in 1888) and world fairs. In what Carla Williams describes as the "National Geographic aesthetic," such photography would "introduce generations of

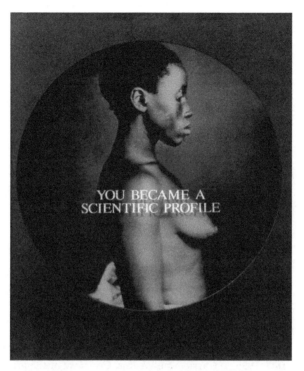

**Figure 5.2a**  Carrie Mae Weems, "Delia," *from From Here I Saw What Happened and I Cried,* 1995. © Carrie Mae Weems. Courtesy of the artist and Jack Shainman Gallery, New York.

American males and females to 'primitive-style' nudity" (Williams, 2002, 187)—a style that encouraged anthropological studies of black female nudes while suppressing its pornographic connections. Such "educational" display of black bodies, linked to pornography, spawned an underground market for this racialized desire and an erotically suppressed reading of such nudity, as Willis and Williams reveal in their historical documentation of countless sexually explicit photographs of black women across the globe. When this colonial historic imagery combines with the more familiar American popular iconography of desexualized, fully clothed mammy images and celebratory imagery of white female beauty, we may be able to more fully comprehend interstices between race and gender that shape our uneasy responses to sexualized visual representations of black women.

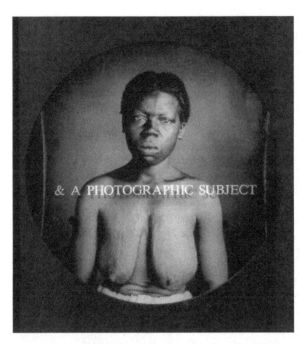

**Figure 5.2b**  Carrie Mae Weems, "Drana," from *From Here I Saw What Happened and I Cried*, 1995. © Carrie Mae Weems. Courtesy of the artist and Jack Shainman Gallery, New York.

Apart from the debacle surrounding Janet Jackson's nudity at the Super Bowl in still and motion pictures, we may recall another scandal involving black nudity in photography decades earlier. I refer here to Vanessa Williams, in which nude photographs of her, published in the July 1984 issue of *Penthouse*, led to her dethroning as Miss America. Just as photographic images of Janet's exposed body made Internet history, so too did Williams's image mark *Penthouse* for success, as that magazine has yet to repeat the record-making sales of that one single issue.

Even before we assess the subject of Williams's photographed body, we should keep in mind how the pictorial realm of magazine ads, World War II–era film reels, and 1950s television programming presented the body of Miss America, whose own historic image changed from Atlantic City burlesque in the 1920s to highly respectable debutante in the 1950s and 1960s. The "whitening" of her image—begun in 1937 when a clause in pageant rules stipulated that contestants must be of the "white race"—shaped an irreproachable ideal of the national body that linked beauty and femininity with racial and virginal purity.[8] In 1968, when mostly white feminists, including Robin Morgan who famously organized with New York Radical Women the first public protest of the pageant (which garnered for mainstream feminists the labeling by the media as "bra burners"), a group of African Americans staged on the same day a "positive protest" by hosting the first Miss Black America pageant. Apart from the involvement of radical black feminist Florynce Kennedy in organizing the anti-beauty-pageant protest, the distinct responses of white and black women to an institutionalized spectacle of feminine beauty suggest, as Barnes notes, that black women's protests "against the exclusion of women of color—rather than the patriarchal structure of the pageant itself—[are a] struggle for black women everywhere to be recognized as women, as feminine subjects" (Barnes, 292).

When Williams became the 1984 Miss America, she not only made history by becoming the first African American woman to win the title, but she also became the first and only woman ever to be dethroned. She also became the first Miss America to receive death threats: a serious reminder that her win was perceived as a viable threat to the system of white supremacy that the pageant was understood to uphold, even as some African Americans debated at the time whether or not Williams, as a light-skinned woman, was "black enough" to represent black womanhood. Such debates, of course, ended when the nude photos of Williams recast her in the historic trajectory of black women's hypersexuality and deviance. Posing alongside a nude white woman, these pictures displayed taboos of both interracial and lesbian sexuality—an occurrence that writer Jackie Goldsby noted was addressed by neither feminist nor queer theorists and activists at the time of the controversy. This silence speaks (no pun intended) to "the historic workings of race in relation to sexuality [that] caused Williams' downfall."[9]

However, we may need to consider, as Dawn Perlmutter asks in her essay, "Miss America: Whose Ideal?": "Was she less beautiful in the nude photos than she was in the bathing suit photos?"[10] When Perlmutter answers her own question with, "No, she was less acceptable to the patriarchal model of the good girl," she mistakenly reduces the issue to one of good girl/bad girl gender roles. When race and sexuality are inserted into the equation, Williams's dethroning as Miss America illustrates that her body became "less acceptable" when her porn image recalled for many the recognizable association between blackness and illicit nudity, as well as "deviant" sexuality, thus turning her beauty queen image, which had already been linked to white purity, into one of utmost incongruity.

Despite these events, Williams's story is hardly viewed as tragic. Indeed, in the PBS documentary, *American Experience: Miss America* (2002), comedian Margaret Cho gloats that Williams has the best revenge story because she is the only Miss America "that we all remember, the only one that became a star." Nonetheless, Williams's subsequent rise to musical and acting stardom depended somewhat on the same hypersexed image that undermined her reign as Miss America, even as her personal life was "redeemed" by heterosexual patriarchy through marriage and motherhood.

This historic crowning and dethroning of a black Miss America presents a complicated reception of a black woman, who might "prove" that black women can indeed be seen as beautiful—albeit with blue-green eyes and long, fair hair—but who might also "prove" that the presence of blackness is enough to tarnish the image of the pure and wholesome Miss America. Similarly, the scandal concerning Janet Jackson at the Super Bowl could also be viewed as the threat of black female sexuality infiltrating the supposedly wholesome terrain of American culture vis-à-vis mainstream white American masculinity (i.e., the football tradition of the Super Bowl and white celebrity, Justin Timberlake, who was once mentored by Janet Jackson). Embedded within these visual representations is the reminder that pictorial "evidence" can undermine black women's movements toward respectability (in the case of Williams) and acceptance (in the case of Janet Jackson) as the specter of history reframes their bodies through familiar tropes.

## Questions of Color

Although Vanessa Williams's 1984 photographic image, both as Miss America and a nude model, incited national debates about racialized beauty and sexuality, we should also take note of the subcultural debates within African American communities about her ability to represent black womanhood. What, for instance, is asserted when she is accused of not being "black enough"? This is especially complicated when we view the history of segregated beauty pageants within black communities of the twentieth century, which typically crowned fair-skinned, longhaired African American women.[11] The charge of "not black enough" subsequently reflects the historic divisions of color that have undermined African American communities, which differentiate between those who are light skinned and those who are dark skinned. More than that, it alludes to a system of privilege that lighter-skinned blacks have accessed over darker-skinned blacks. Nonetheless, this color relativity, while enough to benefit Williams as she won her Miss America title, does little to buttress her when her photographed nude body—cast in the traditional iconography of hypersexed black woman-hood—causes her to relinquish that same title.

Perhaps the insidious stronghold of color consciousness resides in how well it illustrates internalized racism and intra-racial hostility while reinforcing white supremacy. Spike Lee's 1988 film *School Daze* satirically portrays this internalization and hostility; however, although it effectively documents these divisions within black communities, it fails to create a film aesthetic that affirms the full range of blackness represented by these skin color gradations. Somehow, most of the lighter-skinned blacks in the film are reduced to caricatures of "wannabe" whites but for "all that yellow wasted."[12] Whereas, the darker-skinned "Jigaboos" proudly affirm their love of "blackness."

Incidentally, while Lee presents color politics as divisive to the black college community—in a rather sharp condemnation of failures

of the black bourgeoisie in the eighties to maintain Black Nationalism—
he unifies them through a provocative dance called "Da Butt." These
African Americans, who were divided by their skin color and hair tex-
ture differences, can join together on the dance floor and *shake their
thangs*. Unlike the fetishism of black bodies in much of popular culture,
as discussed in chapter 4, the scene reclaims this aspect of the anatomy
for black pride. As bell hooks observes, "The black 'butts' on display are
unruly and outrageous . . . They are not a silenced body. Displayed as
playful cultural nationalist resistance, they challenge assumptions that
the black body . . . is a mark of shame" (1992, 63). Nonetheless, Lee
invokes a certain kind of racial essentialism by reducing blackness to
an anatomy of sameness (assuming, of course, that all black bodies—
regardless of complexion—are endowed in that area) while rejecting
the differences of color and hair. Such a dichotomous portrayal of color
raises the question: Can we envision a non-essentializing blackness that
encompasses skin color variations while also disrupting white supremacy that upholds light-skin privilege?

Fair-skinned and biracial filmmaker Kathe Sandler attempts such
a vision through her 1993 documentary film, *A Question of Color*.
Exploring the impact of color consciousness within African American
communities—including her investigation into the history of these attitudes, as well as its legacy in the present day—Sandler utilizes her own
body within her film to disrupt constructions of blackness and of color
relativity (e.g., her light-skinned sister is cast as dark skinned in comparison to herself). Nonetheless, Sandler seems anxious to "prove" her
blackness by donning Afrocentric attire and dwelling in a predominately
black urban neighborhood. These actions imply that her very fairness,
including her blonde hair and blue eyes, is not enough to establish her
black identity.

In her essay "Light Skinned(ded) Naps," writer Kristal Brent Zook
warns against "blind reversals" in black women's fiction of the late twentieth century that hail brown and dark-skinned black women in attempts

to assert black identity and reverse historic portrayals of virtuous and beautiful light-skinned heroines in early African American literature.[13] In analyzing this practice, Zook recognizes that, because of light-skin privilege, these efforts are critical for black self-representation; however, she has observed limitations in revering both light- and dark-skinned women because these works of fiction continue to view these figures as opposing forces. Using the examples of Gloria Naylor's *The Women of Brewster Place* (1982) and Alice Walker's *The Color Purple* (1982), Zook asserts, "[We] have, for the most part, been denied the opportunity of seeing light skinned Blacks as 'fighters' or as figures who otherwise challenge stereotypical notions of the 'ladylike mulatta'" (Zook, 96n).

Despite these restrictions and inversions of white paradigms of beauty, dominant culture can still render invisible black women's radical color politics. An example of this is the adaptation of Alice Walker's *The Color Purple* into a film by Steven Spielberg in 1985. Walker, who endeavored to give movie casters a physical description of each of her main characters in the novel, portrays an alternative model of beauty to which Hollywood cinema could not relate. Walker thus describes her sensual character, Shug Avery, in the following way:

> She has the requisite 'stout' shape to qualify as sexy and 'womanly' . . . She's gorgeous and knows it, with only positive thoughts about her very black skin—since during this period the black and lighter-skinned black woman had about the same chance with black men. It was the stage shows and early movies produced by whites that began to use 'high yellow' women exclusively in their cabaret and stage dance scenes, thereby encouraging the colorist sexism later exhibited by blacks.[14]

The film casts instead actress Margaret Avery, a slender brown-skinned woman, to portray the dark-skinned, full-figured Shug Avery. Although various issues determine movie casting, in terms of actors' agents, auditions, availability, and interests, we might still conclude that Walker's description of "black beauty" does not correlate with dominant culture's view. Her own account of discrimination against darker-skinned black women in cinematic history—in addition to its later influence on the black community's aesthetic values, whether this is based on fact or not—suggests that Walker's radical revision of black female beauty and sexuality in her work of fiction conflicts sharply with images of beauty perpetuated by mainstream cinema.

Interestingly, Walker also describes Shug Avery as someone who "looks like Pearl Bailey," which reflects a similar preference held by James Baldwin, who, in a review of the 1945 film *Carmen Jones*, berates Hollywood's racial inadequacies from the moment he wishes that "Pearl Bailey [versus a light-skinned Dorothy Dandridge] were playing Carmen." As he puts it, "The 'sexiness,' for example, of Dorothy Dandridge, who plays Carmen, becomes quite largely manufactured and even rather silly the moment Pearl Bailey stands anywhere near her."[15] Baldwin seems harsh in his evaluation of Dandridge, and we may wonder if his rejection of her reflects historic tensions between light-skinned and dark-skinned blacks, as well as judgments about which complexion is more authentically "black" and which black woman better reflects the dark and sensuous Jezebel type. We may presume, however, that Baldwin, like Walker, recognizes a sexiness and femininity in the dark and full-figured black woman that dominant culture, especially as portrayed in Hollywood's mainstream cinema, could not recognize.

A similar fate would befall Toni Morrison's *Beloved* when it too was adapted to film in 1998. Our sensuous titular character, who is described in the novel as "thunder black" and with "midnight skin," is nonetheless portrayed by the copper-colored, biracial actress Thandie Newton, although rumors have suggested that the darker-skinned popular rapper and songstress Lauryn Hill was initially offered the role before turning it down when she became pregnant. This is not to say that a film has to fulfill character descriptions from a novel, neither does it even have to follow the basic plot. Indeed, the actresses who fulfilled these roles gave splendid performances of these characters; however, these adaptations merely illustrate how dominant culture subverts the original intentions of these black women novelists, who created such characters specifically to challenge paradigms of beauty that only pertain to slender, light-and brown-skinned women.

Fortunately, Julie Dash's independent film, *Daughters of the Dust* (1991), provided an alternative representation of black female beauty and sexuality on screen. In contrast to mainstream cinema, Dash affirms the beauty and sensuality of light-, brown-, and dark-skinned black women without privileging one body type over another. As culture critic Greg Tate observes, "Check [Hollywood] history and you'd think that compared to white women or their own lighter-skinned sisters, dark-skinned women had no glamour that any camera could see . . . *Daughters* sent all of that nonsense screaming and kicking to the curb."[16]

Set in 1902, a year marked with hope, progression, new beginnings, and the dawning of what would be called the "New Negro Movement," the time period for this film seems to parallel Dash's own "new beginning" as she pioneered as the first African American woman to have a theatrically released feature-length film. She also broke new ground in her representation of black female bodies, concentrating as she did on a black feminist aesthetic that emphasized the visual richness of such bodies on screen. As Dash admitted to Tate in an interview, she did not "take anything lightly" while painstakingly presenting period costumes and hairstyles representative of African countries such as Senegal, the Ivory Coast, and Madagascar.[17] In view of the initial design of cinematic cameras and lighting to capture translucent qualities of white skin,[18] even Dash's choices, along with those of cinematographer Arthur Jafa, of gold lighting and stock, which film black bodies visually better, become political. Through this gesture as a filmmaker, Dash utilizes the camera—designed to film white bodies—to capture black bodies aesthetically on screen.

Significantly, Dash chooses as her focal point the character Yellow Mary to revise both photographic and cinematic representations. Considering that the New Negro Movement heralded at the turn of the twentieth century images of "mulatta" women as fitting emblems of a dignified New Negro womanhood, Dash's portrayal of a "yellow" woman seems ironic at different moments in the film. Dash may utilize the photographer, Mr. Snead, as a character representing the filmmaker in a self-reflexive motif of her movie camera, but she also signifies her filmmaker role through Yellow Mary. For instance, Dash inserts a point-of-view shot of Yellow Mary gazing through a kaleidoscope, an important scene that builds on Dash's self-reflexivity by suggesting that her film, through one of the oldest camera models, forms multilayered colors and visions that reference a diverse visual culture (the colors in the kaleidoscope, interestingly, form a star design resembling the patterns of the many quilts in the film). Whereas Mr. Snead captures the "realist" picture of the ethnographic film (during which the Gullah family of the Georgia Sea Islands constantly teases him—a teasing in which Dash also engages when she playfully inserts an image of a spiritual character, the Unborn Child, in the line of Mr. Snead's vision while he photographs a group of family men), Yellow Mary's gaze exists beyond the real and toward the mystical and the symbolic.

More than establishing Yellow Mary's mythic gaze, Dash reestablishes her own filmmaker's gaze on Yellow Mary's body to provide a film aesthetic of resistance. As writer Toni Cade Bambara observes of the film's opening shots:

> Standing near the front of the boat is a woman [Yellow Mary] in a long white dress and a large veiled hat. The image is familiar from dominant cinema's colonialism-as-entertainment genre. But we notice that this woman stands hipshot, chin cocked, one arm akimbo. These ebonics signify that filmmaker Dash . . . intends to heal our imperialized eyes. (Dash, xii)

Interestingly, Bambara's description of this film as a "healing" process parallels Yellow Mary's function in *Daughters*, which represents a manifestation of the Yoruba/Cuban Santeria Orisha Yemaya, goddess of healing, waters, secrets, and dreams (Dash, 76).

Through the body of Yellow Mary, this woman who signifies "ebonics" through her posture and attitude in the opening of the film, Dash offers a "new kind of 'oman," as one of the family members describes her, instead of a New Negro woman. The lustrously long and loose hair that Yellow Mary exhibits, which is neither rolled into a conventional and socially acceptable bun of the time period nor is it worn "naturally" through a braided hairstyle like that of the women of her family, indicates that she defies conventions and will create her own sense of aesthetics.[19] Through her hip shaking as she walks in her elaborate dress and veil, Yellow Mary resists the constraints of a corset and redefines her own sexual expression. Finally, through her female companion, Trula, who is never named in the film as her "lover" but is visually identified as such, Yellow Mary formulates her own sexual desires. Ironically, Dash calls attention to the relativity of color identity by depicting Yellow Mary—who is called "yellow" by her Afrocentric family—as "brown-skinned" in complexion, compared to her "high yellow" partner Trula, whose hair is just as unruly (Wilson, 51). Visually, Dash reinterprets black female bodies to disrupt the skin color divisions among black women.

Nonetheless, this "new kind of woman" that Yellow Mary represents still struggles against prescribed roles of Mammy and Jezebel. In an edited scene, Yellow Mary is visually represented as a wet nurse. Simultaneously, as she is nursing a white baby, the father of this baby fondles her other breast, thus recalling a troubled history for black women, whose bodies were often utilized for white male gratification through these mammified and sexualized roles (Dash, 126). As an independent and resourceful woman, Yellow Mary later escapes these limited roles and resists their dual oppression by "fixing the titty," thus preventing her body from being used in this work. As she gains control over her body and, as her exquisite dress indicates, acquires economic wealth, Yellow Mary transforms her self and transcends limited spaces of motherhood and domesticity by traveling the African diaspora from Cuba through the American South on her way to Nova Scotia, Canada. It is she, however, who will eventually remain behind with her great-grandmother Nana on the Gullah islands, as the rest of the family heads north, thus suggesting her deeper attachments to her spiritual heritage and to her ancestors.

The omitted scene of Yellow Mary as a wet nurse parallels another edited scene, in which the enslaved mother of Nana is shown mourning the loss of her child, sold away from her in slavery, as depicted in a close-up of her nipple dripping with milk. Dash describes this scene:

> She is weeping milk tears for the child that has been taken from her rather than just boo-hooing and crying saltwater tears. I really hated not being able to include that in the film because for me . . . I really could not fully understand what it meant to have a child or infant taken from you. (34)

I too lament that such a scene did not remain in the film, not just because of its uniqueness in presenting such an assault on black motherhood under slavery, but for the sheer visual power such an image would evoke when this type of nudity around the breast recalls pain, memory, and frustrated nurturance instead of deviant sexuality—a trope that shaped the scandal surrounding Janet Jackson's exposure at the Super Bowl. In a film that fully dresses every single black female character, and in stark white clothes no less, the suggested nudity of the edited scenes might have expanded upon Dash's revolutionary intent to reframe the black female body for motion pictures. Even then, when we consider that Yellow Mary evokes sex appeal while dressed from head to toe in white, Dash has successfully revamped this iconography.

### Disruptive Beauty

Dash's *Daughters* has been accused of being too beautiful, too romantic, even too much "about hair" (Tate, 72). And, although some critics fault the film for sacrificing a coherent plot for the lush visual treatment of a people, we may recognize how Dash employs an "aesthetic of resistance" that is "often rooted in non-realist, often non-Western or para-Western cultural traditions featuring other historical rhythms, other narrative structures, other views of the body, sexuality, spirituality, and the collective life" (Shohat & Stam, 292). More than providing an alternative aesthetic and narrative structure, Dash imagines for us a historical record of black beauty.

The camera motif in her film signifies not only on the filmmaker's self-reflexivity, but it also serves as a reminder of the black artist in history, via Mr. Snead, who lovingly photographed black people and left a visual record of their simple and elegant humanity.[20] Of course, this historical recovery relies on what film scholar Caroline Brown calls "sentimental progressivism,"[21] an accusation that Brown specifically levels against Dash's portrayal of the sole Native American character in her film, St. Julian Last Child, as a romanticized "noble savage" (Brown, 2). Although we may recognize this indigenous stereotype in Dash's rendering of St. Julian, I would argue that this romantic brush taints all of her characters, even the landscape of the Georgia Sea Islands. Dash's romantic longings for a recovered African American past, interconnected ever so precariously to a Native American presence (best illustrated through St. Julian's romance with Iona, one of the Peazant "daughters"), reflect an ongoing struggle for black self-representation to extricate itself from the larger rubric of Hollywood negations of African American history and black beauty and desirability. Nonetheless, Dash's vision invites further black feminist interventions in visual culture that might disrupt the easy connections made between romance and spirituality with the rural and the dark indigenous body.

A different critical intervention takes place in the cinematic work of Nigerian-born filmmaker Ngozi Onwurah who, raised in the United Kingdom by her Scottish mother while her Nigerian father remained in her war-torn country of origin, constructs a radical and oftentimes disturbing black feminist aesthetic and critique. Her films provide a distinct challenge to the "romance" and "beauty" visualized in the work of Dash. Resisting conventional imagery of the "body beautiful," Onwurah deliberately employs a counter-aesthetic of the body in pain, the body under surveillance. She does so by creating remarkable, *unwatchable* moments in film—somewhat akin to but far less subtle than the "unspeakable" language that Toni Morrison utilizes in a novel like *Beloved*. Onwurah signifies on the "mirror" as motif in her films, thus becoming as self-reflexive as Dash about her role as filmmaker. This is most evident in her first two film shorts—*Coffee Colored Children* (1988) and *The Body Beautiful* (1991)—described by film scholar Gwendolyn Audrey Foster as "auto-ethnographical" approaches to her life story.[22]

One of Onwurah's first unwatchable moments in film occurs when a white supremacist smears excrement on the door of her home in *Coffee Colored Children*, which her mother is forced to wash away. She juxtaposes her mother's action with the proceeding actions of her siblings and herself attempting to "wash" off the blackness of their skins through their use of soap, bleaches, acidic fluids, and cleansing liquids. Ironically, she signifies on the racist European iconography of "washing the Ethiope white." This reference to whiteness as cleanliness and blackness as "bodily waste" is implicit in this particularly jarring ritual of self-hatred (made more unwatchable by the non-diagetically enhanced sounds of the children's scrubbing of their skins). Onwurah depicts recurring scenes of herself, first as a young girl, then as an adolescent, gazing at her mirror image to assess her body image through Western aesthetics, visual shots quite reminiscent of Weems's "Mirror, Mirror."

It is only after Onwurah looks into the mirror and discards her blonde wig, white facial powder, and her "princess" veil that she begins to "wash the real dirt" away from her sense of self: the white supremacist notion of beauty. Thus, she and her brother leave their white porcelain tubs and move toward natural "bathing" locations, such as the ocean and a spring, and "baptize" themselves in the reclamation of their own brown-skinned bodies. They literally "wash themselves" anew in an African aesthetic that values blackness; yet, this water ritual is also accompanied by a fire ritual—a complete destruction of white supremacy. This is represented through their burning of the "trash" that they had indoctrinated: the cleansers and bleaches that they had used to figuratively wash away their blackness, as well as the "snow white" veil that Onwurah used for her dress-up fantasy.

Because of this early struggle to see herself as "beautiful," Onwurah furthers this exploration with her second film, *The Body Beautiful* (1991), in which her body becomes the defined body beautiful, albeit in the exoticized way that black female bodies could be claimed for this category. In one shot, the young Onwurah (played by actress Sian Martin) poses in a red, African-style headdress and sleek gown while she is being photographed as a fashion model. The next shot, however, depicts her white mother (Madge Onwurah playing herself) in the model's place—disfigured because of a mastectomy, aging, and arthritis—who realizes that, unlike her daughter, she cannot "join the elite breed of women penciled in by men who define the sliding scale of beauty that stops at women like [herself]."

Ironically, what makes Onwurah an "exotic beauty" and thus acceptable for the work that she performs as a fashion model, is the mixture of whiteness provided by her mother, which gives her the light skin, long hair, and white features that align her black body within the ranks of this "elite breed." Nevertheless, Onwurah juxtaposes her own body with the body of her mother to reveal these politics of beauty. She lays bare the nude bodies of both women in the opening and closing shots of the film to comment on these representations and—in a direct challenge to Westernized practices of making invisible the "imperfect" body—provides camera close-ups of her mother's missing breast in her relentless depiction of the unwatchable.

Onwurah ventures further by eroticizing her mother's body in a sexual fantasy scene with a young black man, a direct confrontation with mainstream cinema's mandates on which bodies can engage in sexual activity (only the unblemished and unscarred) and which cannot (including interracial and inter-age coupling). Onwurah reminds us of the difficulties of sexualizing the scarred and aged female body—regardless of race—when she interjects in this scene the voice-over of a cold, emotionless male doctor describing the regularity of mastectomies being performed on women. Even as there are "many" bodies undergoing this removal of an essential body part such as the breast, which defines a woman's sense of her femininity, we rarely see such bodies depicted in film. As such, Madge Onwurah is unable to complete her fantasy scene with the absence of visual precursors to suggest the outcome of this particular narrative. It is further interrupted by her daughter's vocal insistence that her young black male lover "touch" her scar.

This film additionally dramatizes the irony of Onwurah's anger toward the black lover in this fantasy, who is first encountered at a pool hall, lasciviously eyeing, presumably, the breasts of a female model in a print advertisement. He has learned to objectify women and fragment their particular body parts, like breasts, through these female models presented for visual display. Onwurah may be a fashion model who gains pleasure in being photographed, but she must also confront the beauty industry that objectifies her body for the pleasures of men and that wants bodies like her mother's "hidden away." In one scene, Onwurah gazes at her mirror image to question the thing that makes her "beautiful"—her breasts—before confronting her mother's body laid bare for viewers to see. Using her own film as a model-turned-filmmaker, she challenges the conventional practice of hiding such bodies and questions the visual orientation of our culture, which defines the body beautiful.

Interestingly, Onwurah proceeded to make the documentary film, *Monday's Girls* (1993), on an annual rite-of-passage ceremony for young Waikiriki girls in a Nigerian rural village. In an attempt to reclaim African aesthetics, Onwurah revisits the country of her origin to film the black body beautiful. Instead of objectifying these young women, however, she juxtaposes the distinct responses of two girls partaking in the ceremony, who provide perspectives on their bodies and communal expectations of their sexuality. Florence, for example, eagerly participates in the ceremony, which includes being paraded publicly in the nude with other initiates—while their elder, Monday Moses, examines their breasts for signs of chastity—as well as a ritual of "fattening," in which the girls emerge five weeks after seclusion in "fattening rooms" to appear before their community as full-bodied beauties. Asikiye, on the other hand, has rejected this ritual, having resided in an urban context, and refuses to bare her breasts before the village, an action that shames her community because she fails to have her virginity tested in public.

Significantly, Onwurah employs a British-sounding white male voice-over to narrate this documentary, a move that film scholar Lisbeth Gant-Britton feels "undercuts" the film by locating "the viewer within a [Westernized] perspective."[23] However, we may recognize Onwurah's provocative invocation of the "colonial" narrative, by her use of this voice-over, to parody a reading of such a film through a lens of "National Geographic" explorations of African village life. As a result, Onwurah undermines this vocal narrative through her visual narrative—a ploy that she has already utilized with utmost irony in *The Body Beautiful* (1991)—to comment on her own stance as an "objective" outsider/observer. At the same time, the supposed objectivity of the white male narrator echoes her own ambiguity as she films both sides that Florence and Asikiye take on the issue of their rite of passage. Onwurah affirms Florence's decision to partake in the communal celebration of fattening girls so that they meet a full-figured beauty ideal, as well as the precolonial, non-Western view of nudity as one of purity instead of illicit sexuality; however, she also affirms Asikiye's refusal to have her village objectify her body, even if we understand her rejection as one cemented in a Western concept of nudity as shame. These differing views complicate African female subjectivity; thus, Onwurah honors the complexities of this postcolonial generation by refusing to reduce African womanhood to a contest of the rural over the urban or the traditional over the modern.

These debates between the "traditional" versus the "modern" body beautiful, as captured in *Monday's Girls,* would culminate in a national strategy eight years later, when Nigeria chose to send the tall and thin fashion model, Agbani Darego, onto the world stage as the country's representative in Miss World 2001. This move departed from the national preference for plump beauty queens; however, Darego captured the Miss World title that year, becoming the first black African to do so. This strategy to create a more "modern," indeed a "global," African beauty image through the slender body obviously proved successful.[24]

On the one hand, this victory diversified the national beauty image, which no longer depended on fattening rituals and in which naturally thin Nigerian women could feel pride. On the other hand, this promotion of Westernized thinness not only undermines a national and West African sense of aesthetics, but it could also encourage a globalizing force in culture and economics that pathologizes healthy, full-figured women. Darego's victory also led to lucrative offers of a modeling career, and she now shares the runway with an international "elite breed of women" to which Onwurah herself once belonged.

Darego's slenderness reflects less of a Nigerian ideal than a Westernized one that has traditionally privileged the extreme slender bodies of East Africans in particular. When we consider that such supermodels as Alek Wek, for instance, survived a refugee camp in the Sudan before being discovered by a model scout or that several of the top African models hail from such famine-stricken countries as Somalia and Ethiopia (most notably Iman, Waris Dirie, Liya Kebede, and Yasmin Warsame), we must question the problematic representation of Darego's win. We might recognize the slender body as a convenient metaphor for underdevelopment—whether through the African female body or the African land itself, even through the underdeveloped body of the idealized adolescent girl in the Euro-American context. As a "primal" space for colonization, the slender female body lies prostrate before the fashion world, which can re-present famine-victim emaciation as chic and exotic supermodel thinness.

Not surprisingly, Darego's exotic slenderness worked in tandem with another image of Nigerian "underdevelopment": that of Amina Lawal, the Muslim woman who was once under threat of being stoned to death by Sharia law, supported by a Nigerian sect of Muslims, for giving birth to an illegitimate child. Even as the nation forged ahead with plans to host the Miss World 2002 pageant, in the wake of Darego's historic win, international protests interrupted their endeavors when several pageant contestants boycotted the event for taking place in such a "barbaric" country that would punish a woman in this way. The irony of these contestants in taking a rather "feminist" stance while failing to make connections between the pageant's objectification of their bodies and the Sharia court's objectification of Lawal, can only be understood when we recognize how Western women often contrast themselves to the "downtrodden" "Third World" female victim, or what Chandra Mohanty has labeled the "Third World difference."[25] This is especially evident in a post-September 11 context, in which Islam and the global south form an image of the "uncivilized" Orient[26] or "darkest Africa."

This same divide between the global north and global south shaped local concerns in Nigeria of an opulent pageant taking precedence over economic struggles and of Western secular "decadence," as represented by scantily clad contestants, colliding with Islamic fundamentalist values. These national conflicts eventually culminated in riots that killed hundreds and displaced thousands from their homes. Nigeria's bid to enter the "Family of Nations" by hosting Miss World subsequently resulted in neocolonial defeat, perhaps best symbolized when the pageant relocated to England.

This disastrous outcome to an historic win is not unlike Vanessa Williams's dethroning after *her* historic win in the 1984 Miss America pageant. Both events remind us that such national and global attempts to hold up "alternative mirrors" on black women's bodies do little but reflect the chaos that forms the metaphorical black holes in our sexual universe. However, while these projects fail, they do reinforce the power of art when filmmakers, such as Onwurah and Dash, see the world differently through their own mirrors.

### Conclusion

In closing, I want to return to the specter of Janet Jackson and imagine her as someone who did not intend for her photographed nude body to circulate beyond her control to a global audience. If innocent of the charges of indecency, how might she defend herself? Unfortunately, black women's vulnerability is not taken for granted, and our raced bodies in photographic imagery have often proven our "guilt" more than our innocence, our grotesquerie more than our beauty. In short, there is a long visual and photographic record that "proves" our hypersexed nature. What is also clear about Janet's possible defense of herself against the visual image is that she, unlike her brother Michael Jackson—charged at the time for child molestation—cannot rely on big brother Jermaine Jackson to invoke the image of a public lynching to gain sympathy.

What black woman could use the same imagery in our defense and be taken seriously? We may note that Willis and Williams's extensive volume on black women's photographic history failed to produce even one photograph of a lynched black woman, even though the nude black female body was instead the "inescapable" motif (Willis & Williams, xix). We know, from the writings of black feminist journalist Ida B. Wells, that black women were also targeted, along with black men and children, for lynching. Yet, we are rarely shown visual imagery of this victimization done to our bodies. What does this suppression reveal about our iconographic history?

Placed in the context of this history, Janet Jackson could not be presumed innocent because no image exists in the public imagination that calls for moral outrage against the combined racism and misogyny that target black women as a specific group. We may recognize the abolitionist imagery studied in the second chapter as an exception, but even then, this iconography still relied on black women's illicit sexuality. Even in a global context, the victimized African female body, whether as "primitive," famine victim, or victim of a brutalizing "Third World" patriarchal culture, tends to incite pity more than outrage. Collectively, the outrageous responses to our image and the outrages done to our bodies reinforce an imperialist global white supremacy that continues to silence black women and un-mirror our visual representation.

In the end, Janet reenacts the flash of her breast in an astute impersonation of then U.S. National Security Advisor Condoleezza Rice on the April 10, 2004 airing of *Saturday Night Live*. In both self-parody and satire of public configurations of black female bodies, Janet defiantly disrobes on her own, without Justin's help, and does the seemingly impossible: She transfers a sexual persona onto the cerebral and desexualized Rice, who had earlier addressed the 9–11 Commission with high resolve and intelligence. It was almost as if Janet had no other recourse but to embrace the charges of sexual indecency and to parody black female intelligence and respectability. Her actions and the subtext of the script remind us that our bodies will always distract from more serious political issues.[27]

In other words, there is still an urgent need for our visual defense in pictures. And even when we attempt breakthroughs in representations, such as the crowning of beauty queens Vanessa Williams or Agbani Darego, the disorder that often ensues in the wake of these hollow victories suggests that blackness is still perceived as existing incongruously with beauty and respectability. It is this defenselessness in popular culture that calls for an alternative mirror in black feminist art, constantly reframing the black female body. Fortunately, the black women photographers and filmmakers discussed in this chapter have taken initial steps in this re-presentation.

---

# REMNANTS OF VENUS: EVOLUTIONS
# OF THE BOOTYLICIOUS BODY

Just days after the 200-year anniversary of the death of Sara Baartman, Britain's *Sun* tabloid announced that international pop star Beyoncé would be writing and starring in a film about Baartman's life.[1] Despite how far-fetched this story seemed, it nonetheless set off a firestorm across the Internet, and the different responses reveal the complex ways that we still react to the bodies of women of African descent. Interesting to unpack is the overwhelming sense of shame in online comments and think pieces, from African Americans puzzling over why someone with the superstar status of Beyoncé would "demean" herself in taking on such a sexualized (and pathologized) role, to South Africans expressing outrage that Baartman, reconfigured as "mother of the nation," would be misrepresented by an iconic black sex symbol from the U.S. One Ghonaqua chief went as far as to proclaim that the pop star was "not worthy" to portray Baartman.[2]

Obviously, both iconic figures from the past and the present had mapped onto each other's bodies in ways that elicited discomfort, even though the British tabloid that sparked the rumors may have humorously been linking the two women simply because they are both renowned for being "bum women," as the news story labeled them. Whether in the freak-show construction of Baartman's "steatopygia" or in Beyoncé's own sonic construction of her body as "bootylicious"— the title of her 2001 hit song with Destiny's Child—The Sun perpetuates an image of racialized sexual spectacle, thus participating in what the Crunk Feminist Collective calls "disrespectability politics." Here, the Collective specifically recalls an earlier time in 2012 when Beyoncé was similarly invoked by an Australian team of scientists who named an insect after the pop star, due to its peculiar rump. As the Collective asserts, "This is a world where disrespectability politics reign, a world where black women's bodies and lives become the load-bearing wall, in the house that race built, a world where the tacit disrespect of Black womanhood is as American as apple pie, as global as Nike. (Just do it. Everybody else is)."[3]

Despite the Sun's attempts at "disrespect," Beyoncé's publicity management released a statement denying reports that she was involved in the making of a film on Baartman while emphasizing that "her story should be told."[4] Incidentally, the controversy also led to the BBC publishing on its website an informative history of Baartman.[5] However, Beyoncé's insistence that Baartman's story needs to be told demonstrates that she herself was not offended at the idea of starring in such a film—even though few people acknowledged the existence of Kechiche's *Venus Noire* from 2010. The year 2016 will be remembered as the pop star's most political and feminist year yet, considering her later releases of the racially-charged Black-Lives-Matter-themed "Formation" music video and the subsequent black feminist visual album *Lemonade*. However, these admirable moments merely followed her bold statement earlier in the year on the life of Sara Baartman.

In the first edition of *Venus in the Dark*, I did not mention Beyoncé and how she fits into the iconography of black female sexuality, a history in which I situated Baartman at the center. However, in providing

a retrospective of the nearly 20 years of the first part of the twenty-first
century, it is difficult *not* to talk of Beyoncé now that she has become
one of the most preeminent symbols of black womanhood in popular
culture. It is fitting that she opened the century by reclaiming a hip-hop
term, "bootylicious," to apply it to her and her fellow group members'
bodies, and other black women by extension. Rapper Snoop Dogg may
be credited with coining the term in a 1993 Dr. Dre track, while music
producer Rob Fusari, who worked on the "Bootylicious" track, has taken
issue with the way Beyoncé has claimed coinage of the term.[6] Nonetheless, it is Beyoncé's hypervisible body that made the term legible for
entry in the Oxford English Dictionary in 2006.

In this chapter, I grapple with how historical echoes from previous
eras map onto highly visible bodies of our own contemporary era,
specifically analyzing fetishistic spectacles of black "booty" in art and
popular culture. These representations sometimes reinforce common
tropes of black female sexuality in contexts of hypersexuality and hyper-
consumption, and at other times flip these scripts in subversive attempts
at a counter-aesthetic. In exploring these issues, I will also foreground
Beyoncé while contextualizing her performances against other artists
and performers and especially within the high-tech environments that
have mediated the ways we consume these images and interact with
popular culture.

First, I provide an overview of the pop star's career and the ways in
which she positioned her voluptuous and light-skinned body for max-
imum visibility that nuances hypersexuality and respectability. I then
examine the spectacles of the "bootylicious" body that she helped to
popularize, specifically assessing how it came to be associated with
edibility and food in both popular culture and art projects. Finally,
I examine Beyoncé's incorporation of feminist politics and racial justice
in her independently produced visual albums and how she advances a
counter-aesthetic for black women's bodies and beauty politics. Beyoncé's prominence indicates that she is well-versed in the iconography of
black women's racial and sexual histories.

## *Body (R)evolutions*

Beyoncé Giselle Knowles released her hit song "Bootylicious" from the album *Survivor* in the early summer of 2001, alongside group members Kelly Rowland and Michelle Williams in the new iteration of Destiny's Child, which no longer included members LaTavia Roberson, Letoya Luckett, and for a brief period Farrah Franklin. Proving that this girl group will have staying power, compared to so many other R&B girl groups that had come and gone during the 1990s, Destiny's Child also overcame the running joke of ever-changing group members, hence the album's titular song "Survivor." The song and video for Bootylicious appeared during a cultural moment that witnessed the global commercialization of hip-hop and a diverse celebration of black women artists in the genre: from Lauryn Hill's critically acclaimed and Grammy-award-winning *The Miseducation of Lauryn Hill;* to rapper Foxy Brown gracing billboards for Calvin Klein denims in major cosmopolitan cities; to innovative producer and rapper Missy Elliott ushering in the "east-west" sound of hip-hop bhangra samplings with her music partner Timbaland in their 2001 hit "Get Ur Freak On," whose music video treats the black booty as frenzied, crunk, energized, and rebelliously free—a representational departure from the conventional fetishism found in "booty" rap videos that reduced video models to their derrières. Such creative music, along with the variety of representations of black women—from the slender and dreadlock-wearing Hill to the heavier Elliott—paved the way for black women's hypervisibility in the pop music scene of the late twentieth and early twenty-first centuries.

While the music of Destiny's Child leans toward R&B, their engagements with hip-hop—as evidenced by their collaboration with Lauryn Hill's former Fugees bandmate Wyclef on their first breakout hit "No, No, No" from 1998—positioned them for crossover audiences. With "Bootylicious" a few years later, thanks to the curvaceous body and provocative dance moves of Beyoncé—or what Aisha Durham calls the regional aesthetic of "Southern booty"[7]—the word proved its longevity, even if the music video seemed far more innocuous. The song itself, featuring a guitar loop from Stevie Nicks's 1982 hit song "Edge of Seventeen," reflected the hip-hop remix practice that had come to shape R&B music, while the music video paid homage to Nicks herself, appearing in the video in neon pink tight pants and on guitar.

Anecdotes about the song's origins suggest that Beyoncé's father, Mathew Knowles who managed the group, was willing to pay hefty copyright fees for the Stevie Nicks sample while he nonetheless objected to the song's title, perhaps recognizing the potential sexualization of a group of teens on the cusp of young womanhood, who had begun their careers with a black Southern-church-girlhood image (Goodman, 2016). The Houston-based Destiny's Child, however, managed to reposition their local regionality for universal appeal. In the "Bootylicious" video, the very slim bodies of twenty-year-old Beyoncé, Kelly, and Michelle, styled by Beyoncé's mother Tina Knowles, suggest only a hint of curves, while they highlighted an ensemble of multiracial dancers, reflecting different shapes and sizes—including heavyset black women—as they recreate a "Soul Train" dance line in raucous and playful shaking of their diverse "bootylicious" bodies. In a role reversal, Destiny's Child counters every rap music video that objectifies and fetishizes women's bodies by instead focusing their female gaze on the raunchy dance moves of bare-chested men in low-riding jeans, whose visible briefs sport the name of the group. The reclamation of "bootylicious," replete with this more playful rather than vulgar display of sensual dancing positioned Destiny's Child as "feminists" promoting women's perspectives and women's independence, a follow-up to their 2000 hit song "Independent Women," featured on the soundtrack of the film reboot of *Charlie's Angels*.

Even in the video, we could see the centrality of Beyoncé, who is often positioned in the middle of the trio while she sports straight blonde hair, which inevitably enhances her light-skinned body that stands out visually from her darker-skinned group members; she also serves as lead singer with songwriting credits. Incidentally, original members LaTavia Roberson and Letoya Luckett, who began singing with Destiny's Child since the early days of the prepubescent Girls Tyme, allegedly left the group because of Mathew Knowles's favoritism for his daughter and Kelly Rowland, the latter raised in the Knowles family. Nonetheless, the girl group prospered both in their harmonic vocals and in their youthful appearance, which appealed to a cross-generation of fans who will eventually grow up alongside lead singer Beyoncé. Knowles's management also demonstrated business acumen, especially when he successfully marketed the group's "Independent Women" for inclusion on the *Charlie's Angels* soundtrack, which enhanced both the hypervisibility and hyperaudibility of Destiny's Child.

This moment at the dawn of the millennium can best be described as celebratory of racial difference. Lauryn Hill had allegedly been recruited for a role in *Charlie's Angels,* which was eventually played by Asian American actress Lucy Liu after the rapper turned it down, thus forcing the film to rely on the music and video of Destiny's Child to enhance its black feminine presence and the racial inclusivity that was an obvious selling point. Indeed, Hill merely demonstrated her eventual retreat from the mainstream with such rejections, as her recording of MTV Unplugged in the summer of 2001 would unleash the following year her rawest and most caustic critique of the superficialities of celebrity culture, which jarred against her artistic values. The singer-rapper's disappearance from mainstream participation signaled a shift in the music landscape, which had already witnessed the sudden death of R&B artist Aaliyah, the false reporting of the death of pop star Whitney Houston by drug overdose (it would take another eleven years before this became an actuality), and the colossal flop of pop diva Mariah Carey's film debut, *Glitter.* All these events might have occupied significant media space had it not been for the tragic events of September 11. However, the aftermath of this terrorist attack on U.S. soil resulted in deeper fears of a once celebratory multiracial landscape that popular culture had signified as the core of American identity, with black culture positioned precariously in its "outsider within" status when a recognizable foreign threat beyond the black body was identified in the Islamic body and the Arab body (often mistaken for the brown body in general, as hate crimes against South Asian Sikhs demonstrated).

Nonetheless, blackness is still mapped onto these bodies of the "Other," such as the "sand nigger" racial epithet used against "enemies" in the war on terror, or even when a white American, John Walker Lindh, was discovered shortly after the war against Afghanistan began, fighting on the Afghan side, and subsequently labeled "the American Taliban." A Newsweek story conveniently described this man's disloyal descent "from hip-hop to Holy War," alleging that Lindh's adolescent interest in rap music eventually led to his discovery of the *Autobiography of Malcolm X* and subsequently Islam, which then led him to terrorist jihad.[8] Here, black masculinity made legible Islamic terrorism via the white male body, subsequently marking racial difference as an inherent threat to American culture. Moreover, the sudden hypervisibility and subsequent exoticization of burqa-clad Afghan women circulated in news media, thus placing in stark relief scantily-clad pop stars bearing cleavages, midriffs, and tight-hugging jeans. Because of this, the sexy fashion style of Destiny's Child along with their harmonic voices positioned black women's bodies as the ligament between exotic blackness and American patriotic fervor, perhaps best represented when their song "Survivor" eventually embodied the nationalist spirit post-September 11. That the cultural landscape further changed with the sudden decline and disappearances of Hill, Houston, Carey, and Aaliyah, left Destiny's Child to fill the vacancy of black female pop stardom, especially once group members embarked on their solo careers.

While Michelle Williams's career path diverged toward gospel music, both Kelly and Beyoncé pursued more secular music in 2002, indeed collaborating with hip-hop artists in the new musical environment merging different black music genres, which had the effect of giving the former group members "street cred" while enabling the mainstream popularity of rappers. Whereas the music video featuring Kelly on rapper Nelly's "Dilemma" follows a conventional good-girl-meets-bad-boy narrative, which finds our good girl sneaking out of the house and ignoring her mother (played by soul-singing legend Patti LaBelle), Beyoncé instead collaborated with Shawn "Jay Z" Carter on a far more bombastic video for "03 Bonnie and Clyde." In the video, the singer plays the Bonnie to Jay Z's Clyde in an outlaw narrative—the song sampling rapper Tupac's ode to his gun, "Me and My Girlfriend"—which finds the lovers on the run from police while crossing state lines and the Mexican border.

Here, Beyoncé is not simply a neighborhood girl getting involved with a bad boy rapper, known for his former drug-dealing past; she is a "ride or die" criminal, conspiring with her artistic and romantic partner and doing so on a global and massive scale. The outsized egos of both artists here suggest that they have met their match and perhaps even signal their future ambitions for world domination through their merging of R&B and hip-hop. The video is often understood as the announcement of these two artists' romantic liaison.

In contrast to his previous darker-skinned partners and musical protegees like Foxy Brown, Jay Z's partnership with Beyoncé is also viewed as an "upgrade" in the colorist objectification standards held by men in hip-hop culture, especially when the pop star crafts a "classy" sexy persona and even made her film debut the same year in *Austin Powers in Goldmember* as the afro-haired Foxxy Cleopatra in obvious satirical Blaxploitation homage to the original Foxy Brown, portrayed by Pam Grier, and Cleopatra Jones, portrayed by Tamara Dobson. As launching pads for her solo album, Beyoncé prepares the public for her more adult transformation, even succumbing to the image of eye-candy trophy-girlfriend-wife-to-be for her future husband twelve years her senior. However, rather than simply reproduce the image of a diminutive blonde-haired "wifey" Faith Evans curled up against the heavier dark-skinned rapper Biggie Smalls—as immortalized on the October 1995 *Vibe* cover—or merely function as the "new Bobby and Whitney" as Jay Z announced in his allusion to what is often assumed to be Whitney Houston's demise when she married the "bad boy" R&B singer Bobby Brown, Beyoncé presents an ego of equals, which burst onto the scene with attitude and swagger when debuting alongside Jay Z her video for her single "Crazy in Love" from her first solo album *Dangerously in Love.* It is here that she visualizes, with far more pizazz and relish than the original Destiny's Child video, the lyrics to "Bootylicious" through her frenzied and hip-shaking choreography: "I don't think you're ready for this jelly/ cause my body is too bootylicious for you babe." Of course, as a respectable "good girl," she is simply acting out of character with her newfound love, as her lyrics suggest: "Your love's got me looking so crazy right now/ looking so crazy in love."

When the pop star emulated the same choreography while performing "Crazy in Love" for the Macy's Fourth of July Fireworks Spectacular show in 2003, she was denounced by conservative groups for her "lascivious" moves and for her "unpatriotic" performance, which took place on Grant's Tomb. The controversy ironically proved that her body really was "too bootylicious." Nonetheless, Beyoncé has proven over the years—up until her politically charged year of 2016—that she knows how to strike a delicate balance between being sexy and being "America's sweetheart."

The year 2003 marked a time when the Dixie Chicks, fellow Texans, and an all-American country music trio, were vilified and banned from country music stations after lead singer Natalie Maines criticized then president George W. Bush for starting the war in Iraq; and just a year later, pop star Janet Jackson was penalized for her "wardrobe malfunction" at the Super Bowl. Against these controversies, Beyoncé nuanced respectability politics and hypersexuality by tempering her black booty with her image of all-American blonde beauty. She would later reveal an alter ego, Sasha Fierce, whom she claimed was birthed from the video "Crazy in Love." This alternate personality, which represented her more aggressive and raunchy side, suggests a deliberate severing of her sexual persona from her respectable self, thus preventing a holistic presentation of black women's sexuality, or as Farah Jasmine Griffin argues in her commentary on Sasha Fierce: "black women have yet to be granted the full privilege of expressing their sexual agency without paying a price."[9]

However, Beyoncé can still be celebrated for embracing her curvaceous body, as comedian and actress Mo'Nique affirmed while hosting the BET Awards show in 2004 and recreating Beyoncé's signature
dance moves from "Crazy in Love" with fellow plus-sized black women
as a gesture to the radical politics of black women's bigger bodies,
even though the pop star is considerably skinnier. What we may recognize here in Mo'Nique's homage is the way Beyoncé mainstreamed
the bootylicious black body in popular culture, especially in a culture
that simultaneously condemned Janet Jackson's sexual spectacle while
rap videos—specifically Nelly's infamous "Tip Drill" video, which dis-
cursively reduced black women to their "ass cause it ain't your face" as
the rapper swiped a credit card through the crevice of a video model's
buttocks—were being protested on the campus of Spelman, a historic
black women's college. Because black women's bodies were routinely
pornified on programs such as BET's raunchy late-night music-video
series *Uncut,* pop stars like Beyoncé had to both compete and still tran-
scend these racial and sexual politics.

The popularity of such images may have forced the pop star to
dichotomize her persona and to strategically retreat into respectability and conservatism, as highlighted when she reunited with Destiny's
Child in 2004 and performed their hit songs "Lose My Breath" and "Soldier" for the National Football League's halftime show on Thanksgiving
Day, which featured an over-the-top celebration of American patriotism
with cheerleaders, a marching band, and several soldiers from different
branches of the military who had recently returned from Iraq. Interestingly, this spectacle became the basis for *Billy Lynn's Long Halftime Walk,*
a novel by Ben Fountain, and later a film by Ang Lee, on our nation's
hypocrisy in heralding war heroes while ignoring such issues as wartime
PTSD. However, such conservative values and spectacles found alternative sexual release in a pornographically-saturated culture that pro-
liferated on the Internet and influenced the pop music industry, which
found provocative ways to sell music once music-sharing online sites
disrupted music sales.

This is the era of the video model, or "video hotties," as Mae G. Henderson describes when observing how such women "effectively redefined female body aesthetics, marking a transition . . . [from] breasts as the principle signifier of femininity to one fashioned by . . . 'bootification.'"[10] While known mostly for their curvaceous bodies, these video models eventually honed their own personalities and cultivated fan communities, including Melyssa Ford, Buffie Carruth, and Karrine Steffans. Indeed, Steffans's *Confessions of a Video Vixen*—which describes a casual sexual encounter with rapper Jay Z—was a bestseller in 2005, the same year that Buffie Carruth, also known as "Buffie the Body," made her debut in hip-hop culture and profited lucratively from posting images of her bikini-clad derrière on her website and performing in rap videos, as she famously did in Tony Yayo and 50 Cent's video "So Seductive." Signifying on the poster-girl image from the film *Shawshank Redemption,* the prison-break narrative of "So Seductive" strategically replaces the classic Hollywood beauty—represented by Rita Hayworth, Marilyn Monroe, and Raquel Welch in the film—with an alternative beauty ideal embodied by Buffie, a dark-skinned "bootylicious" model. While it would take Vogue another nine years before declaring a shift in beauty culture with its 2014 "era of the big booty" article,[11] these aesthetic changes had already begun to quake by the mid-2000s.

Nonetheless, a different cultural shift had already taken place in 2005, with the creation of YouTube earlier that year, Facebook created the previous year, and Twitter created the following year. The photo-based Instagram would arrive in 2010. Where online space was once a lucrative business for models like Buffie Carruth and various web creators and pornographers, this was no longer the case with the evolution into social media. Indeed, Buffie revealed in a video testimony that she needed to seek income elsewhere and found a new market in fitness for women, an audience she cultivated after appearing in 2007 on former supermodel Tyra Banks's talk show in an episode featuring women of color who capitalized on their bodies.[12] Interestingly, Banks confronted paparazzi for body-shaming the size of her own derriere on her show the following year, thus highlighting the different ways black women had carved out their own public platforms to affirm and defend themselves. Such defenses included redefining and proclaiming the desirability of their own voluptuous bodies beyond a white, westernized and heteropatriarchal gaze. However, Banks eventually ended her talk show in 2011, the same year that Oprah Winfrey ended hers.

The market shifted to competitive reality programming, which featured such fare as Banks's *America's Next Top Model,* and was increasingly defined by social-media events, which created alternative public platforms on which various marginalized groups could launch themselves. Inevitably, Beyoncé would follow the market when her music video for "Single Ladies," which premiered on MTV's *Total Request Live* before that show ended, became a YouTube sensation in 2008, the same moment that ushered in Barack Obama as the first black president of the United States. Somehow, the pop star also seemed to exert more freedom, after marrying Jay Z earlier in the year but still steering her solo career before eventually severing ties with her father-manager. The newly married Beyoncé publicly engaged her alter ego with her third solo album, *I Am . . . Sasha Fierce.* After all, Beyoncé Knowles-Carter's marital status may have changed, but Sasha Fierce infamously represented "All the Single Ladies," whose bootylicious body would be mimicked in numerous YouTube recreations of the music video's choreography.

### Consuming the Bootylicious Body

Apart from influencing the culture through the recognized desirability of the "bootylicious" body, the rhetoric of Destiny's Child's hit song also highlights its edibility. This is in keeping with what bell hooks has observed of the phrase "eating the other"; the body that stands in for racial difference is often consumed sexually, as "seasoning that can liven up the dull dish that is mainstream white culture" (hooks, 1992, 21). Interpreting this consumption quite literally, food critic and historian

Fabio Parasecoli has commented on how the term bootylicious suggests "the black body . . . not only as a source of nourishment, but as an edible substance in itself."[13] Here, Parasecoli references the song's use of "jelly," which recalls the earlier rhetoric of blues women such as Ma Rainey and Bessie Smith, who alluded to sex and their bodies through food imagery, not to mention the regularity with which black women's sexualities, as Miller-Young reminds us in her study *A Taste for Brown Sugar: Black Women in Pornography,* are discussed in terms of brown sugar, chocolate, honey, and jelly roll.[14] Moreover, pornographic culture—including hardcore porn, sexually explicit lyrics and videos in pop music, and sex scenes in film and on cable television—has enabled discourses on oral sex that often link sexuality with edibility, hence the literal consumption of the body (including the booty).

Black women's edible sexuality is absurdly depicted in rapper 2 Chainz's music video for his 2012 hit "Birthday Song," which reconfigured his libidinal desire—"all I want for my birthday is a big booty ho"—through a birthday cake in the form of a black-iced booty in thong bikini. In the same video, a black woman lies prostrate on a table, her body smeared in white-iced cake, some of which appears to have been cut into and eaten. That the few black women in the video are reduced to edible substances—indeed, one never reveals her face as she faces a wall and shakes her booty amid a group of beer-guzzling men—while the other racially ambiguous women are given more face time and are visually coded as strippers, suggests a racial hierarchy of sexual objectification and the complete dehumanization of black women since they are literal objects to be consumed.

The edible body, however, takes on a different iteration in performance art, as occurred the same year in a crossdressing blackface performance by Afro-Swedish artist Makode Linde, who ignited international debates when he appeared in a YouTube video as the head of a black-iced elaborate cake in the form of the Paleolithic figure Venus of Willendorf.[15] When the mostly white attendees at this art event in Sweden sliced into the cake, Linde would scream as if he were in agony each time the cake knife cut into the lower "torso." Indeed, the red-velvet cake underneath the black icing evoked the "blood" that flows within the body. That the artwork would later be denounced for its trivialization and recreation of the "Hottentot Venus," as some have interpreted the cake, or even for attempting to "raise awareness" of the "problem" of "female genital mutilation" on the African continent—as others conjectured about the meaning of the performance—confirmed for the artist that people generally react from what he calls their own "prejudice cloud."[16] In other words, Linde suggested that he was not operating from a critique of African womanhood or the African body, but he did note the ways that Africanness had been projected onto the cake itself.

Nonetheless, the artist might be a bit disingenuous here. After all, he not only invited associations with the black body via his blackface and black icing on the cake, but he had also revealed that he had initially planned to create for the occasion a "chocolate Naomi Campbell" (the famous Afro-British supermodel who was once depicted in bikini with her leg draped over a chocolate Playboy bunny logo). This motif of cannibalizing the black body recalls a history of what Vince Woodard describes in *The Delectable Negro* as the cultivation of white desire for black flesh in both U.S. slave and European colonizing cultures.[17] Linde visualizes this desire in his performance and the resulting pain of dehumanization that his performative screams suggest.

Much like the 2 Chainz video, this edibility further evokes a history of the consumption of blackness, especially in advertisements for chocolate, rum, or sugar (incidentally products that stemmed from enslaved black labor in the Americas). The mammy image of Aunt Jemima, in association with pancakes and syrup, or the sexy mulatta on rum labels for *Rhum Negrita* immediately come to mind. A more recent advertisement from our own era by Magnum Chocolate depicted the dark skin of a black model as an outer chocolate crust with the vanilla ice-cream shown beneath the skin surface—alluding to "Washing the Ethiope white."

Linde may have decided to forego the chocolate Naomi Campbell and chose instead to depict the Venus of Willendorf, to focus on European art, but this iconographic redirection does not necessarily remove the association with blackness nor with the Hottentot Venus, whom many identified as the signified history in the artist's performance. Incidentally, earlier French archaeologists from the nineteenth century, such as the Marquis Paul de Vibraye and Edouard Piette, labeled the Paleolithic figurines "Venus" precisely because their prominent breasts and buttocks reminded them of the Khoisan figure from South Africa.[18] These figurines reinforced for Piette the belief in a "primitive" race that once existed in Europe. The Willendorf figurine may have been discovered in Austria in 1908, but her voluptuous figure was nonetheless enveloped in African Venus iconography. There is a reason the ghost of the Hottentot Venus lingers and why the iconography elicits this visceral desire for racial and sexual difference.

Artist Kara Walker worked on a similar "edible" project in 2014 in her first public installation at the old Domino sugar refinery plant in the Williamsburg neighborhood of Brooklyn, before it was demolished to make room for high-rise condominiums. Elaborately titled *A Subtlety, or the Marvelous Sugar Baby: An Homage to the unpaid and overworked Artisans who have refined our Sweet tastes from the cane fields to the Kitchens of the New World on the Occasion of the demolition of the Domino Sugar Refining Plant,* Walker presents a tongue-in-cheek analysis of sugar's legacy, from slavery in the Americas to the exploited labor of the industrial age. The focal point of this ephemeral installation was a 35-foot-tall and 75-foot-long sphinx in the shape of a woman, coated in 40 tons of white sugar donated by the Domino company (Figure 6.1). While the sculpture's severe face juts out with a headscarf covering her head—reminiscent of Aunt Jemima, or as Walker specifically reveals, the Aunt Dinah image once used to sell molasses—the body by contrast is situated in a reclined animalistic pose (suggestive of the part-lion, part-woman sphinx) with an enormous behind and vulva on full display (Figure 6.2).[19]

The sculpture inevitably drew comparisons to the Hottentot Venus,[20] especially when visitors to the exhibit posed with it in sexually provocative selfies later posted on Instagram. Walker herself describes the sculpture as "a bootylicious figure with something paradoxical about her pose.

**Figure 6.1**  *A Subtlety, or the Marvelous Sugar Baby, an Homage to the unpaid and overworked Artisans who have refined our Sweet tastes from the cane fields to the Kitchens of the New World on the Occasion of the demolition of the Domino Sugar Refining Plant, 2014.* Polystyrene foam, sugar. Approx. 35.5 × 26 × 75.5 feet (10.8 × 7.9 × 23 m). A project of Creative Time, Domino Sugar Refinery, Brooklyn, NY, 2014. Photo: Jason Wyche. Artwork © Kara Walker, courtesy of Sikkema Jenkins & Co., New York.

She's both a supplicant and an emblem of power" (cited in Laster, 2014). Appropriating Beyoncé's parlance, Walker also alludes to her creative process, of which Creative Time, the sponsor of the art show, featured a slide show of the artist's early drafts of the installation on its website, including a pictorial collage (Figure 6.3) that fused the head of the Giza Sphinx of Egypt with the derrière of a curvy black model in lingerie.[21] That Walker would associate the booty with an ode to sugar speaks to the link between black female sexuality and brown sugar, and the white supremacist legacy of subjugating and "refining" it for whiteness (Miller-Young, 5).

As Walker observes, "The whole reason for refining sugar is to make it white. Even the idea of becoming 'refined' seems to dovetail with the

**Figure 6.2** *A Subtlety, or the Marvelous Sugar Baby, an Homage to the unpaid and overworked Artisans who have refined our Sweet tastes from the cane fields to the Kitchens of the New World on the Occasion of the demolition of the Domino Sugar Refining Plant, 2014.* Polystyrene foam, sugar. Approx. 35.5 × 26 × 75.5 feet (10.8 × 7.9 × 23 m). A project of Creative Time, Domino Sugar Refinery, Brooklyn, NY, 2014. Photo: Jason Wyche. Artwork © Kara Walker, courtesy of Sikkema Jenkins & Co., New York.

Western way of dealing with the world" (cited in Laster, 2014). How fitting, then, that in analyzing the "ruins" and "waste" represented by a sphinx—an emblem of empire—and the remnants of an old factory plant responsible for the overproduction of an unhealthy substance in the interest of white global capitalism, Walker erects this symbolic "Sugar Baby" to comment on images of excessive sexuality and excessive consumption. This association between sugar and sexuality is reminiscent of such Jamaican planters and enslavers as Thomas Thistlewood, who blamed the sexual proclivities that he projected onto the enslaved women he owned—and with whom he had children—on the eating of too much sugar cane.[22]

**Figure 6.3** Kara Walker *Untitled*, 2014. Collage on board, 16 × 20 inches (40.6 × 50.8 cm). Artwork © Kara Walker, courtesy of Sikkema Jenkins & Co., New York.

As Parasecoli notes, the link between the big booty and food is a deliberate one, not just in the emphasis on "eating the other," but also in the clear connection between excessive sexuality and excessive eating. Indeed, video model Buffie Carruth once addressed rumors that she had resorted to butt injections and plastic surgery by suggesting that her size is not due to artifice but to "calories," hence her rigorous exercise to keep her body in proper proportions lest the fat settles in the wrong place (Carruth, 2012). Because the beauty ideal of a tiny waste and big hips seems impossible for some women to achieve, many had come to question the "realness" of such hourglass figures, especially when rappers like Nicki Minaj and reality stars like Kim Kardashian are rumored to have undergone surgeries to acquire their big behinds. Fascinating to analyze, however, is Buffie's association between big booty size and food, which is further emphasized with the word "Tasty" tattooed on her right butt cheek. As a result, she shuts down rumors that her derrière is fake by suggesting her extra fat is based on extra calories.

The excessive booty as an extension of excessive fat further patholo-gizes women's bodies in general and black women's bodies specifically. Because of high obesity rates in low-income black communities—due to several issues, from lack of access to healthy food to a sedentary lifestyle exacerbated by violent neighborhoods that make it unsafe to engage in outside activities—Michelle Obama chose to raise awareness of child-hood obesity in her role as First Lady and subsequently launched her "Let's Move" campaign. Enlisting the help of Beyoncé, who had already dramatically made her appearance alongside the Obamas when she ser-enaded their first dance at their first Inauguration ball, Obama selected a popular and influential black woman, whose energetic performances embodied the ethos of "Let's Move." Remixing her dance track, "Get Me Bodied," from her 2006 sophomore solo album *B'Day*, into the 2011 fit-ness theme of "Move Your Body," Beyoncé and the first lady helped shift fitness beyond the artificial focus on sex appeal and toward the focus on self-care around healthy food and exercise.

Interestingly, when Beyoncé appeared on Vogue's April 2009 cover not long after her Inaugural performance, the magazine framed her body through the headline, "Real Women Have Curves," an allusion to Patricia Cardoso's 2002 film starring Latina actress America Ferrera and based on the stage play by Josefina Lopez. This association of "curves" with women of color provides stark contrast to the other taglines on Vogue's cover—from "Nip/Tuck: Designing the Perfect Body" to "Weight Obsession: One woman conquers her diet demons"—presumably marking the normative white body. Indeed, the pop star revealed in her interview the extent to which she got in shape for her Vogue cover—she "ate a tiny portion of Honey Nut Cheerios, ran for six miles, and worked out with her trainer"— while also emphasizing that "it's easy for me to gain weight. I'm not a naturally stick-thin girl. I'm not heavy, but I'm not skinny, either."[23]

Such attempts at achieving the slender body belies this so-called cel-ebration of curves, not to mention the scarcity in which black women have landed the Vogue cover, an achievement first accomplished by Beverly Johnson who became its first black cover model in 1974, even though she would later confess to developing an eating disorder in the wake of her success.[24] On the other hand, the relative ease with which, as I had mentioned in chapter 5, the East-African statuesque physique is idealized—as embodied by the dark-skinned beauty and Kenyan actress Lupita Nyong'o, who graced the cover of Vogue, beginning in 2014, on three separate occasions despite her newcomer status in the entertainment world—suggests that black women's size more than skin color might be the real barrier for African-descended women to overcome in achieving the Vogue fashion-model aesthetic.

It is no wonder, then, that Michelle Obama would find a kindred spirit in curvaceous Beyoncé for her "Let's Move" campaign. Indeed, the first lady's political opponents constantly referenced her own voluptuous booty size as "evidence" that she herself did not reflect a "healthy" body ideal and, subsequently, was labeled a "hypocrite" for promoting healthy living. Again, the supposition is made that black women's bodies, due to their big booties, convey excessive eating. Beyoncé would also face criticism when she accepted a $50-million-dollar endorsement deal with the Pepsi company in 2012, which conflicted with her involvement in Obama's "Let's Move" campaign, given the product's sugary ingredients.

Although Michelle Obama and Beyoncé were accused of "hypocrisy" for promoting health and wellness, because the size of their booties presumably canceled out their ability to engender "health" or because they seemed to sanction "unhealthy" commercial projects, Beyoncé's Pepsi endorsement deal nonetheless provided the pop star with an opportunity to headline the Super Bowl halftime show in 2013 and with full creative independence on her subsequent art work. Not surprisingly, her "girl power" spectacle at the Super Bowl—replete with her all-women band, backup singers, and backup dancers—invited both praise for its feminist expression as well as derision for being too raunchy in her energetically sexy choreography, much like the criticism she faced for her

"Crazy in Love" performance at Macy's Fourth of July show. However, as Brittney Cooper argues, "I don't think Beyoncé has aspirations toward respectability . . . She's interested in exploding those categories, in which one can be a wife and mother and still be very sexual."[25]

Certainly, Beyoncé proved this point when she surprised the world with the unexpected digital release via iTunes of her fifth solo album, the self-titled BEYONCÉ Visual Album, on December 13, 2013. With each of her fourteen tracks accompanied by a music video, Beyoncé placed her body front and center and especially mobilized her signature bootylicious moves that gesture toward a holistic integration of her sexuality, which no longer relied on her alter ego Sasha Fierce to express her more forbidden sensual side. As her bonus video "Grown Woman" suggests in the refrain: "I'm a grown woman, and I can do whatever I want," including bypassing expectations from her Columbia music label on the appropriate means for releasing albums or even in disrupting the more traditional forms of commercial promotion that Pepsi attempted.

These rebellious acts further paralleled the unabashed celebration of her curvaceous booty—the subject of her own self-adoration in which the singer constantly invites her love interest (assumed to be her husband) to look at it, to touch it, even to taste it in her raunchier songs "Drunk in Love," "Blow," "Partition," and "Rocket." Such sensual expressions jarred against the values of her staunchest feminist critics, who were made uncomfortable when the pop star deliberately enveloped her booty celebration in feminist discourse. Not only did she sample Adichie's "We Should All Be Feminists" TED Talk on YouTube for the track "Flawless," she also coopted language from the film *The Big Lebowski,* spoken in French on the track "Partition," to question why "feminists" supposedly don't like sex.

Most radical feminists would gladly respond to the pop star by clarifying that they don't like *patriarchal* sex, but what a sexuality liberated from patriarchy looks like is still anyone's guess, even if some—like bell hooks—would argue that Beyoncé's version of sexuality is not particularly feminist in the way she caters to the male gaze and appropriates the blonde-bombshell ideal to articulate black beauty.[26] Nonetheless,

Beyoncé obviously begins with the available sexual images in popular culture and remodels them for her own body, whether in the mimicry of the Parisian exotic dancer in "Partition" or the Houston street walker in "Yoncé," as a way to disrupt the racially essentialist meanings of black femininity. Moreover, in a culture that witnessed younger pop stars such as Miley Cyrus shedding her former Disney image by appropriating big-booty and "twerking" black background dancers and, thus, mobilizing their bodies as props in music videos and performances in attempts at sexual transgression, Beyoncé essentially performed "grown black womanhood" to shut down white-girl imitations and to reclaim the "twerk"—a New Orleans-based street dance within black queer subculture emphasizing rigorous movements of the derrière which, as ethnomusicologist Kyra Gaunt argues, is also a vernacular expression of the Internet that enables displaced New Orleans locals, in the aftermath of Hurricane Katrina, to share their culturally-based dances via YouTube.[27]

We could argue that Beyoncé once again reconstituted the bootylicious body for a different decade in the twenty-first century, as the subject of the booty had again taken on mainstream prominence, which *Vogue* acknowledged in its 2014 article. Jennifer Lopez, the "booty queen" from an earlier era, entered the fray that year when she joined with the latest hip-hop artist, white Australian rapper Iggy Azalea, on a single and video simply titled "Booty." That she would rather collaborate with a curvaceous white rapper than with Nicki Minaj, Beyoncé, or even pop star Rihanna, who wore a daring see-through gown that year inspired by the iconic Josephine Baker, speaks volumes about the Latina's allegiance to white mainstream beauty culture versus black culture. This is ironic, given that hip-hop's aesthetic—driven by black male desire (incidentally, all these women known for their curves had all been romantically linked to black men)—has caused this overall beauty shift.

However, Nicki Minaj received the most backlash and accusations of obscenity when she released a cover art for her single "Anaconda" that featured the rapper in a squat position while sporting a G-string that revealed her ample-sized behind. The cover art served as a preview for the raunchier video that featured varying women of different races with shapely behinds as they twerked against a backdrop of a tropical jungle. While Nicki spoke back to her online critics by posting on her Instagram images of more "acceptable" models—white and slender women similarly wearing G-string bikinis without inviting condemnation, in comparison to her own "unacceptable" image—her video seemed to signify on the longer tradition of colonized and racialized *pornotropic* landscapes (McClintock, 21), in which the bodies of women of color are aligned with the exotic tropical jungle—especially for the Trinidadian rapper, whose bootylicious body in the video (Figure 6.4) inspired a wax replica for Las Vegas's Madame Tussauds Wax Museum.

Within the kitchen space of the video, tropical fruits—from bananas to pineapples to papaya and coconuts—are decorously laid out to convey the edibility of her own body. Nicki literally renders her body delicious/bootylicious by playfully spraying herself with whipped cream, a gesture that is deliberately pornographic but also vaguely comical since she follows this act by violently slicing up a banana, itself a phallic symbol reminiscent of Sir Mix-a-lot's video for the sampling of "Baby Got Back." Nonetheless, the bawdy lyrics in "Anaconda" make explicit

**Figure 6.4**   Still from Nicki Minaj's "Anaconda" music video (2014).

the phrase, "he tossed my salad like his name Romaine," engaging in food metaphors for oral sex, much like Beyoncé singing about "drinking watermelon" or urging her partner to "eat my skittles, it's the sweetest in the middle," from her respective songs "Drunk in Love" and "Blow." All these examples highlight, once again, the edible black booty.

If Beyoncé faced the public's consternation at her hypersexuality, even if confined to the respectable arena of marital sex, Nicki Minaj's single status subjected her to harsher critique, which was also the result of her non-slender body being too outrageous, too cartoonish (as various social media memes of the cover art suggested), and just "too bootylicious." This is not surprising when we consider Beyoncé's own attempts at respectability with her revelations in her behind-the-scenes YouTube video that suggested her need to "get her body back"—referring to the weight she had gained while pregnant with her daughter Blue Ivy Carter, who was born in January 2012—and to do so in a much more sexualized way than in previous manifestations in her earlier videos and performances.[28] Despite the newly evolved "grown woman," her behind-the-scenes video highlights the pop star expressing coyness at the thought of either her husband or her mother watching her sexy videos. If anything, such confessions suggest that a black woman—no matter how "grown" she is— is all too conscious of the way her sexuality is subject to respectability policing within our own communities or the public at large. Nonetheless, Beyoncé's later collaborations with Nicki Minaj—including a remix of her feminist-themed "Flawless" and the fun-filled song and video, "I'm Feeling Myself"—demonstrate the complex ways that she continues to disrupt the arbitrary lines between sexiness and respectability.

### Encounters with History

Despite the respectability police, Beyoncé continues to push the envelope both sexually and politically. Having already staked a claim in feminism, the pop star expanded her political lens to comment on racial justice.[29] However, her acts on behalf of the Black Lives Matter movement—launched with the #BlackLivesMatter Twitter hashtag in the wake of the unjust killing of black teenager Trayvon Martin at the hands of a vigilante citizen—provoked a much more hostile reaction from the public, especially from police unions that called for a boycott of her concerts, as had occurred in the wake of her provocative music video and Super Bowl performance of her 2016 hit single "Formation." In the music video, the first image we see is Beyoncé atop a New Orleans police cruiser, partly submerged in flood water, which she will later sink at video's end. At once invoking the tragedy of post-Katrina devastation and police brutality—both extensions of state violence against black lives—Beyoncé strategically positions her body, clad in a country-style red and white dress, at the site of political resistance.

This is not the first instance of Beyoncé employing imagery of Louisiana. Indeed, Daphne Brooks notes the way her 2006 album, *B'Day,* invoked "the specter of Gulf Coast culture"[30] at a time when she and Destiny's Child had remained silent in the aftermath of Hurricane Katrina, which devastated New Orleans in 2005. While rapper Kanye West openly criticized President Bush for failing to respond to the disaster, Destiny's Child focused their efforts toward charity for displaced families in the region.

Tellingly, the video for "Formation" not only remixes the voice of the dead—as heard in the opening audio, featuring the late Messy Mya, a local personality—but also the sounds of the storm (thunder rolls are audible). The final audio of the video includes the voice of New Orleans native and Katrina survivor Kimberly Rivers Roberts, from the documentary film *Trouble the Water* (2008). It is almost as if the pop star's political voice had been suppressed for ten years—as Brooks argues, there are "more metaphorical than literal ties to Katrina on *B'Day*" (Brooks, 193)—and has finally found the occasion to vocalize and visualize dissent, made manifest with sampled footage from Abteen Bagheri's bounce-music documentary, *That B.E.A.T.* (2014), featuring the remnants of post-Katrina devastation and black queer men from New

Orleans reclaiming and queering the booty through feminine/femme/ queen moves in the employment of local "bounce" music (including an audio sampling from Big Freedia, the "queen" of bounce music, whose audacity as a gay black man supplies Beyoncé with a voice of defiance: "I came to slay, bitch!").

Such queer representations precede a preacher man in a local church, which is immediately followed by the prominent image of Beyoncé adorned in sacred black attire, jewelry, and wide-brimmed hat, channeling the Vodou loa Maman Brigitte, guardian of the souls of the dead who loves to curse and drink rum with hot peppers. Here is no clearer example of the pop star's insistence on blurring the boundaries between the heteronormative and the queer, between the hypersexual and the respectable, between the sacred and the profane, and especially between Christianity and African religion. It is no coincidence that her first line, "Y'all haters corny with that illuminati mess," both doubles as a refutation of Internet conspiracy theories proclaiming her involvement with a secret Satanic society called the Illuminati, as well as an embrace of an African cosmology that has long been demonized by church communities. Regardless of such denouncements, Beyoncé reclaims all the aspects of black life that have been relegated to the margins.

The video presents a catalog of visuals signifying Southern blackness, with echoes of the African Diaspora and the post-industrial world, as well as the historical. Empty swimming pools and parking lots suggest abandonment (perhaps in the aftermath of Hurricane Katrina) and an opportunity for rebuilding and resurrection. The pop star also gives her ancestral pedigree rooted in the Gulf region—"My daddy Alabama, Mama Louisiana/You mix that Negro with that Creole make a Texas bama"—against the backdrop of a parlor where portraits of an African king and queen hang from the walls.

The ladies in the parlor that Beyoncé and her group of women embody exist ambiguously between the respectability of "New Negro womanhood" from the turn-of-the-twentieth-century era and the less reputable positioning of "Creole" courtesans and concubines that birthed the multiple colors of blackness in the Louisiana heritage of plaçage, in which mixed-race women entered concubinage with European and Euro-American men. Specifically, the pop star alludes to photographer E.J. Bellocq's Storyville prostitutes in early-twentieth-century New Orleans, from the thigh-high striped stockings and corseted romper to the boudoir setting. As Griffin notes, Beyoncé routinely visualizes "commercial sexual culture" (Griffin, 140), referencing Beyoncé's music video for her 2006 song "Déjà Vu," which is alluded to in "Formation" with a "déjà vu" echo of the corseted "mulatta concubine" (Figure 6.5).

Regarding the mulatta concubine, Lisa Ze Winters has placed this historical figure at the center of the African Diaspora: "Light-skinned,

**Figure 6.5**   Still from Beyoncé's "Formation" music video (2016).

female, and always beautiful . . . her body [is] evidence of . . . the violence of white male desire . . . so central to economies of American slavery."[31] Intriguingly, Beyoncé signifies through her light-skinned body this mixed-raced Creole sexual history. This historical presence in "Formation" further suggests an ancestral backdrop to the more present-day twerking of the red-clad dancers who are seen gyrating in the hallway of a decorous home. These women already disrupt respectability politics by donning mutton sleeves, pearls, and booty-hugging bodysuits that emphasize their raunchy sexiness.

Beyoncé's battle cry to the "ladies"—"Let's get in formation"—triples as a call to "get information," a call to perfect the dance, and a call to militarize, to come together in collective defense of their bodies, their families, their neighborhoods, and their communities. The "twerk," far from being raucous and unruly—as is often depicted in both vernacular and choreographed dance moves—is instead presented as disciplined movement, in which black women are focused on their embodied power as they thrust their behinds with precision and controlled effect. When their very bodies were once enslaved and continue to be criminalized, Beyoncé suggests through this precise choreography how such women could enact mastery of the body and the styling of that body in a bid for liberation. Dance as a way of exhibiting control of the black body maintains centrality in black popular culture. Indeed, a young boy at video's end dances effortlessly and with power and freedom before a line of police in riot gear who eventually surrender to his artistic prowess. These images—including a graffitied message on the wall, "Stop Shooting Us," intended for both police and civilians—reinforce the political ethos of the value and precarity of black life.

That her "Formation" choreography made an appearance during the halftime show at the Super Bowl—replete with thirty black women backup dancers clad in Black-Panther style leather and berets while Beyoncé herself channeled Michael Jackson, sporting a jacket like the one he wore during his Super Bowl performance—demonstrates that the pop star is seriously grappling with the power and influence she must now yield to affirm black life. The video for "Formation," directed by Melina Matsoukas, featured cinematography by Malik Sayeed and Arthur Jafa, the latter renowned for his work on Julie Dash's *Daughters of the Dust.* That Dash's remastered version of her film on its twenty-fifth anniversary coincided with Beyoncé's release of her sixth album *Lemonade,* which premiered on the premium cable channel HBO during its free promotion weekend before it was made available on her co-owned music-streaming site Tidal, gestures toward a new black feminist filmic moment and a worthy successor to the earlier film. Not since *Daughters of the Dust* have black women looked dreamier, more glorious, more haunting, more celebrated, and more revered.

The different singles on the visual album of *Lemonade* are delivered cohesively as a complete musical and film narrative, held together expertly by both the striking visuals and especially by the poetry of Somalian British poet Warsan Shire, performed as spoken-word voice-overs that Beyoncé delivers in elusive pronouncements and whispers. Shire's added voice expands the global and transnational context for the local texts Beyoncé signifies through her construction of Southern black womanhood. *Lemonade* begins with the pop star in profile, her face hidden in an extreme close-up on her blondish cornrows, gold-studded earlobe, and an elaborate fur coat, all foreshadowing the verse "beautiful mane, I am the lion" from the song "Don't Hurt Yourself." The image— used as the cover art for the visual album—deliberately morphs Beyoncé into an animal-like force, with the "lion's mane"-like fur framing her body. We will come to this imagery again in a segment titled "Anger." Such an emphasis on "gold"—the fur, the earrings, the golden braids— will culminate in her embodiment of the Yoruba Orisha Oshun.

This is the goddess of fertility, wealth, and love, whose trademark yellow also recalls the color of lemonade: a "sweet water" for which Oshun is also known and which mixes the sweet and the sour—both literally and figuratively—as expressed in the "grandmother" wisdom of the narrative. Before we are provided with further context, however, the next shot depicts a chain hanging from the side of a wooden cabin, with a mossy tree towering just above it. Because of its black-and-white imagery, which contrasts with the earlier color shot, this scene invokes the past, as the chain and cabin both represent slavery, as does the following color shot of an ancient wall emerging from the cane fields.

Given that scenes from *Lemonade* were filmed on location at the Madewood and Destrehan plantations in Louisiana, this allusion to slavery is significant to the narrative, which on its most surface level follows the emotional journey of a woman betrayed by an unfaithful husband. Interweaving history with the present, and the personal with the political, Beyoncé broadens the scope of such marital betrayal—a common theme in black women's music, from the blues to R&B—to encompass a critique of the society at large, in which women have been betrayed by lovers, husbands, and a nation that once enslaved them but now subjects them to state violence, as referenced by the inclusion of the mothers of slain sons Trayvon Martin, Michael Brown and Eric Garner, who make an appearance in the climax of the album narrative. These women, often referred to as "Mothers of the Black Lives Matter Movement," alongside the spirits of the enslaved ancestors, situate the world of *Lemonade* in an Afrofuturism—based in black speculative fictions—that defies our temporal plane.

In such a world, Beyoncé provides stark contrast to the material dispossession that shaped the lives of enslaved black women—apart from those involved in plaçage—by fashioning their bodies, filmed both in color and black-and-white, in the glamour of Victorian steampunk haute couture. Because the women embody both present-day trends (tattoos and hairstyles) and period-costuming from the past, they effortlessly blur these historical lines. Indeed, in the first segment, "Intuition," Beyoncé narrates in voiceover a verse from Shire's poetry—"the past and future merge to meet us here"—while she emerges from an antique bathtub, presumably within the ancient walls earlier shown, and dons a *tignon* covering her head, a relic from New Orleans' past when laws required free mixed-race women to cover their hair to downplay their beautification hair rituals and, especially, to racially distinguish them from white women. That these women then transformed the obligatory tignon into its own aesthetic practice—which Beyoncé visualizes as a fashion statement—testifies to the legacy of black women's resistance, indeed turning "lemons" into "lemonade."

Given the conflict driving the narrative—her partner's infidelity with a "sidechick," later dismissed as "Becky with the good hair" (alluding to a white woman)—such historical imagery takes on deeper meaning. We need not interpret the narrative as autobiographical, as some of Beyoncé's fans have done in an online hunt for "Becky," even though earlier songs like "Resentment," "Ring the Alarm," and "Jealous" suggest an ongoing struggle with a cheating partner. Nonetheless, the significance of "Becky with the good hair" as both "sidechick" and oppressive feminine signifier of whiteness serves more as a figurative struggle for black women against the sexism and racism of the culture. Indeed, "Becky" as a moniker for white womanhood—whose origins reside in the opening of Sir Mix-a-Lot's "Baby Got Back" music video, which depicts two white women (one of whom is called Becky) derisively commenting on the size of a black woman's behind—symbolizes the antithesis to black beauty and femininity.

When Beyoncé first sings "Pray You Catch Me," the opening song, she is dressed in black and kneeling on a theatrical stage, her song highlighted as a meta-performance of desperation and melancholy. That she drifts among the cane fields before emerging on the rooftop of a city building suggests geographical dislocation and the timelessness of pain that drives her to suicide. Leaping from the roof, Beyoncé literally embodies Ntozake Shange's "colored girls who have considered suicide"; however, rather than hit the pavement below, the camera cuts to her diving shot into the underwater world of Oshun.

It is here that she encounters her dormant self, unconscious, not yet "woke," submerged in the demands of love, to try "to be soft, prettier . . . less awake." This segment, appropriately titled "Denial," struggles for voice, consciousness, and rage, which manifests in the underwater La Sirene figure resurrecting as Oshun, bedecked in an elaborate yellow gown with gushing waters accompanying her entrance as she opens the doors of a city hall, ready to exact her revenge. Threatening to flood the city streets, like Hurricane Katrina (already referenced in her "Formation" video), she is both lover scorned and a Hebrew-like "jealous God" who rains down the great flood onto her disobedient devotees and/or her unfaithful husband. For the featured song, a reggae-based "Hold Up," Beyoncé sets about destroying cars and store windows in her path with a baseball bat, all while gleefully smiling and laughing, thus signifying Oshun at her most dangerous, as well as the material work of Pipilotti Rist's audiovisual art, Ever is Over All. Not only does the pop star unleash the power of the Orishas but, through art, she signals her dismantling of the dominant gaze—best reflected in her destruction of a police surveillance camera and the music video camera itself.

Her destructive bat—labeled "hot sauce" in homage to Southern local flavors and domestic power, representing her hidden strength—is reminiscent of the one used in her music video for "Pretty Hurts," the opening song and narrative featured on her *BEYONCÉ* album that raged against the demands of beauty culture. There is a reason "Oshun" utilizes her bat to destroy the store window that advertises "free facials" and displays colored wigs. She especially targets symbols of power—busting open a water hydrant and liberating her waters from this state-controlled fixture, which takes on even deeper meaning with the water crisis in the predominately black town of Flint, Michigan (where the pop star has donated funds from her Formation world tour to bring clean water to the region) and hijacking a monster truck to destroy cars, a sign of masculine virility.

This otherworldly scene nonetheless fades into a scene from the "real" world for the next segment, "Anger," a reality signified through documentary footage of a black high school band performing elaborate choreography in the streets of a New Orleans neighborhood. Here, too, Beyoncé's spoken-word voiceover takes on double meaning, in which she sarcastically reassures her partner that she will emulate the other woman: "If this is what you truly want, I can wear her skin over mine . . . her hair over mine." These lines are delivered just as we catch a glimpse of the black dancing girls in the band, the lightest-skinned one with long hair positioned at the front while the darker-skinned girls appear at the back. That they are all subject to wearing "nude" hosiery intended for white complexions invites an association between the cheating narrative and a critique of the wider racist and colorist society.

Indeed, the scene cuts to the subterranean space of a parking garage, where black women outfitted in overlong sleeves as they struggle to free themselves, exist in the literal shadows and margins. Incidentally this is located near the Superdome stadium in New Orleans, the site for atrocious abandonment in the post-Katrina aftermath. Here, the Beyoncé from the opening scene, in her cornrows and fur coat, emerges alongside three other black women, coded as sex workers in their pose and style of dress. This is the pop star at her angriest, and the underground location suggests that this rage has been repressed.

Among the ghostly images of marginal black women is another specter—a bleached shot of a goddess-like woman, who will appear later in red, quietly sitting in a ring of fire. Here is Beyoncé, "the dragon breathing fire," declaring "when you hurt me, you hurt yourself." Not only does she voice her anger in "Don't Hurt Yourself," but she remixes a sample of Malcolm X's voice for feminist critique: "The most disrespected person in America is the black woman/ the most unprotected person in America is the black woman/ the most neglected person in America is the black woman."

Much like Nicki Minaj's controversial appropriation of Malcolm X's infamous "By any means necessary" photo to promote her violent "Looking-Ass Nigga" single raging against the male gaze, Beyoncé's remix of Malcolm X's speech utilizes masculine authority to validate gender-based oppression. However, she is not simply letting Malcolm X speak for himself. Invoking the voice of the dead, Beyoncé speaks through him: "Call me Malcolm X!" That she further samples Led Zeppelin's "When the Levees Break" for this song—which also features blues-rock artist Jack White—speaks volumes about her coupling racial concerns (with its inevitable allusion to Katrina) with sexual politics and musical legacies. The sample is itself a rendition of blues woman Memphis Minnie singing of the Great Flood of 1927 in the Gulf Coast region.

This sample also represents what Brittany Spanos calls Beyoncé's "important nod to the . . . forgotten place black women had in inspiring and forming the genre [of rock music]."[32] Given the subterranean location of these discarded women—the sex worker, the exiled goddess, the abandoned Katrina survivor, the forgotten black women of rock—Beyoncé's rage through song vows to break the silence, to break the barriers much like the hurricane winds of Katrina broke the levees in New Orleans. Noting how "Don't Hurt Yourself" transitions to a music-box rendition of Tchaikovsky's "Swan Lake," mournfully following the echoing cymbals of a black woman's drum set, Gaunt suggests the ballet's themes of heartbreak and dehumanization—specifically the heroine Odette's cursed entrapment in swan form, whose spell can only be broken by a faithful prince—are Beyoncé's "attempt[s] at restoring black women to their human form."[33]

Beyoncé restores the full humanity of black womanhood in multi-faceted ways. There is the sacred body artwork of Nigerian artist Laolu Senbanjo, which renders the bodies of the dancers, who appear in the black-and-white segment titled "Apathy," through the mystical. While featuring the song "Sorry," Beyoncé situates black women on a "party bus" and simultaneously intercuts these images with tennis champion Serena Williams gliding down an elegant staircase of a plantation home in heels while twerking in a bodysuit outlining her curvaceous body. In these ways, Beyoncé depicts joyously free and unbothered black women transgressing spaces once existing as sites of oppression—the Jim-Crow-era segregation of public transportation and the plantation house of the slave era—which have now become sites of liberation.

That "Sorry" closes on a dismissive to her husband—"you better call Becky with the good hair"—while Beyoncé sports intricate and stunningly gorgeous Nefertiti-style braids further upends the racial meanings of "good hair." Indeed, a transitional scene of women donning similar hairstyles resembles a coven of witches, nude and walking in a trance into the wilderness, thus signaling their departure from the white patriarchal world. This is immediately followed by Beyoncé's re-embodiment of our underground goddess, now shown in all her glory in an extravagant red gown, surrounded by flames. She makes manifest the "God [who was] in the room" during lovemaking.

She is Isis, the Egyptian moon goddess, or perhaps the Haitian Vodou loa and love goddess Erzulie, summoned in the segments "Emptiness" and "Loss" by the power of the Vodou priestess Marie Laveau, another Creole manifestation (alluded to in a scene depicting Beyoncé-turned-priestess, bathed in red light, who hypnotically swings a lightbulb in circular motion among a group of women). Beyoncé further embodies a sex worker in the featured song, "6 Inch," much like the "Creole Lady Marmalade" whom Patti LaBelle once serenaded, also harking back to the Storyville prostitute. Through the power of her sexuality and her rage, this "sacred whore" burns down the big house on the plantation—oppressive with its memories of black women's roles as house slaves, servants, and concubines.

Other African goddesses abound: from Oya-Yansa, warrior goddess of the storms, represented by Beyoncé's multicolored attire set against a stormy sky, to Yemaya, healing goddess summoning her women devotees entering her waters. In the segments "Resurrection" and "Hope," different groups of black women across generations, color complexions and hair textures gather together and build community away from the big house in the plantation space and on the grounds inhabited by enslaved ancestors, still haunting us like the women in the mossy trees: symbols of longevity and lineage. The French-Cuban musical duo and twins Ibeyi, who make a cameo appearance in *Lemonade*, conjured similar black-and-white tree imagery in their Santeria-inspired song and video "Oya."

Beyoncé has assembled and interwoven an eclectic collection, including her country song, "Daddy Lessons," whose origins in black music are reclaimed. The powerful "Freedom" remixes a Puerto Rican sixties psychedelic band, Kaleidoscope, with beats from blues songs collected by Alan Lomax, while the reggae-based song "All Night," which is featured in the final segment, "Redemption," suggests a Bob-Marl-eyesque redemption theme. That these songs hail from an era of civil rights and anti-colonialism indicate Beyoncé's attempts at intersecting present-day struggles with the past, while also highlighting a multiracial and transnational musical legacy. In connecting her reconciliation with her husband Jay Z—appearing in the segment, "Forgiveness," which features the ballad "Sandcastles"—with a montage of various heterosexual, gay, black, white, and interracial couples and families featured for the finale song "All Night," Lemonade gestures toward the universal, even as it is grounded in the black feminist proclamation that "the personal is political" and that "black lives matter." Here is a woman proclaiming "Freedom," a climactic song that Beyoncé sings before her collective community of black women—past and present—and choosing the multimedia platforms for her music distribution all while announcing her full autonomy.

### Conclusion: Body Politics

It was inevitable, after such bold political statements, that Beyoncé would eventually enter the fray of the 2016 election season. She made an appearance at a Hillary Rodham Clinton rally in Cleveland, Ohio, aimed to get out the vote. There, she, and her women backup dancers, wore pantsuits in homage to Clinton's signature style while the pop star highlighted her role as a mother who sees a woman president representing "limitless possibilities" for her daughter. Moreover, Beyoncé boldly reclaimed in a digital collage Clinton's "baked cookies" remark from 1992, for which the presidential candidate had been vilified over the years for daring to be an ambitious woman entering the political sphere while refuting domestic expectations.

However, the backlash against Beyoncé's provocative performances perhaps foreshadowed the victory of Donald J. Trump over Clinton on Election Day. Several voters had tired of the racial and feminist progress that the pop star fully embraced, and Beyoncé has entered unchartered territory as a politicized mainstream artist instead of an All-American sweetheart willing to subjugate her black identity. The cultural landscape was changing but not fast enough, considering that—despite Clinton's ability to win the popular vote—she could not secure a historic win as the first woman president of the United States.

Nonetheless, as women throughout the U.S. and the world mobilized massive protests through social media and on the streets, in the wake of Trump's presidential inauguration, and resisted the misogyny, racism, and xenophobia that his campaign ignited, Beyoncé embodied a different protest on the stage of the 2017 Grammy Awards show. After pictorially announcing on her Instagram that she was pregnant with twins, Beyoncé again summoned the goddess Oshun, bearing her pregnant belly—perhaps to preemptively strike against any potential rumors of a "fake" pregnancy, as had plagued her pregnancy with her daughter Blue Ivy. As Kameelah L. Martin argues, Beyoncé is "head priestess in charge" who "gathers her womenfolk to commence a ritual healing with her artistic hoodoo,"[34] as she boldly did on the Grammy stage.

Reminding the audience that bootylicious bodies like hers are the source of life, she implores them through Shire's poetry to "remember the hips that cracked" for our collective births—thus connecting the sexuality of conception to the pain of childbirth. In the televised performance, Beyoncé digitally syncretizes Oshun, the Virgin Mary, and the Hindu goddess Durga while also multiplying her image alongside her mother Tina Knowles, her daughter, and other women. Moreover, in a cultural and political climate that routinely seeks to regulate and legislate against women's reproductive rights and that constantly denigrates the bodies of black and brown women, the pop star's daring display of black beauty and maternal divination subverts the political reinstatement of white supremacy and masculine power.

Knowing how the ancestors work, perhaps the spirit of Baartman seized the occasion of her bicentennial anniversary to ensure that her name would be invoked alongside one of the biggest pop stars in the world. Perhaps she knew before the rest of us what Beyoncé had in mind for 2016; that the pop star indeed was already involved in spirit work and would seek both artistic and divine intervention, by way of Oshun, to heal our past and remind us of our collective power. As Joan Morgan argues, "Of all the tools Oshun is said to carry, perhaps the most powerful one is her mirror. The layperson mistakes this for a sign of her vanity . . . [but] Oshun holds up [the mirror] to our faces when she requires us to do the difficult work of really seeing ourselves."[35]

Through this African Venus, Beyoncé lauds the collective black body politic, encompassing Baartman, our enslaved ancestors, and present-day black women in the process. She reminds us of the spirits that continue to shape our ways of seeing and being seen. Whether we call her Black, Sable, or "Hottentot," this Venus insists on holding up her mirror of resistance so that we may all see her beauty and ours, that we may reflect on our own brilliance and embrace our full humanity. Only then could we recognize our divinity and proclaim our dignity.

# EPILOGUE

As we have seen, beauty ideology is deeply rooted in cultural ideologies of race, gender, and sexuality—views that have supported the subjugation of women and people of African descent. Because of this, we may be compelled to define works that re-present black female bodies in contexts of beauty and desirability as examples of political resistance. Subsequently, access to media and knowledge production, which privilege marginalized groups, remains a significant struggle in dismantling the intersections of racism and sexism. Thus, our understanding of present-day power dynamics in aesthetic practices, as well as an awareness of historical practices of visual oppression—as Sara Baartman's story attests—may signal an important step in the direction of social change.

Nevertheless, it is unlikely that black women will find their liberation in "higher" echelons of society—the academy, law, medicine, science, or mass media—as long as most black bodies are still reduced to objects of poverty, violence, and consumerism, with a few black bodies "tokenized" in these higher arenas. In fields of art and media, where black women artists and writers stand the best chance of transforming representations of blackness and beauty, class limitations also combine with race and gender restrictions in determining both the production and accessibility of black women's creative work.[1] Because of this, Audre Lorde has famously commented that:

> A room of one's own may be a necessity for writing prose, but so are reams of paper, a typewriter [or computer for our current period], and plenty of time. The actual requirements to produce the visual arts also help determine, along class lines, whose art is whose. In this day of inflated prices for material, who are our sculptors, our painters, our photographers? When we speak of a broadly based women's culture, we need to be aware of the effect of class and economic differences on the supplies available for producing art. (Lorde, 116)[2]

By highlighting the economies of aesthetic production, Lorde reminds us that intersections of race, class, and gender oppression limit the creative options of black women and other marginalized groups. Moreover, she calls attention to the ways in which art—an important tool in revisions of aesthetics and productions of images—can be classified and valued, or undervalued, by these means. Categorizations of certain art as "high" or "low" depend very much on the class of the artist; thus Lorde concludes that "poetry is not a luxury" because it functions for most women and people of color as "the most economical" art form that "requires the least physical labor, the least material, and the one which can be done between shifts" (116).[3]

Not only is black women's participation in artistic productions necessary for transformations of images, so is their access to media, which make these productions available to the public. As Michele Wallace suggests, the challenge is to transform the roles of black people, especially black women, and other people of color from consumers to participatory producers in fields of culture and communication. She thus comments:

> [People of color] neither own nor manage—except in the case of marginal institutions—publishing companies, magazines, television stations, film studios, museums, theatres. . . . Blacks are discouraged from service as writers, editors, curators, and directors. . . . As perpetual

objects of contemplation, contempt, derision, appropriation, and
marginalization, Afro-Americans are kept too busy to ever become
producers. (Wallace, 98)

Because people of color have been prevented on a grand scale from
access to these managerial positions, societal expectations position
them as objects and passive consumers, which collude in this exclusion. Moreover, within the context of the information age, these concerns are reflected in their access to computers and the Internet, where
fewer women and people of color participate, in comparison to men and
white people, as web users, let alone as web designers and writers. This is
especially significant since the Internet provides an alternative space for
creative work beyond traditional media outlets, which is more so in the
context of social media.

Fortunately, those few black women artists and writers who do have
access to visual and literary tools of media have attempted re-presentations of black female bodies and have resisted the objectification efforts
of dominant culture, even as they suggest that struggles persist in transforming this iconography. In addition, they expand their struggles to
privilege black women's experiences across the globe and across time
periods.

Within this framework, efforts made by indigenous African groups
and African American women thinkers on this side of the Atlantic to
memorialize and politicize the history of Baartman reflect a larger issue.
Namely, these diverse communities have exercised their power and
awareness of their self-worth through these political demands. With such
late-twentieth-century developments as movements for Civil Rights,
women's rights, and "Third World" liberation, the fight for Baartman's
return, burial, and memorial represents an extension of these struggles
and reconciliation with an oppressive past.

Our ability as marginalized subjects to identify with other marginalized peoples on this planet thus depends upon our acknowledgment of
our direct or indirect support of a global economy and world community

that render most African people and other people of color on the lowest rung of the economic and social ladder. This awareness could clear the way for more than an "imagined alliance" between African American women and non-Western women.

The term "imagined alliance" is taken from an essay by Wahneema Lubiano, who suggests the following: "'Imagining alliances'... requires that we look carefully at the difficulties, at the obstacles to alliances; otherwise, the powerful *attractiveness* [emphasis added] of alliance possibilities will hide the very pitfalls that frequently disrupt those alliance possibilities."[4] Here, Lubiano specifically refers to the lack of criticism, on the part of African American women, of national privileges that African Americans possess when they are used in the military, for example, to further U.S. foreign policies. Although Lubiano recognizes the economic limitations of African Americans that lead them to join the armed services, she nonetheless urges a critical analysis of how these positions prohibit alliance possibilities. She also suggests ways that African American feminism, in particular, can begin the process of self-criticism through the example of the vocal group known as Sweet Honey in the Rock. Their political song, "Are My Hands Clean?" (1985), questions how a working-class black woman purchasing a blouse on sale at a U.S. department store perpetuates the oppression of women in developing countries who provided the labor to make that blouse. Through our consumerist positions, even if we may be poor, we assist U.S. global policies and strengthen its system of power, dominance, and exploitation, thus reinforcing global and patriarchal white supremacy—the very structure at the heart of our struggles. Neither consumerism nor romanticism respects depth, complexity, or solidarity. Thus, if we can resist these imperialist impulses, perhaps we might then develop a worldview that is not an extraction from a culture of the past, giving us solace in a timeless, ahistorical "Africa," or a distant, exotic "Third World," with imagined solidarity based on skin color or reproductive organs, the latter curtailed even further around a presumed cisgender experience.

One black feminist text that manages to complicate yet affirm the transnational connections of black women's lives is Edwidge Danticat's 1994 novel *Breath, Eyes, Memory*.[5] Through an exploration of the mother-daughter relationship, as well as through invocations of the local flavor of Haitian Vodou, the novel interweaves the local and the global, the urban and rural, the modern and traditional. She also signifies on black diasporic identity through humor and irony. For instance, Danticat renders our protagonist Sophie's African American guru-therapist, Rena, in ironic terms. Described as a "gorgeous black woman who was an initiated Santeria priestess . . . [and who served] two years in the Peace Corps in the Dominican Republic" (Danticat, 206), Rena represents the African American spiritual consumer who appropriates from the "Third World" her own brand of Afrocentric identity even as she participates within U.S. imperialist forces. However, Rena, in her "brightly colored prints, noisy bangles, and open sandals" (206), is both therapist and spiritualist. She disrupts the professional divide between the sacred and the secular in ways that can be seen as empowering and affirming of an African diasporic identity. Rena's body also becomes a site for alternative aesthetic practices. Such identities are also formed through Sophie's involvement in group therapy with fellow multiracial and multinational women immigrants in New York, whom she meets through Rena, which complements her connections with the women of Haiti. Within these groups, Sophie comes to accept and confront, especially through invocation of Vodou's love goddess Erzulie (a Black Venus figure), her troubled sexual history alongside the sexual histories of the women in her representative groups.

Such narratives remind us of the power of the word and the image to affirm and critique black feminist thought and aesthetics. Subsequently, we may recognize Danticat's novel as an act of resistance and articulation of a transnational black feminism. This understanding and awareness incorporate antiracist and antisexist ideologies to reevaluate meanings of black womanhood. Thus, prevailing images and stereotypes of black femininity in dominant culture are confronted, interrogated, and eventually subverted in various efforts to re-present black female bodies in cultural productions.

Beyond Diasporic literature is the arena of beauty and fashion. Indeed, pop stars like Robyn Rihanna Fenty—another Caribbean transplant who repositions her local Barbadian regionality for transnational appeal—have enhanced the visibility of black women's bodies when launching her cosmetics line, *Fenty Beauty* through Sephora, in the fall season of 2017. By marketing toward women of color consumers, perhaps best represented with Sudanese-Australian model Duckie Thot featured in the opening of the advertisement, Rihanna emphasized the inclusivity of *all* women (including white, Asian, hijab-wearing brown women, and Latina women shown in the ad), thus making her product, which offers forty different shades of foundation, the most diverse and inclusive thus far in the cosmetics industry. Given the widespread use of skin-bleaching creams on the African continent and in countries like India, this inclusivity marketing is quite a feat and one that we can imagine could only be conceived by a woman of African descent, even one who benefits from lighter-skin privilege. The various shades of brown women, who are then anchored by the pop star herself closing out the ad for *Fenty Beauty* suggests that Rihanna—much like the first black millionaire and beauty entrepreneur Madam C.J. Walker a century before her—is aligned with her consumer-audience and not just standing aloof as a would-be wealthy capitalist selling a product. This may explain why the darkest shades of her cosmetics line sold out within days of its opening.

Proving that she is more than a singer and trendsetter, Rihanna is also poised to co-star with Lupita Nyong'o in a potential heist movie, to be directed by African American filmmaker Ava DuVernay and based on a script to be written by black rising star Issa Rae. This concept, developed by black women on the social media sites Tumblr and Twitter, may come to fruition with reports that the streaming site company Netflix secured a deal at the 2017 Cannes Film Festival to develop this film project. The social-media concept developed from a photograph featuring the well-dressed duo sitting side by side at a 2014 Miu Miu fashion show in Paris, which naturally excited African American women who viewed the Barbadian and Kenyan celebrities as representing a transnational beauty ideal that captures the elegance and richness of both light-brown and darker-brown shades of black womanhood.

Black feminist aesthetics, then, in transforming images as well as arenas in which such imagery is produced, can be situated in a praxis, which, according to Patricia Hill Collins, "views the world as a dynamic place where the goal is not merely to survive or to fit in or to cope; rather, it becomes a place where we feel ownership and accountability" (Collins, 1990, 237). This worldview insists on viewing black feminist work as not just creating agency and subjectivity in art and media but in perpetuation of lived experiences that move beyond mere survival toward fulfillment. Such theory and practice will continue to challenge beauty hegemonies and create alternative aesthetics. This is no small feat, as we only need to remember Sara Baartman to realize that a slogan such as "Black is beautiful" is never superficial and always political.

# NOTES

## Foreword

1. Priscilla Netto, "Reclaiming the Body of the 'Hottentot' The Vision and Visuality of the Body Speaking with Vengeance in Venus Hottentot 2000," *European Journal of Women's Studies* 12, no.2 (2005): 149–163; Mansell Upham, "From the Venus Sickness to the Hottentot Venus, Part Two," *Quarterly Bulletin of the National Library of South Africa* 61, no.2 (2007): 74–82; Deborah Willis, ed., *Black Venus 2010: They Called Her "Hottentot"* (Philadelphia: Temple University Press, 2010); Harvey Young, *Embodying Black Experience: Stillness, Critical Memory, and the Black Body* (Ann Arbor: University of Michigan Press, 2010); Natasha Gordon-Chipembere, ed., *Representation and Black Womanhood: The Legacy of Sarah Baartman* (New York: Palgrave Macmillan, 2011); Simone Kerseboom, "Grandmother-Martyr-Heroine: Placing Sara Baartman in South African Post-Apartheid Foundational Mythology," *Historia* 56, no.1 (2011): 63–76; Rachel Holmes, *African Queen: The Real Life of the Hottentot Venus* (New York: Random House, 2007); Clifton Crais and Pamela Scully, *Sara Baartman and the Hottentot Venus: A Ghost Story and a Biography* (Princeton: Princeton University Press, 2010).
2. This listing refers to the following creative works: Brooklyn-based burlesque dancer Akynos's erotic variety show *Thick* (2010); the paintings *Birth of Venus Hottentot* by Beth Consetta Rubel (2010), an untitled portrait of Baartman by Frederick Mpuuga (2013), *The Ghost of the Hottentot Venus* by Brian Kirhagis (2014), and *Hottentot Venus* by Camil Williams (2015). Plays include *Venus' Daughter* by Meghan Swaby (2016) and *Hottentotted* by Charly Evon Simpson (2016).
3. Natasha Maria Gordon-Chipembere, "'Even with the Best of Intentions': The Misreading of Sarah Baartman's Life," Agenda: Empowering Women for Gender Equity, 68 (2006): 54–62; Tavia Nyong'o, "The Body in Question," *International Journal of Communication* 1 (2007): 27–31.
4. Paul Gilroy, *The Black Atlantic: Modernity and Double Consciousness* (Cambridge: Harvard University Press, 1993).
5. Cited in Janell Hobson, "Black Women's Histories: A Conversation with Mireille Miller-Young," *Ms. Magazine Blog* (February 3, 2015), available: http://msmaga zine.com/blog/2015/02/03/black-womens-histories-a-conversation-with-mireille-miller-young.

6. Cleuci de Oliveira, "Saartjie Baartman: The Original Booty Queen," *Jezebel* (November 14, 2014), available: http://jezebel.com/saartje-baartman-the-original-booty-queen-1658569879.
7. Gail Dines, "Nicki Minaj: Little More Than a Big Butt?" *Huffington Post* (September 27, 2014), available: http://www.huffingtonpost.co.uk/gail-dines/nicki-minaj_b_5629232.html.
8. Bettina Judd, *Patient. Poems* (New York: Black Lawrence Press, 2014), 61.
9. *Venus Noire,* directed by Abdellatif Kechiche, distributed by MK2 Productions, 2010.
10. Clifton Crais and Pamela Scully were historical consultants on the film.
11. Katrina Dyonne Thompson, "'Some were Wild, some were Soft, some were Tame, and some were Fiery': Female Dancers, Male Explorers, and the Sexualization of Blackness, 1600–1900," *Black Women, Gender, and Families* 6, no. 2 (2012): 1–28.
12. "South Africa Anger after Sarah Baartman's Grave Defaced," BBC News (April 28, 2015), available: http://www.bbc.com/news/world-africa-32499070.

# Chapter 1

1. Saartjie is Dutch for "little Sarah," which has been contested in postcolonial South African discourse that refers to Baartman as "Sara," to distinguish from the Dutch moniker, often interpreted as derogatory. While I had chosen to use the name Saartjie Baartman in the earlier stages of my writing, since it had appeared first in the historical record, I will use "Sara" for the purposes of this study.
2. This is a reference to the term "esthetic of resistance," used in Ella Shohat and Robert Stam, *Unthinking Eurocentrism: Multiculturalism and the Media* (New York: Routledge, 1994), 292, and coined by Mikhail Bakhtin in *Rabelais and His World,* translated by Hélène Iswolsky (Bloomington: Indiana University Press, 1984); both hereafter cited in text.
3. Using the term "West," or "Western," is already problematic. I refer here to generalizations that concur when speaking of a culture or ideology as "Western" or emerging from the "West." The term not only serves to reinforce Euro-centric ideas that geographically distinguish Euro-based nations from their "Far Eastern" or "Middle Eastern" neighbors—such as Asia and Arab nations—as they locate themselves to the "West" of these cultures, but it also conflates a diverse range of European and North American cultures as somehow maintaining similar worldviews and cultural practices. At the same time, I use the term "Western" and other variants to suggest that, through a belief in the shared "whiteness" of predominantly white nations from Europe and North America, a commonality of ideas and practices can be recognized in opposition to worldviews that emerge from cultures that resist or that existed before colonization by "Western" nations. Thus, it may be more appropriate to refer to white-dominated cultures—with ideologies that have been shaped by white supremacy—as dominant cultures and to locate black women studied in this project within this dominance as they try to redefine their subordinated positions.
4. This is in reference, respectively, to Bernth Lindfors, "'The Hottentot Venus' and Other African Attractions in Nineteenth-Century England," *Australasian Drama Studies* 1, no. 2 (1983): 100, and Z. S. Strother, "Display of the Body Hottentot," in *Africans on Stage,* edited by Bernth Lindfors (Bloomington: Indiana University Press, 1999), 1; both hereafter cited in text.

5. See the following examples: Yvette Abraham, "Images of Sara Baartman: Sexuality, Race, and Gender in Early-Nineteenth-Century Britain," in *Nation, Empire, Colony: Historicizing Gender and Race,* edited by Ruth Roach Pierson, Nupur Chaudhuri, and Beth McAuley (Bloomington: Indiana University Press, 1998); bell hooks, *Black Looks: Race and Representation* (Boston: South End Press, 1992); Kimberly Wallace-Sanders, *Skin Deep, Spirit Strong: The Black Female Body in American Culture* (Ann Arbor: University of Michigan Press, 2002); and Deborah Willis and Carla Williams, *The Black Female Body: A Photographic History* (Philadelphia: Temple University Press, 2002). All references are hereafter cited in text.

6. Nancy Hartsock, "The Feminist Standpoint: Developing the Ground for a Specifically Feminist Historical Materialism," in *Discovering Reality: Feminist Perspectives on Epistemology, Metaphysics, Methodology, and Philosophy of Science,* edited by Sandra Harding and Merrill B. Hintikka (Dordrecht: Reidel, 1983), 283–310; Sandra Harding, *Whose Science, Whose Knowledge? Thinking from Women's Lives* (Ithaca: Cornell University Press, 1991); Patricia Hill Collins, *Black Feminist Thought: Knowledge, Consciousness, and the Politics of Empowerment* (New York: Routledge, 1990). All references are hereafter cited in text.

7. Uma Narayan, *Dislocating Culture: Identities, Traditions, and Third World Feminism* (New York: Routledge, 1997).

8. Audre Lorde, *Sister Outsider: Essays and Speeches* (Freedom, CA: The Crossing Press, 1984), 115–16; hereafter cited in text.

9. Kimberly Wallace-Sanders, who taught this seminar at Emory University in spring 1999, has since published an anthology of the same title (2002).

10. "Body politic" is understood to mean a people constituting a collective unit. Throughout this book, I refer to the "body politic" specifically to disrupt this political, social, and cultural collectivity by calling attention to its normative constructions of race and gender, as well as to the ways that this unit posits bodily difference.

11. I am grateful to Namita Goswami, fellow Emory doctoral student at the time, who accompanied me on this research trip as we furthered our studies on Baartman.

12. T. Denean Sharpley-Whiting, *Black Venus: Sexualized Savages, Primal Fears, and Primitive Narratives in French* (Durham, NC: Duke University Press, 1999), 24; hereafter cited in text.

13. This is not to suggest that men do not have concerns about physical attractiveness, especially African American men who, because of their racial difference, are often reduced in visual culture to their bodies.

14. Preface to Barbara Summers, *Skin Deep: Inside the World of Black Fashion Models* (New York: Amistad Press, 1998).

15. Ben Arogundade, *Black Beauty: A History and Celebration* (New York: Thunder's Mouth Press, 2000), 144–45; hereafter cited in text.

16. Michel Foucault, *Discipline and Punish: The Birth of the Prison,* translated by Alan M. Sheridan-Smith (New York: Vintage Books, 1979), 217; hereafter cited in text.

17. Toni Morrison, *Playing in the Dark: Whiteness and the Literary Imagination* (Cambridge, MA: Harvard University Press, 1992), 38; hereafter cited in text.

18. Noël Carroll, "Ethnicity, Race, and Monstrosity: The Rhetoric of Horror and Humor," in *Beauty Matters,* edited by Peggy Zeglin Brand (Bloomington: Indiana University Press, 2000), 38.

19. Mikhail Bakhtin, *The Dialogic Imagination,* edited by Michael Holquist and translated by Caryl Emerson and Michael Holquist (Austin: Texas University Press, 1981), 159.

20. Rosemarie Garland Thomson, *Extraordinary Bodies: Figuring Disability in American Culture and Literature* (New York: Columbia University Press, 1997), 46; hereafter cited in text.

21. Sander Gilman, "Black Bodies, White Bodies: Toward an Iconography of Female Sexuality in Art, Medicine, and Literature," in *"Race," Writing, and Difference,* edited by Henry Louis Gates Jr. (Chicago: University of Chicago Press, 1986), 231; hereafter cited in text.

22. Iris Marion Young, *Throwing Like a Girl and Other Essays in Feminist Philosophy and Social Theory* (Bloomington: Indiana University Press, 1990), 153.

23. See Jennifer L. Morgan, "'Some Could Suckle over Their Shoulder': Male Travelers, Female Bodies, and the Gendering of Racial Ideology, 1500–1770," *William and Mary Quarterly* 54 (1997): 167–92, and Winthrop Jordan, *White over Black: American Attitudes toward the Negro, 1550–1812* (Chapel Hill: The University of North Carolina Press, 1968), 39; both hereafter cited in text.

24. See Jan Todd, "Bring on the Amazons: An Evolutionary History," in *Picturing the Modern Amazon,* edited by Joanna Frueh, Laurie Fierstein, and Judith Stein (New York: Rizzoli, 2000), 48–61.

25. Cited in Nell Painter, *Sojourner Truth: A Life, a Symbol* (New York: W. W. Norton & Co., 1996); hereafter cited in text.

26. Painter argues that Truth did not have this number of children and that either Gage inserted this number in her account, or that Truth made a symbolic gesture in linking her body with the bodies of other enslaved women.

27. Jacqueline E. Brady, "Pumping Iron with Resistance: Carla Dunlap's Victorious Body," in *Recovering the Black Female Body,* edited by Michael Bennett and Vanessa D. Dickerson (New Brunswick, NJ: Rutgers University Press, 2001), 253–54.

28. Preface to Henry Louis Gates Jr., *The Signifying Monkey: A Theory of African-American Literary Criticism* (New York: Oxford University Press, 1988).

29. Lorraine O'Grady, "Olympia's Maid: Reclaiming Black Female Subjectivity," *Afterimage* 20, no. 1 (1992): 14; hereafter cited in text.

30. Evelynn Hammonds, "Black (W)holes and the Geometry of Black Female Sexuality," *Differences* 6, no. 2–3 (1995): 141; hereafter cited in text.

31. Hortense Spillers, "Interstices: A Small Drama of Words," in *Pleasure and Danger: Exploring Female Sexuality,* edited by Carole Vance (London: Pandora, 1989), 74.

32. Here, Hammonds expands on the metaphor of the black hole, first referenced by black feminist Michele Wallace in her *Invisibility Blues: From Pop to Theory* (New York: Verso, 1990); hereafter cited in text.

33. See Yvette Abraham (1998); Anne Fausto-Sterling, "Gender, Race, and Nation: The Comparative Anatomy of 'Hottentot' Women in Europe, 1814–1817," in *Deviant Bodies,* edited by Jennifer Terry and Jacqueline Urla (Bloomington: Indiana University Press, 1995), 19–48; and Karla Holloway, *Codes of Conduct: Race, Ethics, and the Color of Our Character* (New Brunswick, NJ: Rutgers University Press, 1995). All references are hereafter cited in text.

# Chapter 2

1. Georges Cuvier, "Extrait d'observations Faites sur le cadavre d'une femme connue à Paris et à Londres sous le nom de Venus Hottentote" (Observation Extracts Made on the Cadaver of a Young Female Known in Both Paris and London by the Name of Hottentot Venus) in *Notes of Museum d'Histoire Naturelle* (Paris, 1817).

Extracts of this document are also included in Frederic Cuvier and Geoffroy St. Hilaire's *Histoire naturelle des mammifères* (Paris: A. Berlin, 1824–27). This English translation is provided in Sander Gilman, *Difference and Pathology* (Ithaca: Cornell University Press, 1985).

2. Here, I refer to concepts of racial othering as explored in Frantz Fanon's *Black Skin, White Masks,* translated by Charles L. Markmann (New York: Grove Press, 1967).

3. See Gilman (1985) and E. Frances White, *Dark Continent of Our Bodies: Black Feminism and the Politics of Respectability* (Philadelphia: Temple University Press, 1999); both hereafter cited in text.

4. See Zine Magubane, "Which Bodies Matter? Feminism, Poststructuralism, Race, and the Curious Theoretical Odyssey of the 'Hottentot Venus,'" *Gender and Society* 15, no. 6 (2001): 816–34; hereafter cited in text.

5. Strother argues that, historically, "Hottentots" were regarded as "reserved" or "undersexed" because the men only possessed one testicle and the women's *tablier,* or aprons, provided a "barrier of flesh guarding their modesty" (39).

6. Excerpts from Cuvier's description are translated into English in Anne Fausto-Sterling (1995, 37–38) and T. Denean Sharpley-Whiting (1999, 24).

7. Cited in Paul Edwards and James Walvin, *Black Personalities in the Era of the Slave Trade* (Baton Rouge: Louisiana State University Press, 1983), 172; hereafter cited in text.

8. See Kim F. Hall, *Things of Darkness: Economies of Race and Gender in Early Modern England* (Ithaca, NY: Cornell University Press, 1995); Jacob Lassner, *Demonizing the Queen of Sheba* (Chicago: University of Chicago Press, 1993); and Jan Nederveen Pieterse, *White on Black: The Image of Africa and Blacks in Western Popular Culture* (New Haven, CT: Yale University Press, 1992). All references are hereafter cited in text.

9. In addition to Jordan's 1968 study, see also Paula Giddings, *When and Where I Enter* (New York: William Morrow & Co., 1984).

10. For more on the connections between sexual and imperial conquest, see Anne McClintock, *Imperial Leather: Race, Gender, and Sexuality in the Colonial Conquest* (New York: Routledge, 1994). For feminist interpretations of native American women's history, see Paula Gunn Allen, *The Sacred Hoop: Recovering the Feminine in American Indian Traditions* (Boston: Beacon Press, 1986); hereafter cited in text.

11. Some examples include La Malinche of Mexico, Barbi on the Caribbean island of St. Kitts, Pocahontas and Sacagawea in U.S. history, and Truganini of Australia.

12. Cited in Bryan Edwards, The History, Civil and Commerce, of the British Colonies of the West Indies, vol. 2 (London, 1794).

13. Cited in Hugh Honour, *The Image of the Black in Western Art.* vol. 4, pt. 2. (Cambridge, MA: Harvard University Press, 1989), 13.

14. Londa Schiebinger, *Nature's Body: Gender in the Making of Modern Science* (Boston: Beacon Press, 1993), 127; hereafter cited in text.

15. Jenny Sharpe, *Ghosts of Slavery: A Literary Archaeology of Black Women's Lives* (Minneapolis: University of Missouri Press, 2003), 49; hereafter cited in text.

16. Peter Kolb, *The Present State of the Cape of Good Hope,* 2 vols, translated by Guido Medley. (London, 1731).

17. Pieterse includes an eighteenth-century illustration from Britain, titled "The Orang-Outang Carrying off a Negro Girl," 38. See also Deborah Gray White, who quotes Thomas Jefferson as having said that the orangutan preferred "the black

woman over those of his own species," in *A'r'n't I a Woman? Female Slaves in the Plantation South* (New York: W. W. Norton & Co., 1985), 30.

18. See also Fausto-Sterling and Thomson.

19. Saidiya V. Hartman, *Scenes of Subjection: Terror, Slavery, and Self-Making in Nineteenth-Century America* (New York: Oxford University Press, 1997).

20. John Gabriel Stedman, *Narrative of a Five Years' Expedition against the Revolted Negroes of Surinam* (London, 1796), 266.

21. John Burdick, *Blessed Anastácia: Women, Race, and Popular Christianity in Brazil* (New York: Routledge, 1998).

22. Sara Baartman's ethnic origin is up for dispute. Georges Cuvier (1817), who dissected Baartman's cadaver, described her as belonging to the "*Bushman* race," known as San. Strother believes that the Hottentots, referenced in European travel narratives, describe the Khoikhoi tribe. Biographical accounts of Baartman are provided by Gilman (1985), Sharpley-Whiting, and the 1998 film *The Life and Times of Sara Baartman*, directed by Zola Maseko.

23. In a paper presented at the African Studies Association meeting in November 2004, historian Pamela Scully suggests that the accepted story of Baartman's life might be radically different than most of us have imagined, when we focus on her experiences at the Cape in colonial South Africa instead of her life in Europe. This includes evidence that Baartman may have been older by a decade, and one of her exhibitors, Hendrik Cezar, was a free man of color.

24. Alexander Dunlop, who was originally included in the contract as an exhibitor, later backed out, fearing that Baartman would not be an attraction. See *The Life and Times of Sara Baartman* (1998). However, he re-enters the picture and begins to have a more prominent position in comparison to Hendrik Cezar (Clifton and Crais, 97).

25. Cuvier declared in his writings that Baartman died of small pox, which was complicated by alcoholism.

26. Similar interpretations of this cartoon are made by Maseko and Sharpley-Whiting.

27. Although the "scramble for Africa" between European powers is recognized as taking place during the late nineteenth and early twentieth centuries, I use this phrase to remind us of the colonizing forces already unfolding on the continent in the late eighteenth and early nineteenth centuries.

28. Richard Altick, *The Shows of London* (Cambridge, MA: Harvard University Press, 1978), 269; hereafter cited in text.

29. The Irish, especially with the battle against English annexation of Ireland, have long existed within British culture as perpetual outsiders, so we should find Cezar's analogous construction particularly striking.

30. An interesting debate, featured in Maseko's film, discusses Baartman's agency to speak on her own behalf.

31. A copy of this baptism certificate exists at the Musée de l'Homme in Paris.

32. A translation of this play, originally titled *La Venus Hottentote; ou la haine aux françaises*, is included in the Appendix of Sharpley-Whiting's *Black Venus: Sexualized Savages, Primal Fears, and Primitive Narratives in French* (1999). In addition, the second chapter in this book provides a close reading of this play.

33. "La Venus Hottentote," *Journal des dames et des modes* (January 25, 1815): 37–40.

34. This description is quite similar to reactions from some observers in London of Baartman's show on Piccadilly Circus. See Altick, 269–70. See also Edwards and Walvin, 172.

35. This is from "callipygous," meaning "beautiful backside." This is a specific representation of the Greco-Roman Venus.
36. This is my translation. This newspaper account is also included in Maseko's film.
37. Baartman was already drinking heavily, suggesting her resistance to human exhibition through self-medication.
38. In particular, Blainville compared Baartman to a monkey when she pouted her lips. In his account—"Sur une femme de la race hottentote" *Bulletin des sciences par la Sociètè Philomatique de Paris* (1816): 183–190—it was clear that Baartman disapproved of him, especially when he tried to uncover her handkerchief so that he could get a full view of her "Hottentot apron."
39. See Blainville's "Sur une femme de la race hottentote"; Cuvier's report on his dissection in the *Notes of Museum d'Histoire Naturelle* (1817); and Cuvier and St. Hilaire's *Histoire naturelle des mammifères* (1824–27).
40. See Diana Axelsen, "Women as Victims of Medical Experimentation: J. Marion Sims' Surgery on Slave Women, 1845–1850," *Sage* 2, no. 2 (1985): 10–13; Terri Kapsalis, *Public Privates: Performing Gynecology from Both Ends of the Speculum* (Durham, NC: Duke University Press, 1997).
41. See Jennifer DeVere Brody, *Impossible Purities: Blackness, Femininity, and Victorian Culture* (Durham, NC: Duke University Press, 1998).
42. See Frances Smith Foster, *Witnessing Slavery: The Development of Ante-Bellum Slave Narratives,* 2nd ed. (Madison: The University of Wisconsin Press, 1979).
43. We may concur that, because of dominant culture's attempts to deny black women their womanhood, such abuses would have proven that they were not women. To black men who were asserting their manhood in their narratives, however, this emphasis on crimes against black women illustrated that they were also interested in asserting black women's right to femininity and thus their call to their readers for outrage against such acts against the "fairer sex."
44. Frederick Douglass, *Narrative of Frederick Douglass* (1845), reprinted in *Classic Six Slave Narratives,* edited by Henry Louis Gates Jr. (New York: Penguin, 1987), 259; hereafter cited in text.
45. Louisa Picquet "Louisa Picquet, the Octoroon: A Tale of Southern Slave Life (1861)," in *Collected Black Women's Narratives,* introduction by Anthony G. Barthelemy, ed. (New York: Oxford University Press, 1988).
46. Harriet Jacobs, *Incidents in the Life of a Slave Girl* (Cambridge, MA: Harvard University Press, 1987, 1861); hereafter cited in text.
47. Recent scholarship on this event include Robert W. Rydell's *The Reason Why the Colored American Is Not at the World's Columbian Exposition* (Urbana: University of Illinois Press, 1999, 1893); Christopher Robert Reed's *All the World Is Here: The Black Presence at White City* (Bloomington: Indiana University Press, 2000); and Deborah Willis and Carla Williams's *The Black Female Body: A Photographic History* (2002).

# Chapter 3

1. Lisa Jones, *Bulletproof Diva: Tales of Race, Sex, and Hair* (New York: Anchor Books, 1995), 76.
2. Stephen Jay Gould, "The Hottentot Venus," in *The Flamingo's Smile: Reflections in Natural History* (New York: Norton Press, 1985), 291–92. Gould describes his encounter

at the Musée de l'Homme with Baartman's genitalia, stored in a fluid-filled jar, which sat on a shelf above a jar featuring scientist Paul Broca's brain. Gould also describes another jar featuring a disheveled foot, labeled as belonging to a woman from China.

3. Gayatri Spivak, "Can the Subaltern Speak?" in *Marxism and the Interpretation of Culture,* edited by Cary Nelson and Lawrence Grossberg (Urbana: University of Illinois Press), 308.

4. Mark Reinhardt, "Who Speaks for Margaret Garner? Slavery, Silence, and the Politics of Ventriloquism," *Critical Inquiry* 29 (autumn 2002): 84; hereafter cited in text.

5. Elizabeth Alexander, *Venus Hottentot* (Charlottesville: University Press of Virginia, 1990), 3–7.

6. Darlene Clark Hine, "Rape and the Inner Lives of Black Women in the Middle West: Ruminations on the Culture of Dissemblance," in *Words of Fire: An Anthology of African American Feminist Thought,* edited by Beverly Guy-Sheftall (New York: The New Press, 1995), 380–87.

7. Paula Giddings, "The Last Taboo," in *Race-ing Justice, En-gendering Power,* edited by Toni Morrison (New York: Pantheon Books, 1992), 456.

8. Toni Morrison, *Beloved* (New York: Alfred A. Knopf, 1987), 43–44; hereafter cited in text.

9. Expanding on this theme in *Beloved* is Rachel Adam, "The Black Look and 'the Spectacle of Whitefolks': Wildness in Toni Morrison's *Beloved,*" in *Skin Deep, Spirit Strong: The Black Female Body in American Culture,* edited by Kimberly Wallace-Sanders (Ann Arbor: University of Michigan Press, 2002), 153–81.

10. Suzan-Lori Parks, *Venus* (New York: Theatre Communications Group, 1997), 36; hereafter cited in text.

11. Jean Young, "The Re-Objectification and Re-Commodification of Saartjie Baartman" in Suzan-Lori Parks's *Venus: African American Review* 31, no. 4 (winter 1997): 702–3.

12. Ben Brantley, "'Venus' Recalls a Woman's Fortune, and Her Ruin," in New York Times (May 15, 2017), available: https://www.nytimes.com/2017/05/15/theater/venus-review.html?mcubz=1.

13. Barbara Chase-Riboud, *The Hottentot Venus: A Novel* (New York: Doubleday, 2003), 11; hereafter cited in text.

14. In particular, Oyeronke Oyewumi criticizes the work of Alice Walker in "Alice in the Motherland: Reading Alice Walker on Africa and Screening the Color 'Black,'" *Jenda: A Journal of Culture and African Women Studies* 1, no. 2 (2001); hereafter cited in text.

15. This is an allusion to Eve Ensler's widely popular *Vagina Monologues,* which has been criticized for its reduction of "Third World" women—such as the women in Afghanistan, post-September 11, and Mexican women in Juarez, who have been murdered since 1993—as solely "victims" in the Western feminist viewpoint.

16. B. E. Meyers, "What Is My Legacy? Transient Consciousness and the 'Fixed' Subject in the Photography of Renee Cox," in *Gendered Visions,* edited by Salah M. Hassan (Trenton, NJ: Africa World Press, 1997), 30.

17. This is from "Artist's Statement," included on Carla Williams's website (September 2002), http://www.carlagirl.net/photos.html. *This website is no longer available.*

18. Laura Mulvey, "Visual Pleasure and Narrative Cinema," in *Issues in Feminist Film Criticism,* edited by Patricia Erens (Bloomington: Indiana University Press, 1990), 28–40.

19. Coco Fusco, *English Is Broken Here* (New York: The New Press, 1995), 37–63.
20. Coco Fusco, *The Bodies That Were Not Ours and Other Writings* (New York: Routledge, 2001), 188.
21. Mara Verna's website (2002), http://www.hottentotvenus.com.
22. Donna Haraway, *Simians, Cyborgs and Women: The Reinvention of Nature* (New York: Routledge, 1991).
23. On a more personal note, I see no problems with the Musée de l'Homme holding onto the cast that Cuvier molded from Baartman's likeness. Although I agree with both Verna and Chief Coetzee that such actions pose a threat to race relations if the cast is further subjected to scientific study, it holds *historical* value and, rather than destroy it, we must preserve it with an understanding of the oppressive past that it reflects. Perhaps it should be reframed in a permanent exhibit that warns of the dangers of racist science, instead of preserving it for the purposes of "science."
24. M. A. Jaimes Guerrero, "Savage Hegemony: From Endangered Species to Feminist Indiginism," in *Talking Visions: Multicultural Feminism in a Transnational Age,* edited by Ella Shohat (Cambridge, MA: MIT Press, 1998), 427; hereafter cited in text.
25. Clea Koff, *The Bone Woman: A Forensic Anthropologist's Search for Truth in the Mass Graves of Rwanda, Bosnia, Croatia, and Kosovo* (New York: Random House, 2004).
26. Ann DuCille, "Where in the World Is William Wells Brown? Thomas Jefferson, Sally Hemings, and the DNA of African-American Literary History," *American Literary History* 12, no. 3 (fall 2000): 446.

# Chapter 4

1. See Natasha Barnes, "Face of the Nation: Race, Nationalisms, and Identities in Jamaican Beauty Pageants," in *Daughters of Caliban: Caribbean Women in the Twentieth Century,* edited by Consuelo López Springfield (Bloomington: Indiana University Press, 1997), 290; hereafter cited in text.
2. Steeve O. Buckridge, *The Language of Dress: Resistance and Accommodation in Jamaica, 1760–1890.* (Kingston, Jamaica: University of West Indies Press, 2004), 75.
3. Carmel Schrire, "Native Views of Western Eyes," in *Miscast: Negotiating the Presence of Bushmen,* edited by Pippa Skotness (Cape Town, South Africa: University of Cape Town Press, 1996), 351.
4. Charles L. Perdue, Jr., Thomas E. Barden, and Robert K. Phillips, eds. *Weevils in the Wheat: Interviews with Virginia Ex-Slaves* (Charlottesville: University Press of Virginia, 1976), 48–49. See also Hélène Lecaudey, "Behind the Mask: Ex-Slave Women and Interracial Sexual Relations," in *Discovering the Women in Slavery: Emancipating Perspectives on the American Past,* edited by Patricia Morton (Athens: University of Georgia Press, 1996), 272; both hereafter cited in text.
5. I refer here to the mythical view in much of Western and other cultural traditions in which female genitalia was imagined as possessing "teeth," thus threatening male castration. For a provocative critique of this myth and the criminalization of the historical figure of Sukie, see Hershini Bhana Young's "Inheriting the Criminalized Black Body: Race, Gender, and Slavery in Gayl Jones' *Eva's Man,*" presented at the Collegium for African American Research Conference in April 2005.

6. Cited in Painter (140), who further comments on this incident as one of numerous legends and myths that creates a hyperbolic figure of Truth. Whether this event of Truth revealing her breasts is based on fact or fabrication, the structure of the narrative posits Truth as witty, defiant, and dignified in the face of racist detractors, as well as able to re-present her body in opposition to the forces that wish to reduce her to spectacle and objectification.

7. Kariamu Welsh Asante, "Images of Women in African Dance: Sexuality and Sensuality as Dual Unity," *Sage* 8, no. 2 (1994): 16–19; hereafter cited in text.

8. Belinda Edmondson, "Public Spectacles: Caribbean Women and the Politics of Public Performance," *Small Axe* 13 (March 2003): 5. See also Pamela R. Franco, "Dressing Up and Looking Good: Afro-Creole Female Maskers in Trinidad Carnival," *African Arts* 31, no. 2 (spring 1998): 62–67, 91, 95–96.

9. Patience Abenaa Kwakwa, "Dance and African Women," *Sage* 8, no. 2 (1994): 10.

10. Wendy Martin, "Remembering the Jungle: Josephine Baker and Modernist Parody," *Prehistories of the Future: The Primitivist Project and the Culture of Modernism,* edited by Elazar Barkan and Ronald Bush (Stanford, CA: Stanford University Press, 1995), 311.

11. Phyllis Rose, *Jazz Cleopatra: Josephine Baker in Her Time* (New York: Doubleday, 1989), 34–38.

12. Carole Marks and Diana Edkins, *The Power of Pride: Stylemakers and Rulebreakers of the Harlem Renaissance* (New York: Crown Publishers, 1999), 34–35.

13. See Michel Fabre, "International Beacons of African-American Memory: Alexandre Dumas Pere, Henry O. Tanner, and Josephine Baker as Examples of Recognition," in *History and Memory in African-American Culture,* edited by Geneviève Fabre and Robert O'Malley (New York: Oxford University Press, 1994), 128.

14. "Protest on Jo Baker as Queen," *Chicago Defender* (April 11, 1931), 5. See also Rose, 1989, 23.

15. Anthea Kraut, "Between Primitivism and Diaspora: The Dance Performances of Josephine Baker, Zora Neale Hurston, and Katherine Dunham," *Theatre Journal* 55 (2003): 433–50.

16. Katherine Dunham performed a decade after Baker, reaching her height in the 1940s and 1950s and Pearl Primus in the 1960s and 1970s, when she became a prominent choreographer.

17. See Jean-Paul Goude, *Jungle Fever* (New York: Xavier Moreau, 1981); Miriam Kershaw, "Postcolonialism and Androgyny: The Performance Art of Grace Jones," *Art Journal* 97, no. 56 (winter 1997): 19–25.

18. This is an allusion to *Legs,* a popular song and music video by ZZ Top in the early 1980s.

19. Latinos/as have recently been recognized and made visible in contemporary discourse as a third "racial" category, despite the fact that their various communities encompass racial shades of "white" and "black."

20. Imani Perry, "Who(se) am I? The Identity and Image of Women in Hip-Hop," in *Gender, Race, and Class in Media: A Text-Reader,* 2nd ed., edited by Gail Dines and Jean M. Humez (Thousand Oaks, CA: Sage Publications, 2003), 137.

21. This is an allusion to Carolyn Cooper, *Noises in the Blood: Orality, Gender, and the Vulgar Body of Jamaican Culture* (Durham, NC: Duke University Press, 1995).

22. Tricia Rose, "Never Trust a Big Butt and a Smile," *Camera Obscura* 23 (1990): 124–25.

23. Available online: http://www.airbubble.com/your_revolution.html. *This website is no longer available.*

24. Gwendolyn Pough, *Check it While I Wreck it: Black Womanhood, Hip-Hop Culture, and the Public Sphere* (Boston: Northeastern University Press, 2004), 187.
25. Kristina Rodulfo, "Dior's 'We Should All Be Feminists' Shirts Will Benefit Rihanna's Charities" (February 28, 2017), *Elle,* available: http://www.elle.com/fashion/news/a43431/dior-we-should-all-be-feminists-shirt-rihanna-charity.
26. Jamia Wilson, "Turning the Tables" (April-May 2017), *Bust,* available: http://bust.com/feminism/192922-solange-knowles-digs-deep-and-opens-up-about-life-as-a-woman.html.
27. The interview of this dancer is included in the video *Women's Work* (1996), directed by Jawole Willa Jo Zollar, Marianne Henderson, and Bruce Berryhill.
28. Asantewaa's review (1998) is available at http://www.danceonline.com/rev/bush.html.
29. See preface to Ntozake Shange, *For Colored Girls Who Have Considered Suicide/ When the Rainbow Is Enuf* (New York: Simon & Schuster, 1977).
30. *Daughters of the Dust,* directed by Julie Dash, Kino International, 1992.

## Chapter 5

1. See Ben Charny, "Janet Jackson's Flash Dance Tops Web Search" (February 11, 2004), http://news.com.com/2100-10265153330.html. *This website is no longer available.*
2. After the Super Bowl incident, Justin Timberlake issued a public statement in which he infamously coined this term to project his undressing of Janet's body onto *her* body and wardrobe choice.
3. Mary Ann Doane, "Film and Masquerade: Theorising the Female Spectator," *Screen* 23, no. 3–4 (1982): 74–88.
4. Jane Gaines, "White Privilege and Looking Relations: Race and Gender in Feminist Film Theory," *Screen* 29, no. 4 (1988): 12–17.
5. Lisa Gail Collins, *The Art of History: African American Women Artists Engage the Past* (New Brunswick: Rutgers University Press, 2002), 23; hereafter cited in text.
6. In addition to Lisa Gail Collins and Willis and Williams, see also Alison Griffiths, *Wondrous Difference: Cinema, Anthropology, and Turn-of-the-Century Visual Culture* (New York: Columbia University Press, 2002), and Brian Wallis, "Black Bodies, White Science: Louis Agassiz's Slave Daguerreotypes," *American Art* 9, no. 2 (summer 1995): 38–61.
7. I am grateful to Robin Blaetz for this interpretation of early film and photography's impact on paintings of the late nineteenth and early twentieth centuries during a lecture at Emory University in the spring semester of 1999.
8. See *Miss America* video, directed by Lisa Ades, 2002.
9. Jackie Goldsby, "Queen for 307 Days," in *Afrekete: An Anthology of Black Lesbian Writing,* edited by Catherine E. McKinley and L. Joyce DeLaney (New York: Anchor Books, 1995), 173.
10. Dawn Perlmutter, "Miss America: Whose Ideal?" in *Beauty Matters,* edited by Peg Zeglin Brand (Bloomington: Indiana University Press, 2000), 160–162.
11. See A Question of Color: Color Consciousness in Black America, directed by Kathe Sandler, 1993.
12. This expression from African American Southern culture suggests that lighter-skinned blacks benefited little from the white supremacist caste system, thus the idea that the "yellowness" of the "yellows" is truly a waste.

13. Kristal Brent Zook, "Light Skinned(ded) Naps," in *Making Face, Making Soul,* edited by Gloria Anzaldua (San Francisco: Aunt Lute Books, 1990), 93; hereafter cited in text.

14. Walker's film notes are recorded in *The Same River Twice* (New York: Scribner, 1996), 52.

15. James Baldwin, *"Carmen Jones:* The Dark Is Light Enough," in *Notes of a Native Son* (New York: Dial Press, 1963), 44. Pearl Bailey also appeared in this film, which starred Dorothy Dandridge and Harry Belafonte.

16. In Julie Dash, *Daughters of the Dust: The Making of an African American Woman's Film* (New York: New Press, 1992), 70; hereafter cited in text.

17. Greg Tate, "Of Homegirl Goddesses and Geechee Women: The Africentric Cinema of Julie Dash," *The Village Voice* 36, no. 23 (June 4, 1991): 72.

18. See Richard Dyer, *White* (New York: Routledge, 1997), 89.

19. Judith Wilson offers a similar reading of black hair in this film in her essay, "Beauty Rites: Towards an Anatomy of Culture in African American Women's Art," *International Review of African American Art* 11, no. 2 (1994): 11–18, 47–55.

20. Mr. Snead might also double as early twentieth-century African American photographer James Van Der Zee, a great influence on Dash's film.

21. Brown acknowledges her colleague, Linda Dittmar of the University of Massachusetts Boston, for familiarizing her with this term. See Caroline Brown, "The Representation of the Indigenous Other in *Daughters of the Dust* and *The Piano*," *NWSA Journal* 15, no. 1 (spring 2003): 2.

22. Foster borrows this term from Bill Nichols's 1994 *Blurred Boundaries: Questions of Meaning in Contemporary Culture* (Bloomington: Indiana University Press, 1994). See Gwendolyn Audrey Foster, *Women Filmmakers of the Asian and African Diaspora* (Carbondale: Southern Illinois University Press, 1997), 27.

23. Lisbeth Gant-Britton, "African Women and Visual Culture: a Sample Syllabus," *Camera Obscura* 36 (September 1995): 96.

24. Norimitsu Onishi, "Globalization of Beauty Makes Slimness Trendy," *New York Times* (October 3, 2002): A4.

25. Chandra Mohanty, "Under Western Eyes: Feminist Scholarship and Colonial Discourses," in *Third World Women and the Politics of Feminism,* edited by Chandra Mohanty, Ann Russo, and Lourdes Torres (Bloomington: Indiana University Press, 1991), 53.

26. This is an allusion to Edward Said, *Orientalism* (New York: Random House, 1979).

27. We need only examine the ways in which Condoleezza Rice, now serving as U.S. Secretary of State, still manages to elicit comments from the media on her mode of dress and hairstyle, while her diplomatic approaches in her current role become secondary concerns.

## Chapter 6

1. Dan Wootton, "Beyoncé has bot[h] her eyes on winning an Oscar for film about lady with giant rear," *The Sun* (January 2, 2016), available: https://www.thesun.co.uk/archives/bizarre/934423/beyonce-has-bot-her-eyes-on-winning-an-oscar-for-film-about-lady-with-giant-rear.

2. Cited in Justin Carissimo, "South African Chief says Beyoncé is 'not worthy' to make Saartjie Baartman film," *The Independent* (January 5, 2016), available: http://www.independent.co.uk/arts-entertainment/films/south-african-chief-says-beyonc-is-not-worthy-to-make-saartjie-baartman-film-a6798151.html.

3. Crunk Feminist Collective, "Disrespectability Politics: On Jay-Z's Bitch, Beyoncé's 'Fly' Ass, and Black Girl Blue," *Crunk Feminist Collective* (January 19, 2012), available: http://www.crunkfeministcollective.com/2012/01/19/disrespectability-politics-on-jay-zs-bitch-beyonces-fly-ass-and-black-girl-blue.

4. Cited in Adelle Platon, "Beyoncé 'In No Way Tied' to Saartjie Baartman Film," *Billboard* (January 5, 2016), available: http://www.billboard.com/articles/columns/hip-hop/6828940/beyonce-saartjie-baartman-film.

5. Justin Parkinson, "The Significance of Sarah Baartman," *BBC News* (January 7, 2016), available: http://www.bbc.com/news/magazine-35240987.

6. Jessica Goodman, "Inside the Making of Destiny's Child's 'Bootylicious' 15 Years Later," *Entertainment Weekly* (May 20, 2016), available: http://ew.com/article/2016/05/20/destinys-child-bootylicious-15th-anniversary.

7. Aisha Durham, "'Check on It': Beyoncé, Southern Booty, and Black Femininities in Music Video," *Feminist Media Studies* 12, no.1 (2012): 35–49.

8. Evan Thomas, "A Long, Strange Trip to the Taliban," *Newsweek* (December 16, 2001), available: http://www.newsweek.com/long-strange-trip-taliban-148503.

9. Farah Jasmine Griffin, "At Last . . .? Michelle Obama, Beyoncé, Race & History," *Daedalus* 140, no. 1 (winter 2011): 138.

10. Mae G. Henderson, "About Face, or What is this 'Back' in B(l)ack Popular Culture? From Venus Hottentot to Video Hotties," in *Understanding Blackness through Performance: Contemporary Arts and the Representation of Identity,* 159–179, Anne Cremieux, Xavier Lemoine, and Jean-Paul Rocchi, eds. (New York: Palgrave Macmillan, 2013), 160.

11. Patricia Garcia, "We're Officially in the Era of the Big Booty," *Vogue* (September 9, 2014), available: http://www.vogue.com/1342927/booty-in-pop-culture-jennifer-lopez-iggy-azalea. *This website is no longer available.*

12. Buffie Carruth, "Buffie the Body: Is My Butt Fake and Why I Left the Hip Hop Industry," YouTube Video (September 18, 2012), available: https://www.youtube.com/watch?v=-i6kPii-iac.

13. Fabio Parasecoli, "Bootylicious: Food and the Female Body in Contemporary Black Popular Culture," *Women's Studies Quarterly* 35, no. 1/2 (2007): 111.

14. Mireille Miller-Young, *A Taste for Brown Sugar: Black Women in Pornography* (Durham: Duke University Press, 2014).

15. Available (April 16, 2012): https://www.youtube.com/watch?v=rCK6zvWEN_Q.

16. Cited in Johan Palme, "Makode Linde – the 'Swedish Cake' Artist – Explains Himself," *Africa is a Country* (April 24, 2012), available: http://africasacountry.com/2012/04/africa-is-a-country-interview-with-makode-linde.

17. Vincent Woodard, *The Delectable Negro: Human Consumption and Homoeroticism within U.S. Slave Culture* (New York: NYU Press, 2014).

18. Randall White, "The Women of Brassempouy: A Century of Research and Interpretation," *Journal of Archaeological Method and Theory* 13, no. 4 (2006): 250–303.

19. Cited in Paul Laster, "Kara Walker Interview," *Time Out* (May 5, 2014), available: https://www.timeout.com/newyork/art/kara-walker-interview-the-whole-reason-for-refining-sugar-is-to-make-it-white.

20. Vanessa Newman, "The Tragic Genius of Kara Walker's 'Sugar Baby' Exhibit," *Moodie Mills: Catalyzing Culture, Capital, and Community through Media, Policy, and Advocacy* (June 22, 2014), available: http://moodiemills.com/2014/06/the-tragic-genius-of-kara-walkers-sugar-baby-exhibit. *This website is no longer available.*

21. Creative Time, "*Creative Time* Presents Kara Walker," *Creative Time* Pages (May 10-July 6, 2014), available: http://creativetime.org/projects/karawalker/inspiration.

22. Trevor Burnard, *Mastery, Tyranny, and Desire: Thomas Thistlewood and His Slaves in the Anglo-Jamaican World* (Chapel Hill: University of North Carolina Press, 2004), 175.

23. Jonathan Van Meter, "Beyoncé: Fierce Creature," *Vogue* (April 1, 2009), available: http://www.vogue.com/article/beyonc233-fierce-creature.

24. Cited in Ryan Buxton, "Beverly Johnson's Scary Diet: As Supermodels in the '70s, 'We Thought Water was Fattening,'" *The Huffington Post* (September 12, 2014), available: http://www.huffingtonpost.com/2014/09/12/beverly-johnson-diet-mod els_n_5810160.html. See also Dodai Stewart, "How Offensive is Beyoncé's Vogue Cover? Let Us Count the Ways," *Jezebel* (March 16, 2009), available: http://jezebel.com/5170632/how-offensive-is-beyonces-vogue-cover-let-us-count-the-ways.

25. Cited in Janell Hobson, "Beyoncé's Fierce Feminism," *Ms. Magazine* (spring 2013): 44.

26. bell hooks, Keynote Address Delivered at the National Women's Studies Association Annual Meeting, San Jan, Puerto Rico, November 14, 2014.

27. Kyra Gaunt, "A Time Signature of Black Bottomlines (1936–2016): Compounding Gender Stratification on YouTube from Race Records to Rap Songs," lecture delivered at the University at Albany, December 5, 2016.

28. Beyoncé Knowles-Carter, "Self-Titled, Part 4: Liberation," YouTube Video (January 13, 2014), available: https://www.youtube.com/watch?v=0eZ0mzI37-A.

29. Beyoncé and Jay Z, who once distracted from a peace rally for Trayvon Martin that they attended in Brooklyn, began discreetly bailing out protesters in Ferguson, Missouri in 2014 and Baltimore, Maryland, in 2015. Their music-streaming company, Tidal, which was launched in 2014, also donated financially to the Black Lives Matter movement.

30. Daphne Brooks, "'All That You Can't Leave Behind': Black Female Soul Singing and the Politics of Surrogation in the Age of Catastrophe," *Meridians: feminism, race, transnationalism* 8, no. 1 (2008): 193.

31. Lisa Ze Winters, *The Mulatta Concubine: Terror, Intimacy, Freedom, and Desire in the Black Transatlantic* (Athens: University of Georgia Press, 2016), 14.

32. Brittany Spanos, "How Beyoncé's 'Lemonade' Reclaims Rock's Black Female Legacy," *Rolling Stone* (April 26, 2016), available: http://www.rollingstone.com/music/news/how-beyonces-lemonade-reclaims-rocks-black-female-legacy-20160426.

33. Kyra Gaunt, "Beyoncé's Lemonade is Smashing," *TEDFellows* Blog (May 12, 2016), available: https://fellowsblog.ted.com/beyonc%C3%A9s-lemonade-is-smashing-1cc 70bda2197.

34. Kameelah L. Martin, *Envisioning Black Feminist Voodoo Aesthetics: African Spirituality in American Cinema* (London: Lexington Books, 2016).

35. Joan Morgan, "Beyoncé, Black Feminist Art, and this Oshun Bidness," *Genius* (April 30, 2016), available: https://genius.com/a/beyonce-black-feminist-art-and-this-oshun-bidness.

# Epilogue

1. In the realm of filmmaking, for instance, it had taken Julie Dash thirteen years to produce *Daughters of the Dust* (1992), from the time she had conceived of the story to the time that the film was released in theaters. Filmmaking is perhaps one of the most expensive art forms, which might explain why few people of color and women work within this industry and also why representations of these groups—based on white hegemonic patriarchal ideologies—prevail in mainstream American cinema.
2. See also Alice Walker's *In Search of Our Mothers' Gardens: Womanist Prose* (San Diego: Harcourt Brace & Co., 1984). Walker also poses similar questions concerning class limitations in producing art, as well as alternative artworks that have been created, such as her working class mother's artistic creation of a "garden" or a slave woman's "quilt."
3. Lorde has also observed that poets tend not to be taken as seriously as prose writers and novelists, which is reflected in its economically accessible form.
4. Wahneema Lubiano, "Talking about the State and Imagining Alliances," *Talking Visions: Multicultural Feminism in a Transnational Age,* edited by Ella Shohat (Cambridge, MA: MIT Press, 1998), 442.
5. Edwidge Danticat, *Breath, Eyes, Memory* (New York: Vintage Books, 1994); hereafter cited in text.

# BIBLIOGRAPHY

Abraham, Yvette. "Images of Sara Baartman: Sexuality, Race, and Gender in Early-Nineteenth-Century Britain." In *Nation, Empire, Colony: Historicizing Gender and Race,* eds. Ruth Roach Pierson, Nupur Chaudhuri, and Beth McAuley, 220–36. Bloomington: Indiana University Press, 1998.

Adam, Rachel. "The Black Look and 'the Spectacle of Whitefolks': Wildness in Toni Morrison's *Beloved.*" In *Skin Deep, Spirit Strong: The Black Female Body in American Culture,* ed. Kimberly Wallace-Sanders, 153–81. Ann Arbor: University of Michigan Press, 2002.

Alexander, Elizabeth. *Venus Hottentot.* Charlottesville: University Press of Virginia, 1990.

Allen, Paula Gunn. *The Sacred Hoop: Recovering the Feminine in American Indian Traditions.* Boston: Beacon Press, 1986.

Altick, Richard. *The Shows of London.* Cambridge, MA: Harvard University Press, 1978.

"Are My Hands Clean?" Composed by Bernice Johnson Reagon. Songtalk Publishing, 1985. Performed by Sweet Honey in the Rock. *Live at Carnegie Hall.* Flying Fish Records, 1988.

Arogundade, Ben. *Black Beauty: A History and Celebration.* New York: Thunder's Mouth Press, 2000.

Asante, Kariamu Welsh. "Images of Women in African Dance: Sexuality and Sensuality as Dual Unity." *Sage* 8, no. 2 (1994): 16–19.

Asantewaa, Eva Yaa. "Upbeat Program Shakes Its Batty: Urban Bush Women, Aaron Davis Hall, NYC, February 12–14, 1998." Dance Online, Inc., http://www.dance online.com/rev/bush.html.

*Austin Powers in Goldmember.* Dir. Jay Roach. Los Angeles: New Line Cinema, 2002.

Axelsen, Diana E. "Women as Victims of Medical Experimentation: J. Marion Sims' Surgery on Slave Women, 1845–1850." *Sage* 2, no. 2 (1985): 10–13.

"Baby Got Back." Performed by SirMixaLot. *Mack Daddy.* Los Angeles: Warner Brothers, 1992.

Bakhtin, Mikhail M. *The Dialogic Imagination,* ed. Michael Holquist. Trans. Caryl Emerson and Michael Holquist. Austin: Texas University Press, 1981.

———. *Rabelais and His World.* Trans. Hélène Iswolsky. Bloomington: Indiana University Press, 1984.

Baldwin, James. *"Carmen Jones:* The Dark Is Light Enough." In *Notes of a Native Son,* 43–50. New York: Dial Press, 1963.

Barnes, Natasha. "Face of the Nation: Race, Nationalisms, and Identities in Jamaican Beauty Pageants." In *Daughters of Caliban: Caribbean Women in the Twentieth Century,* ed. Consuelo López Springfield, 285–306. Bloomington: Indiana University Press, 1997.

*Beloved.* Dir. Jonathan Demme. Los Angeles: Touchstone Pictures, 1998.

*The Big Lebowski.* Dirs. Joel and Ethan Coen. Polygram Filmed Entertainment, 1998.

*Billy Lynn's Long Halftime Walk.* Dir. Ang Lee. Los Angeles: Bona Film Group, 2016.

Blainville, Henri de. "Sur une femme de la race hottentote." *Bulletin des sciences par la Sociétè Philomatique de Paris* (1816): 183–190.

*The Body Beautiful.* Dir. Ngozi Onwurah. New York: Women Make Movies, 1991.

Brady, Jacqueline E. "Pumping Iron with Resistance: Carla Dunlap's Victorious Body." In *Recovering the Black Female Body,* eds. Michael Bennett and Vanessa D. Dickerson, 253–78. New Brunswick, NJ: Rutgers University Press, 2001.

Brantley, Ben. "'Venus' Recalls a Woman's Fortune, and Her Ruin." *New York Times* (May 15, 2017). Available: https://www.nytimes.com/2017/05/15/theater/venus-review.html?mcubz=1.

Brody, Jennifer DeVere. *Impossible Purities: Blackness, Femininity, and Victorian Culture.* Durham, NC: Duke University Press, 1998.

Brooks, Daphne. "'All That You Can't Leave Behind': Black Female Soul Singing and the Politics of Surrogation in the Age of Catastrophe." *Meridians: feminism, race, transnationalism* 8, no. 1 (2008): 180–204.

Brown, Caroline. "The Representation of the Indigenous Other in *Daughters of the Dust* and *The Piano.*" *NWSA Journal* 15, no. 1 (spring 2003): 1–19.

Buckridge, Steeve O. *The Language of Dress: Resistance and Accommodation in Jamaica, 1760–1890.* Kingston, Jamaica: University of West Indies Press, 2004.

Burdick, John. *Blessed Anastácia: Women, Race, and Popular Christianity in Brazil.* New York: Routledge, 1998.

Burnard, Trevor. *Mastery, Tyranny, and Desire: Thomas Thistlewood and His Slaves in the Anglo-Jamaican World.* Chapel Hill: University of North Carolina Press, 2004.

Buxton, Ryan. "Beverly Johnson's Scary Diet: As Supermodels in the '70s, 'We Thought Water was Fattening.'" *The Huffington Post* (September 12, 2014). Available: http://www.huffingtonpost.com/2014/09/12/beverly-johnson-diet-models_n_5810160.html.

Carissimo, Justin. "South African Chief says Beyoncé is 'not worthy' to make Saartjie Baartman film," in *The Independent* (January 5, 2016). Available: http://www.independent.co.uk/arts-entertainment/films/south-african-chief-says-beyonc-is-not-worthy-to-make-saartjie-baartman-film-a6798151.html.

Carroll, Nëel. "Ethnicity, Race, and Monstrosity: The Rhetoric of Horror and Humor." In *Beauty Matters,* ed. Peggy Zeglin Brand, 37–56. Bloomington: Indiana University Press, 2000.

Carruth, Buffie. "Buffie the Body: Is My Butt Fake and Why I Left the Hip Hop Industry." YouTube Video (September 18, 2012). Available: https://www.youtube.com/watch?v=-i6kPii-iac.

"The Censorship of Sarah Jones." (2003). Available online: http://www.airbubble.com/your_revolution.html. *This website is no longer available.*

*Charlie's Angels*. Dir. McG. Los Angeles: Columbia Pictures, 2000.

Charny, Ben. "Janet Jackson's Flash Dance Tops Web Search." (February 11, 2004). CNET News.com, http://news.com.com/2100-1026-5153330.html. *This website is no longer available.*

Chase-Riboud, Barbara. *The Hottentot Venus: A Novel*. New York: Doubleday, 2003.

*Coffee Colored Children*. Dir. Ngozi Onwurah. New York: Women Make Movies, 1988.

Collins, Lisa Gail. *The Art of History: African American Women Artists Engage the Past*. New Brunswick, NJ: Rutgers University Press, 2002.

Collins, Patricia Hill. *Black Feminist Thought: Knowledge, Consciousness, and the Politics of Empowerment*. New York: Routledge, 1990.

*The Color Purple*. Dir. Steven Spielberg. Los Angeles: Warner Brothers, 1985.

Cooper, Carolyn. *Noises in the Blood: Orality, Gender, and the Vulgar Body of Jamaican Culture*. Durham, NC: Duke University Press, 1995.

Crais, Clifton and Pamela Scully. *Sara Baartman and the Hottentot Venus: A Ghost Story and a Biography*. Princeton: Princeton University Press, 2010.

Creative Time. "*Creative Time* Presents Kara Walker." *Creative Time* Pages (May 10–July 6, 2014). Available: http://creativetime.org/projects/karawalker/inspiration.

Crunk Feminist Collective. "Disrespectability Politics: On Jay-Z's Bitch, Beyoncé's 'Fly' Ass, and Black Girl Blue." *Crunk Feminist Collective* (January 19, 2012). Available: http://www.crunkfeministcollective.com/2012/01/19/disrespectability-politics-on-jay-zs-bitch-beyonces-fly-ass-and-black-girl-blue.

Cuvier, Frederic and Geoffroy St. Hilaire. *Histoire naturelle des mammifères*. Paris: A. Berlin, 1824–27.

Cuvier, Georges. "Extrait d'observations faites sur le cadavre d'une femme connue à Paris et à Londres sous le nom de Venus Hottentote." In *Notes of Museum d'Histoire Naturelle*. Paris, 1817.

*Dancehall Queen*. Dirs. Rick Elgood and Don Letts. Los Angeles: Lion's Gate Films, 1997.

Danticat, Edwidge. *Breath, Eyes, Memory*. New York: Vintage Books, 1994.

*The Darker Side of Black*. Dir. Isaac Julien. New York: Filmmakers' Library, 1994.

Dash, Julie. *Daughters of the Dust: The Making of an African American Woman's Film*. New York: New Press, 1992.

*Daughters of the Dust*. Dir. Julie Dash. New York: Kino International, 1992.

Dines, Gail. "Nicki Minaj: Little More Than a Big Butt?" *Huffington Post* (September 27, 2014). Available: http://www.huffingtonpost.co.uk/gail-dines/nicki-minaj_b_562 9232.html.

Doane, Mary Ann. "Film and Masquerade: Theorising the Female Spectator." *Screen* 23, no. 3–4 (1982): 74–88.

Douglass, Frederick. *Narrative of Frederick Douglass*, 1845. In *Classic Six Slave Narratives*, ed. Henry Louis Gates Jr., 243–331. New York: Penguin, 1987.

DuCille, Ann. "Where in the World Is William Wells Brown? Thomas Jefferson, Sally Hemings, and the DNA of African-American Literary History." *American Literary History* 12, no. 3 (fall 2000): 443–62.

Durham, Aisha. "'Check on It': Beyoncé, Southern Booty, and Black Femininities in Music Video." *Feminist Media Studies* 12, no.1 (2012): 35–49.

Dyer, Richard. *White*. New York: Routledge, 1997.

Edmondson, Belinda. "Public Spectacles: Caribbean Women and the Politics of Public Performance." *Small Axe* 13 (March 2003): 1–16.

Edwards, Bryan. *The History, Civil and Commerce, of the British Colonies of the West Indies*, vol. 2. London, 1794.

Edwards, Paul and James Walvin. *Black Personalities in the Era of the Slave Trade*. Baton Rouge: Louisiana State University Press, 1983.

*Eve's Bayou*. Dir. Kasi Lemmons. Los Angeles: Lion's Gate Films, 1997.

Fabre, Michel. "International Beacons of African-American Memory: Alexandre Dumas Pere, Henry O. Tanner, and Josephine Baker as Examples of Recognition." In *History and Memory in African-American Culture*, 122–29. eds. Geneviève Fabre and Robert O'Malley. New York: Oxford University Press, 1994.

Fanon, Frantz. *Black Skin, White Masks*. Trans. Charles L. Markmann. New York: Grove Press, 1967.

Fausto-Sterling, Anne. "Gender, Race, and Nation: The Comparative Anatomy of 'Hottentot' Women in Europe, 1814–1817." In *Deviant Bodies*, eds. Jennifer Terry and Jacqueline Urla, 19–48. Bloomington: Indiana University Press, 1995.

Foster, Frances Smith. *Witnessing Slavery: The Development of Ante-Bellum Slave Narratives*, 2nd ed. Madison: The University of Wisconsin Press, 1979.

Foster, Gwendolyn Audrey. *Women Filmmakers of the African and Asian Diaspora*. Carbondale: Southern Ilinois University Press, 1997.

Foucault, Michel. *Discipline and Punish: The Birth of the Prison*. Trans. Alan M. Sheridan-Smith. New York: Vintage Books, 1979.

Fountain, Ben. *Billy Lynn's Long Halftime Walk*. New York: Ecco Press, 2012.

Franco, Pamela R. "Dressing Up and Looking Good: Afro-Creole Female Maskers in Trinidad Carnival." *African Arts* 31, no. 2 (spring 1998): 62–67, 91, 95–96.

*Full Metal Jacket*. Dir. Stanley Kubrick. Los Angeles: Warner Brothers, 1987.

Fusco, Coco. *English Is Broken Here*. New York: The New Press, 1995.

——. *The Bodies That Were Not Ours and Other Writings*. New York: Routledge, 2001.

Gaines, Jane. "White Privilege and Looking Relations: Race and Gender in Feminist Film Theory." *Screen* 29, no. 4 (1988): 12–17.

Gant-Britton, Lisbeth. "African Women and Visual Culture: A Sample Syllabus." *Camera Obscura* 36 (September 1995): 85–117.

Garcia, Patricia. "We're Officially in the Era of the Big Booty." *Vogue* (September 9, 2014). Available: http://www.vogue.com/1342927/booty-in-pop-culture-jennifer-lopez-iggy-azalea. *This website is no longer available.*

Gates, Henry Louis Jr. *The Signifying Monkey: A Theory of African-American Literary Criticism*. New York: Oxford University Press, 1988.

Gaunt, Kyra. "Beyoncé's Lemonade is Smashing." *TEDFellows Blog* (May 12, 2016). Available: https://fellowsblog.ted.com/beyonc%C3%A9s-lemonade-is-smashing-1cc70bda2197.

——. "A Time Signature of Black Bottomlines (1936–2016): Compounding Gender Stratification on YouTube from Race Records to Rap Songs." Lecture at the University at Albany, December 5, 2016.

Giddings, Paula. *When and Where I Enter*. New York: William Morrow & Co., 1984.

——. "The Last Taboo." In *Raceing-Justice, En-gendering Power*, ed. Toni Morrison, 441–63. New York: Pantheon Books, 1992.

Gilman, Sander. *Difference and Pathology: Stereotypes of Sexuality, Race, and Madness*. Ithaca: Cornell University Press, 1985.

————. "Black Bodies, White Bodies: Toward an Iconography of Female Sexuality in Art, Medicine, and Literature." In "*Race,*" *Writing, and Difference,* ed. Henry Louis Gates Jr., 223–61. Chicago: University of Chicago Press, 1986.

Gilroy, Paul. *The Black Atlantic: Modernity and Double Consciousness.* Cambridge: Harvard University Press, 1993.

Goldsby, Jackie. "Queen for 307 Days." In *Afrekete: An Anthology of Black Lesbian Writing,* eds. Catherine E. McKinley and L. Joyce DeLaney, 165–88. New York: Anchor Books, 1995.

Goodman, Jessica. "Inside the Making of Destiny's Child's 'Bootylicious' 15 Years Later." *Entertainment Weekly* (May 20, 2016). Available: http://ew.com/article/2016/05/20/destinys-child-bootylicious-15th-anniversary.

Gordon-Chipembere, Natasha Maria. "'Even with the Best of Intentions': The Misreading of Sarah Baartman's Life." *Agenda: Empowering Women for Gender Equity,* 68 (2006): 54–62.

Gordon-Chipembere, Natasha, ed. *Representation and Black Womanhood: The Legacy of Sarah Baartman.* New York: Palgrave Macmillan, 2011.

Goude, Jean-Paul. *Jungle Fever.* New York: Xavier Moreau, 1981.

Gould, Stephen Jay. "The Hottentot Venus." In *The Flamingo's Smile: Reflections in Natural History,* 291–305. New York: Norton Press, 1985.

Griffin, Farah Jasmine. "At Last . . .? Michelle Obama, Beyoncé, Race & History." *Daedalus* 140, no. 1 (winter 2011): 138.

Griffiths, Alison. *Wondrous Difference: Cinema, Anthropology, and Turn-of-the-Century Visual Culture.* New York: Columbia University Press, 2002.

Guerrero, M. A. Jaimes. "Savage Hegemony: From Endangered Species to Feminist Indiginism." In *Talking Visions: Multicultural Feminism in a Transnational Age,* ed. Ella Shohat, 413–29. Cambridge, MA: MIT Press, 1998.

Hall, Kim F. *Things of Darkness: Economies of Race and Gender in Early Modern England.* Ithaca: Cornell University Press, 1995.

Hammonds, Evelynn. "Black (W)holes and the Geometry of Black Female Sexuality." *Differences* 6, no. 2–3 (1995): 126–45.

Haraway, Donna. *Simians, Cyborgs and Women: The Reinvention of Nature.* New York: Routledge, 1991.

Harding, Sandra. *Whose Science, Whose Knowledge? Thinking from Women's Lives.* Ithaca, NY: Cornell University Press, 1991.

Hartman, Saidiya V. *Scenes of Subjection: Terror, Slavery, and Self-Making in Nineteenth-Century America.* New York: Oxford University Press, 1997.

Hartsock, Nancy. "The Feminist Standpoint: Developing the Ground for a Specifically Feminist Historical Materialism." In *Discovering Reality: Feminist Perspectives on Epistemology, Metaphysics, Methodology, and Philosophy of Science,* eds. Sandra Harding and Merrill B. Hintikka, 283–310. Dordrecht: Reidel, 1983.

Henderson, Mae G. "About Face, or What is this 'Back' in B(l)ack Popular Culture? From Venus Hottentot to Video Hotties." In *Understanding Blackness through Performance: Contemporary Arts and the Representation of Identity,* 159–179. Anne Cremieux, Xavier Lemoine, and Jean-Paul Rocchi, eds. New York: Palgrave Macmillan, 2013.

Hine, Darlene Clark. "Rape and the Inner Lives of Black Women in the Middle West: Ruminations on the Culture of Dissemblance." In *Words of Fire: An Anthology of*

*African American Feminist Thought,* ed. Beverly Guy-Sheftall, 380–87. New York: New Press, 1995.

Hobson, Janell. "Beyoncé's Fierce Feminism," *Ms. Magazine* (spring 2013): 42–45.

———. "Black Women's Histories: A Conversation with Mireille Miller-Young." *Ms. Magazine Blog* (February 3, 2015). Available: http://msmagazine.com/blog/2015/02/03/black-womens-histories-a-conversation-with-mireille-miller-young.

Holloway, Karla. *Codes of Conduct: Race, Ethics, and the Color of Our Character.* New Brunswick, NJ: Rutgers University Press, 1995.

Holmes, Rachel. *African Queen: The Real Life of the Hottentot Venus.* New York: Random House, 2007.

Honour, Hugh. *The Image of the Black in Western Art.* Vol. 4, Pt. 2. Cambridge, MA: Harvard University Press, 1989.

hooks, bell. *Black Looks: Race and Representation.* Boston: South End Press, 1992.

———. Keynote Address. National Women's Studies Association Annual Meeting, San Jan, Puerto Rico, November 14, 2014.

Jacobs, Harriet. *Incidents in the Life of a Slave Girl.* Cambridge, MA: Harvard University Press, 1987, 1861.

Jefferson, Thomas. *Notes on the State of Virginia.* 1784. Chapel Hill: University of North Carolina Press, 1954.

Jones, Lisa. *Bulletproof Diva: Tales of Race, Sex, and Hair.* New York: Anchor Books, 1995.

Jordan, Winthrop. *White over Black: American Attitudes toward the Negro, 1550–1812.* Chapel Hill: University of North Carolina Press, 1968.

Judd, Bettina. *Patient. Poems.* New York: Black Lawrence Press, 2014.

Kapsalis, Terri. *Public Privates: Performing Gynecology from Both Ends of the Speculum.* Durham, NC: Duke University Press, 1997.

Kerseboom, Simone. "Grandmother-Martyr-Heroine: Placing Sara Baartman in South African Post-Apartheid Foundational Mythology." *Historia* 56, no.1 (2011): 63–76.

Kershaw, Miriam. "Postcolonialism and Androgyny: The Performance Art of Grace Jones." *Art Journal* 97, no. 56 (winter 1997): 19–25.

Knowles-Carter, Beyoncé. *B'Day.* Parkwood Entertainment/Columbia Records, 2006.

———. *BEYONCÉ: The Visual Album.* Parkwood Entertainment/Columbia Records, 2013.

———. "Self-Titled, Part 4: Liberation." YouTube Video (January 13, 2014). Available: https://www.youtube.com/watch?v=0eZ0mzI37-A.

———. *Lemonade.* Parkwood Entertainment/Columbia Records, 2016.

Koff, Clea. *The Bone Woman: A Forensic Anthropologist's Search for Truth in the Mass Graves of Rwanda, Bosnia, Croatia, and Kosovo.* New York: Random House, 2004.

Kolb, Peter. *The Present State of the Cape of Good Hope,* 2 vols. Trans. Guido Medley. London, 1731.

Kraut, Anthea. "Between Primitivism and Diaspora: The Dance Performances of Josephine Baker, Zora Neale Hurston, and Katherine Dunham." *Theatre Journal* 55 (2003): 433–50.

Kwakwa, Patience Abenaa. "Dance and African Women." *Sage* 8, no. 2 (1994): 10–15.

Lassner, Jacob. *Demonizing the Queen of Sheba.* Chicago: University of Chicago Press, 1993.

Laster, Paul. "Kara Walker Interview," *Time Out* (May 5, 2014). Available: https://www.timeout.com/newyork/art/kara-walker-interview-the-whole-reason-for-refining-sugar-is-to-make-it-white.

Lecaudey, Hélène. "Behind the Mask: Ex-Slave Women and Interracial Sexual Relations." In *Discovering the Women in Slavery: Emancipating Perspectives on the American Past*, ed. Patricia Morton, 260–277. Athens: University of Georgia Press, 1996.

Le Vaillant, François. *Voyage de François Le Vaillant dans l'intérieur de l'Afrique*. Paris, 1790.

*The Life and Times of Sara Baartman*. Dir. Zola Maseko. New York: First Run/Icarus Films, 1998.

Lindfors, Bernth. "'The Hottentot Venus' and Other African Attractions in Nineteenth-Century England." *Australasian Drama Studies* 1, no. 2 (1983): 82–104.

Lorde, Audre. *Sister Outsider: Essays and Speeches*. Freedom, CA: The Crossing Press, 1984.

Lubiano, Wahneema. "Talking about the State and Imagining Alliances." In *Talking Visions: Multicultural Feminism in a Transnational Age*, ed. Ella Shohat, 441–49. Cambridge, MA: MIT Press, 1998.

Machera, Mumbi. "Opening a Can of Worms: A Debate of Female Sexuality in the Lecture Theatre." In *Re-thinking African Sexualities in Africa*, ed. Signe Arnfred, 157–72. Uppsala, Sweden: The Nordic Africa Institute, 2004.

Magubane, Zine. "Which Bodies Matter? Feminism, Poststructuralism, Race, and the Curious Theoretical Odyssey of the 'Hottentot Venus.'" *Gender and Society* 15, no. 6 (2001): 816–34.

Marks, Carole and Diana Edkins. *The Power of Pride: Stylemakers and Rulebreakers of the Harlem Renaissance*. New York: Crown Publishers, 1999.

Martin, Kameelah L. *Envisioning Black Feminist Voodoo Aesthetics: African Spirituality in American Cinema*. London: Lexington Books, 2016.

Martin, Wendy. "Remembering the Jungle: Josephine Baker and Modernist Parody." In *Prehistories of the Future: The Primitivist Project and the Culture of Modernism*, eds. Elazar Barkan and Ronald Bush, 310–25. Stanford, CA: Stanford University Press, 1995.

McClintock, Anne. *Imperial Leather: Race, Gender, and Sexuality in the Colonial Conquest*. New York: Routledge, 1994.

Mercer, Kobena, Catherine Ugwu, and David A. Bailey. *Mirage: Enigmas of Race, Difference, and Desire*. London: Institute for Contemporary Art, 1995.

"Me So Horny." Performed by 2 Live Crew. *As Nasty as They Wannabe*. New York: Jay Records, 1989.

Meter, Jonathan Van. "Beyoncé: Fierce Creature." *Vogue* (April 1, 2009). Available: http://www.vogue.com/article/beyonc233-fierce-creature.

Meyers, B. E. "What Is My Legacy? Transient Consciousness and the 'Fixed' Subject in the Photography of Renee Cox." In *Gendered Visions*, ed. Salah M. Hassan, 27–37. Trenton, NJ: Africa World Press, 1997.

Miller-Young, Mireille. *A Taste for Brown Sugar: Black Women in Pornography*. Durham: Duke University Press, 2014.

*Miss America*. Dir. Lisa Ades. Burbank, CA: PBS American Experience, 2002.

Mohanty, Chandra. "Under Western Eyes: Feminist Scholarship and Colonial Discourses." In *Third World Women and the Politics of Feminism*, eds. Chandra Mohanty, Ann Russo, and Lourdes Torres, 51–80. Bloomington: Indiana University Press, 1991.

*Monday's Girls*. Dir. Ngozi Onwurah. New York: Women Make Movies, 1993.

Morgan, Jennifer L. "'Some Could Suckle over Their Shoulder': Male Travelers, Female Bodies, and the Gendering of Racial Ideology, 1500–1770." *William and Mary Quarterly* 54 (1997): 167–92.

Morgan, Joan. "Beyoncé, Black Feminist Art, and this Oshun Bidness." *Genius* (April 30, 2016). Available: https://genius.com/a/beyonce-black-feminist-art-and-this-oshun-bidness.

Morrison, Toni. *Beloved.* New York: Alfred A. Knopf, 1987.

———. *Playing in the Dark: Whiteness and the Literary Imagination.* Cambridge, MA: Harvard University Press, 1992.

Mulvey, Laura. "Visual Pleasure and Narrative Cinema." In *Issues in Feminist Film Criticism,* ed. Patricia Erens, 28–40. Bloomington: Indiana University Press, 1990.

Narayan, Uma. *Dislocating Culture: Identities, Traditions, and Third World Feminism.* New York: Routledge, 1997.

Netto, Priscilla. "Reclaiming the Body of the 'Hottentot': The Vision and Visuality of the Body Speaking with Vengeance in Venus Hottentot 2000." *European Journal of Women's Studies* 12, no. 2 (2005): 149–163.

Newman, Vanessa. "The Tragic Genius of Kara Walker's 'Sugar Baby' Exhibit." Moodie Mills: Catalyzing Culture, Capital, and Community through Media, Policy, and Advocacy (June 22, 2014). Available: http://moodiemills.com/2014/06/the-tragic-genius-of-kara-walkers-sugar-baby-exhibit. *This website is no longer available.*

Nichols, Bill. *Blurred Boundaries: Questions of Meaning in Contemporary Culture.* Bloomington: Indiana University Press, 1994.

Nyong'o, Tavia. "The Body in Question." *International Journal of Communication* 1 (2007): 27–31.

O'Grady, Lorraine. "Olympia's Maid: Reclaiming Black Female Subjectivity." *Afterimage* 20, no. 1 (1992): 14–20.

Oliveira, Cleuci de. "Saartjie Baartman: The Original Booty Queen." *Jezebel* (November 14, 2014). Available: http://jezebel.com/saartjie-baartman-the-original-booty-queen-1658569879.

Onishi, Norimitsu. "Globalization of Beauty Makes Slimness Trendy." *New York Times,* (October 3, 2002): A4.

Oyewumi, Oyeronke. "Alice in the Motherland: Reading Alice Walker on Africa and Screening the Color 'Black.'" *Jenda: A Journal of Culture and African Women Studies* 1, no. 2 (2001): Available online: http://www.jendajournal.com/vol1.2/oyewumi.html. *This website is no longer available.*

Painter, Nell. *Sojourner Truth: A Life, a Symbol.* New York: W. W. Norton & Co., 1996.

Palme, Johan. "Makode Linde – the 'Swedish Cake' Artist – Explains Himself." *Africa is a Country* (April 24, 2012). Available: http://africasacountry.com/2012/04/africa-is-a-country-interview-with-makode-linde.

Parasecoli, Fabio. "Bootylicious: Food and the Female Body in Contemporary Black Popular Culture." *Women's Studies Quarterly* 35, no. 1/2 (2007): 110–125.

Parks, Suzan-Lori. *Venus.* (First performed in 1996.) New York: Theatre Communications Group, 1997.

Perdue, Charles L., Jr., Thomas E. Barden, and Robert K. Phillips, eds. *Weevils in the Wheat: Interviews with Virginia Ex-Slaves.* Charlottesville: University Press of Virginia, 1976.

Perlmutter, Dawn. "Miss America: Whose Ideal?" In *Beauty Matters,* ed. Peg Zeglin Brand, 155–68. Bloomington: Indiana University Press, 2000.

Perry, Imani. "Who(se) am I? The Identity and Image of Women in Hip-Hop." In *Gender, Race, and Class in Media: A Text-Reader,* 2nd ed., eds. Gail Dines and Jean M. Humez, 136–48. Thousand Oaks, CA: Sage Publications, 2003.

Picquet, Louisa. "Louisa Picquet, the Octoroon: A Tale of Southern Slave Life (1861)." In *Collected Black Women's Narratives,* ed. Anthony G. Barthelemy. New York: Oxford University Press, 1988.

Pieterse, Jan Nederveen. *White on Black: Images of Africa and Blacks in Western Popular Culture.* New Haven, CT: Yale University Press, 1992.

Platon, Adelle. "Beyoncé 'In No Way Tied' to Saartjie Baartman Film." *Billboard* (January 5, 2016). Available: http://www.billboard.com/articles/columns/hip-hop/6828940/beyonce-saartjie-baartman-film.

Pough, Gwendolyn. *Check it while I Wreck it: Black Womanhood, Hip-Hop Culture, and the Public Sphere.* Boston: Northeastern University Press, 2004.

Prince, Mary. "The History of Mary Prince," (1831). In *Classic Six Slave Narratives,* ed. Henry Louis Gates, Jr., 183–242. New York: Penguin, 1987.

"Protest on Jo Baker as Queen." *Chicago Defender,* (April 11, 1931): 5.

A *Question of Color: Color Consciousness in Black America.* Dir. Kathe Sandler. San Francisco: California Newsreel, 1993.

Reed, Christopher Robert. *All the World Is Here: The Black Presence at White City.* Bloomington: Indiana University Press, 2000.

Reinhardt, Mark. "Who Speaks for Margaret Garner? Slavery, Silence, and the Politics of Ventriloquism." *Critical Inquiry* 29 (autumn 2002): 81–119.

Rodulfo, Kristina. "Dior's 'We Should All Be Feminists' Shirts Will Benefit Rihanna's Charities." (February 28, 2017). *Elle.* Available: http://www.elle.com/fashion/news/a43431/dior-we-should-all-be-feminists-shirt-rihanna-charity.

Rose, Phyllis. *Jazz Cleopatra: Josephine Baker in Her Time.* New York: Doubleday, 1989.

Rose, Tricia. "Never Trust a Big Butt and a Smile." *Camera Obscura* 23 (1990): 109–131.

Rydell, Robert W., ed. *The Reason Why the Colored American Is Not at the World's Columbian Exposition.* Urbana: University of Illinois Press, 1999, 1893.

Said, Edward. *Orientalism.* New York: Random House, 1979.

Schiebinger, Londa. *Nature's Body: Gender in the Making of Science.* Boston: Beacon Press, 1993.

*School Daze.* Dir. Spike Lee. Los Angeles: Columbia Pictures, 1988.

Schrire, Carmel. "Native Views of Western Eyes." In *Miscast: Negotiating the Presence of Bushmen,* ed. Pippa Skotness, 343–53. Cape Town, South Africa: University of Cape Town Press, 1996.

Scully, Pamela. "Sara Baartman and the Boundaries of African History." Paper authored by Scully and presented by Clifton Cais at the African Studies Association Conference, New Orleans. November 11, 2004.

Shange, Ntozake. *For Colored Girls Who Have Considered Suicide/When the Rainbow Is Enuf.* New York: Simon & Schuster, 1977.

Sharpe, Jenny. *Ghosts of Slavery: A Literary Archaeology of Black Women's Lives.* Minneapolis: University of Minnesota Press, 2003.

Sharpley-Whiting, T. Denean. *Black Venus: Sexualized Savages, Primal Fears, and Primitive Narratives in French.* Durham, NC: Duke University Press, 1999.

*The Shawshank Redemption.* Dir. Frank Darabont. Los Angeles: Castle Rock Entertainment, 1994.

Shelley, Mary. *Frankenstein: or, the Modern Prometheus*. Ed. M. K. Joseph. New York: Oxford University Press, 1969, 1818.

Shiva, Vandana. *Staying Alive: Women, Ecology, and Development*. London: Zed Books, 1988.

Shohat, Ella and Robert Stam. *Unthinking Eurocentrism: Multiculturalism and the Media*. New York: Routledge, 1994.

Skotness, Pippa, ed. *Miscast: Negotiating the Presence of Bushmen*. Cape Town, South Africa: University of Cape Town Press, 1996.

*Soul Food*. Dir. George Tillman Jr. Los Angeles: Fox 2000 Pictures, 1997.

"South Africa Anger after Sarah Baartman's Grave Defaced." *BBC News* (April 28, 2015). Available: http://www.bbc.com/news/world-africa-32499070.

Spanos, Brittany. "How Beyoncé's 'Lemonade' Reclaims Rock's Black Female Legacy." *Rolling Stone* (April 26, 2016). Available: http://www.rollingstone.com/music/news/how-beyonces-lemonade-reclaims-rocks-black-female-legacy-20160426.

Spillers, Hortense. "Interstices: A Small Drama of Words." In *Pleasure and Danger: Exploring Female Sexuality*, ed. Carole Vance, 73–100. London: Pandora, 1989.

Spivak, Gayatri. "Can the Subaltern Speak?" In *Marxism and the Interpretation of Culture*, eds. Cary Nelson and Lawrence Grossberg, 271–313. Urbana: University of Illinois Press.

Stedman, John Gabriel. *Narrative of a Five Years' Expedition against the Revolted Negroes of Surinam*. London, 1796.

Stewart, Dodai. "How Offensive is Beyoncé's Vogue Cover? Let Us Count the Ways." *Jezebel* (March 16, 2009). Available: http://jezebel.com/5170632/how-offensive-is-beyonces-vogue-cover-let-us-count-the-ways.

Strother, Z. S. "Display of the Body Hottentot." In *Africans on Stage*, ed. Bernth Lindfors, 1–61. Bloomington: Indiana University Press, 1999.

Summers, Barbara. *Skin Deep: Inside the World of Black Fashion Models*. New York: Amistad Press, 1998.

Tate, Greg. "Of Homegirl Goddesses and Geechee Women: The Africentric Cinema of Julie Dash." *The Village Voice* 36, no. 23 (June 4, 1991): 72.

*That B.E.A.T.* Dir. Abteen Bagheri. Vimeo Video (2014). Available: https://vimeo.com/58423297.

Thealon, Marie-Emmanuel-Guillaume-Marguerite, Armand Dartois, and Brasier. *La Vénus Hottentote, ou haine aux françaises* (The Hottentot Venus, or Hatred of French Women), 1814. Translated and reprinted in *Black Venus: Sexualized Savages, Primal Fears, and Primitive Narratives in French*, ed. T. Denean, Sharpley-Whiting, appendix. Durham, NC: Duke University Press, 1999.

Thomas, Evan. "A Long, Strange Trip to the Taliban." *Newsweek* (December 16, 2001). Available: http://www.newsweek.com/long-strange-trip-taliban-148503.

Thompson, Katrina Dyonne. "'Some were Wild, some were Soft, some were Tame, and some were Fiery': Female Dancers, Male Explorers, and the Sexualization of Blackness, 1600–1900." *Black Women, Gender, and Families* 6, no. 2 (2012): 1–28.

Thomson, Rosemarie Garland. *Extraordinary Bodies: Figuring Disability in American Culture and Literature*. New York: Columbia University Press, 1997.

Todd, Jan. "Bring on the Amazons: An Evolutionary History." In *Picturing the Modern Amazon*, eds. Joanna Frueh, Laurie Fierstein, and Judith Stein, 48–61. New York: Rizzoli, 2000.

Toole-Stott, R. *Circus and Allied Arts: A World Bibliography*, 1500–1962. Derby, U.K.: Harpur, 1962.

*Triplets of Belleville.* Dir. Sylvain Chomet. Sony Pictures Classics, 2003.

*Trouble the Water.* Dirs. Carl Deal and Tia Lessin. Elsewhere Pictures, 2008.

Upham, Mansell. "From the Venus Sickness to the Hottentot Venus, Part Two." *Quarterly Bulletin of the National Library of South Africa* 61, no. 2 (2007): 74–82.

"La Venus Hottentote." *Journal des dames et des modes* (January 25, 1815): 37–40.

*Venus Noire.* Dir. Abdellatif Kechiche. MK2 Productions, 2010.

Verna, Mara. "Mara Verna Pages." (2002). http://www.hottentotvenus.com.

Walker, Alice. *In Search of Our Mothers' Gardens: Womanist Prose.* San Diego: Harcourt Brace & Co., 1984.

———. *The Same River Twice.* New York: Scribner, 1996.

Wallace, Michele. *Invisibility Blues: From Pop to Theory.* New York: Verso, 1990.

Wallace-Sanders, Kimberly, ed. *Skin Deep, Spirit Strong: The Black Female Body in American Culture.* Ann Arbor: University of Michigan Press, 2002.

Wallis, Brian. "Black Bodies, White Science: Louis Agassiz's Slave Daguerreotypes." *American Art* 9, no. 2 (summer 1995): 38–61.

White, Deborah Gray. *Ar'n't I a Woman? Female Slaves in the Plantation South.* New York: W. W. Norton & Co., 1985.

White, E. Frances. *Dark Continent of Our Bodies: Black Feminism and the Politics of Respectability.* Philadelphia: Temple University Press, 1999.

White, Randall. "The Women of Brassempouy: A Century of Research and Interpretation." *Journal of Archaeological Method and Theory* 13, no. 4 (2006): 250–303.

Williams, Carla. "Artist's Statement." (September 2002). http://www.carlagirl.net/photos.html. *This website is no longer available.*

———. "Naked, Neutered, Noble: The Black Female Body in America and the Problem of Photographic History." In *Skin Deep, Spirit Strong: The Black Female Body in American Culture,* ed. Kimberly Wallace-Sanders, 182–200. Ann Arbor: University of Michigan Press, 2002.

Willis, Deborah, ed. *Black Venus 2010: They Called Her "Hottentot."* Philadelphia: Temple University Press, 2010.

Willis, Deborah and Carla Williams. *The Black Female Body: A Photographic History.* Philadelphia: Temple University Press, 2002.

Wilson, Jamia. "Turning the Tables." (April–May 2017). *Bust.* Available: http://bust.com/feminism/192922-solange-knowles-digs-deep-and-opens-up-about-life-as-a-woman.html. *This website is no longer available.*

Wilson, Judith. "Beauty Rites: Towards an Anatomy of Culture in African American Women's Art." *International Review of African American Art* 11, no. 2 (1994): 11–18, 47–55.

Winters, Lisa Ze. *The Mulatta Concubine: Terror, Intimacy, Freedom, and Desire in the Black Transatlantic.* Athens: University of Georgia Press, 2016.

*Women's Work.* Dirs. Jawole Willa Jo Zollar, Marianne Henderson, and Bruce Berryhill. Richmond: Virginia Museum of Fine Arts, 1996.

Woodard, Vincent. *The Delectable Negro: Human Consumption and Homoeroticism within U.S. Slave Culture.* New York: NYU Press, 2014.

Wootton, Dan. "Beyoncé has bot[h] her eyes on winning an Oscar for film about lady with giant rear." *The Sun* (January 2, 2016). Available: https://www.thesun.co.uk/archives/bizarre/934423/beyonce-has-bot-her-eyes-on-winning-an-oscar-for-film-about-lady-with-giant-rear.

Young, Harvey. *Embodying Black Experience: Stillness, Critical Memory, and the Black Body.* Ann Arbor: University of Michigan Press, 2010.

Young, Hershini Bhana. "Inheriting the Criminalized Black Body: Race, Gender, and Slavery in Gayl Jones' *Eva's Man.*" Paper presented at the Collegium for African American Research Conference on April 21, 2005.

Young, Iris Marion. *Throwing Like a Girl and Other Essays in Feminist Philosophy and Social Theory.* Bloomington: Indiana University Press, 1990.

Young, Jean. "The Re-Objectification and Re-Commodification of Saartjie Baartman in Suzan-Lori Parks's *Venus.*" *African American Review* 31, no. 4 (winter 1997): 699–708.

Zook, Kristal Brent. "Light Skinned(ded) Naps." In *Making Face, Making Soul,* ed. Gloria Anzaldua, 85–96. San Francisco: Aunt Lute Books, 1990.

# INDEX

# Taylor & Francis eBooks

---

## Helping you to choose the right eBooks for your Library

Add Routledge titles to your library's digital collection today. Taylor and Francis ebooks contains over 50,000 titles in the Humanities, Social Sciences, Behavioural Sciences, Built Environment and Law.

**Choose from a range of subject packages or create your own!**

**Benefits for you**

» Free MARC records
» COUNTER-compliant usage statistics
» Flexible purchase and pricing options
» All titles DRM-free.

**Benefits for your user**

» Off-site, anytime access via Athens or referring URL
» Print or copy pages or chapters
» Full content search
» Bookmark, highlight and annotate text
» Access to thousands of pages of quality research at the click of a button.

**REQUEST YOUR FREE INSTITUTIONAL TRIAL TODAY**

**Free Trials Available**
We offer free trials to qualifying academic, corporate and government customers.

## eCollections – Choose from over 30 subject eCollections, including:

| | |
|---|---|
| Archaeology | Language Learning |
| Architecture | Law |
| Asian Studies | Literature |
| Business & Management | Media & Communication |
| Classical Studies | Middle East Studies |
| Construction | Music |
| Creative & Media Arts | Philosophy |
| Criminology & Criminal Justice | Planning |
| Economics | Politics |
| Education | Psychology & Mental Health |
| Energy | Religion |
| Engineering | Security |
| English Language & Linguistics | Social Work |
| Environment & Sustainability | Sociology |
| Geography | Sport |
| Health Studies | Theatre & Performance |
| History | Tourism, Hospitality & Events |

For more information, pricing enquiries or to order a free trial, please contact your local sales team:
**www.tandfebooks.com/page/sales**